CAE
Advantage
Teacher's Guide

Roy Kingsbury   Felicity O'Dell   Guy Wellman

Roy Kingsbury
is a freelance ELT materials writer and consultant.

Felicity O'Dell
is a Senior Teacher at Eurocentre, Cambridge, and Chief Examiner for the Writing Paper of the CAE Examination.

Guy Wellman
is Principal of BEET Language Centre, Bournemouth.

Overview of the CAE Examination

PAPER	TIME	% OF MARKS	SECTIONS	BRIEF OUTLINE OF QUESTIONS/PHASES
One READING	1 hour	20%	Four texts	The questions on the texts involve matching, gap-filling and multiple-choice. The candidates' ability to skim read is tested.
Two WRITING	2 hours	20%	A Compulsory question	Candidates must read one or more pieces and then write about 250 words based on what they have read.
			B Choice of topic	Candidates must choose one of four tasks and write about 250 words. The tasks include letters, reports, articles, competition entries, etc.
Three ENGLISH IN USE	1 hour 30 mins.	20%	A Blank-filling: two questions	Two texts with blanks to be filled in. With the first multiple-choice options are provided to choose from.
			B Editing: two questions	In the first question mistakes have to be corrected in, for example, grammar or spelling.
				In the second a piece of writing has to be changed from one style to another e.g. from a formal to an informal style.
			C Text completion: two questions	In the first question there is a text with a number of gaps, each indicating that a sentence or part of a sentence is missing. Under the text there is a list of options: candidates must choose which option fits each of the gaps.
				In the second question candidates are given some notes which must be written out in full.
Four LISTENING	approx. 45 mins.	20%	A Monologue B Monologue C Two or more speakers D Short extracts	Candidates hear every section twice *except* Section B. In all the sections candidates may be asked to tick boxes, complete plans, label diagrams, choose from multiple-choice options, and so on. The Paper therefore employs a wide range of testing techniques.
Five SPEAKING	approx 15 mins.	20%	Phase A	The two candidates must introduce themselves to the examiners and perhaps also introduce themselves to each other.
			Phase B	The two candidates take turns in looking at a picture (or diagram) of some kind and talking about it for a minute or so.
			Phase C	The two candidates are given a problem of some kind to discuss together. After a few minutes they must come to a common solution, or agree to differ. They then report what they think to the examiners.
			Phase D	The two examiners use this last phase to talk to both candidates again in order to finalise their assessments.

Contents

Introduction

Background information
---

1 Who the course is for

CAE Advantage was written primarily for students preparing for the Cambridge Certificate in Advanced English (CAE). The course is equally suitable for students in their own countries who will take a year's course (perhaps four to six lessons per week) leading to the CAE and for those on an intensive (perhaps three-month) course in Britain.

As an integrated advanced skills development course, however, *CAE Advantage* can be used with students who simply want to continue to improve their English beyond FCE and who have no intention of taking an examination.

The content of the course assumes that students will be adults and young adults in full or part-time education or studying independently.

2 Entry point

The course assumes that students embarking on *CAE Advantage* will have successfully completed an upper intermediate course and will most probably have passed the FCE or other examination(s) in English at an equivalent level.

3 Time allocation

a Long-term CAE courses

Assuming an academic year in many schools to consist of 30 weeks with something like four to six hours per week to devote to English for the CAE, it will be possible to complete an average of three-quarters of a Unit of the course per week. In such circumstances, the course should take 140-160 hours to complete. It must be remembered, however, that not all Units are exactly the same length and some will require more classroom time than others.

If the class has no more than four hours or lessons, you may find it necessary to set more of the material as homework.

Time should always be allowed towards the end of the course and before the exam itself for general revision and use of Practice Exams material (*Longman Practice Exams for the CAE,* 1991).

b Short-term intensive CAE courses

The course will be found to be ideal as the basic coursebook around which to build a full CAE programme on short-term (three or six-month) intensive courses leading to the CAE in private or other language institutes. To take an example, students on a twelve-week intensive course with some 20 (45 to 50-minute) lessons per week should be able to cover the course easily by completing an average of two Units per week. In these circumstances, the course should take 120 to 140 hours to complete. Such a timetable would also still allow the programme to include additional practice material.

4 The needs of CAE students

The needs of learners aiming to take the CAE exam are those of any learners at post-FCE level, but with the additional requirements of the exam itself. First, what are some of the needs of *any* post-FCE learners?

- Students at this level need particularly to consolidate their understanding and active use of structure and build up their range of vocabulary.
- They need to acquire a feeling for when a certain register, style or mode of speech is appropriate or inappropriate.
- They need to develop greater competence in all four skills while developing competence in integrated skills.
- Because students often seem to reach a 'learning plateau' at around FCE level and their English tends to contain a number of ingrained errors, they need to be made aware of such errors and need to learn to be more self-critical. More important still, they have to be prepared to 're-learn' certain things in order to eradicate errors.
- Many students at this level need to work towards using English at a professional level since they are often setting their sights on a job or career which will of necessity involve the use of English at a reasonably high level.
- They need to work with material (themes, topics and subjects) which will catch their interest and which they relate and respond to.

- They need to be encouraged to enjoy English beyond the classroom.

And what are the additional, specific needs of CAE students?

In short, they have to bring their English up to the level which will allow them to pass the exam. This means becoming proficient in English in all four skills and integrated skills up to a level between FCE and CPE as defined by the Cambridge Syndicate, and becoming thoroughly familiar with all the testing techniques employed in all five Papers of the CAE. (See the Overview of the CAE Examination on the page opposite Contents.)

5 Aims of the course

- To help students broaden or expand their knowledge of and proficiency in general English.
- To give equal prominence and practice in all four main skills with, at the same time, considerable practice in integrated skills.
- To provide practice in reading and listening to authentic English.
- To help students revise, consolidate and extend their command of English grammar and vocabulary.
- To help students broaden their ability to function in English in a variety of spoken and written situations.
- To help students acquire some appreciation of style, register and appropriacy — with particular reference to those style and register tasks which occur in the exam (e.g. in Papers 2 and 3).
- To provide material which attempts to balance practice in basic language structure with communicative use of the language.
- To present students with a variety of universal subjects or topics which will engage their interest.
- To provide materials and suggested classroom management strategies which will not only promote maximum student participation in the classroom, but which will also be of value when they are taking the exam.
- To provide ample opportunities to discuss and practise all the tasks or testing techniques which they are likely to meet in the exam so that they are perfectly familiar with the format of the exam Papers.

Course components

CAE Advantage consists of:
A Coursebook
This Teacher's Guide
A set of two cassettes

1 The Coursebook contains:

A brief overview of the CAE examination
Contents
20 Units
Unit-by-Unit Grammar Commentary
Listening Tapescripts (tapescripts or transcripts of all Listening material *except* Exam Practice recordings)

2 This Teacher's Guide contains:

A comprehensive Introduction (see Contents)
An Overview of the CAE examination
Course Skills and Language Syllabus
Teaching Notes for all 20 Units, including Tapescripts for Exam Practice (Paper 4 Listening) tasks

3 The recorded material consists of:

Two cassettes to accompany the Coursebook. They contain recordings for all Listening phases throughout the course, including Exam Practice (Paper 4 Listening). (There are no repetitions on the cassettes.)

Course structure

1 20 Units

The course consists of 20 Units which are designed to ensure that learners gradually and steadily increase their knowledge and control of the language to a point where they will have every chance of success in the exam.

2 Special features of the course

- All four skills are practised in a Unit and there is considerable emphasis on integrated skills.
- At the same time, each Unit has a certain 'bias' towards an exam Paper. (See 'Exam preparation cycle' and 'Description of a Unit' below.)
- Each Unit closes with an 'Exam Practice' section or phase which not only includes a sample task (or 'test'), but which also provides an opportunity to discuss what the task involves and how best to tackle it.
- Topics are universal — the kind of topics that might appear in a wide range of publications across the world — and alternate between light and serious.
- A considerable proportion of the written texts are authentic and have been culled from a variety of

newspapers, magazines and other sources. This reflects the practice of the CAE exam.

- A certain amount of the listening material is also authentic and includes real-life interviews with, or speeches by, famous names including Prince Charles, John Tusa (Managing Director of the BBC World Service), Sir Yehudi Menuhin and Alan Sugar (founder of Amstrad Computers).
- Each of the last five Units contains a Tip Strip which gives tips on doing one of the exam Papers.
- Immediately following Unit 20 is the Grammar Commentary. This is *not* a full-blown grammar of English. Each page is devoted to comments on the grammar practised mainly in the 'Language focus' section of the Unit, although from time to time it also comments on language practised in other phases in the Unit.
- The final pages of the Coursebook contain the Tapescripts for all listening phases and activities *except* those for Exam Practice (Paper 4 Listening). These appear only in this Teacher's Guide.

3 Exam preparation cycle

The preparation necessary for each of the Papers of the CAE exam is cycled four times in *CAE Advantage* :

Paper 1 Reading:	Units 1, 6, 11 and 16
Paper 2 Writing:	Units 2, 7, 12 and 17
Paper 3 English in Use:	Units 3, 8, 13 and 18
Paper 4 Listening:	Units 4, 9, 14 and 19
Paper 5 Speaking:	Units 5, 10, 15 and 20

The Exam Practice phase at the end of each Unit prepares students specifically for the kinds of task they will meet in the exam itself while Warm-up activities and/or the initial or presentation Unit text (written or spoken) also reflect the skills bias of the Unit.

The Exam Practice phases are not simply 'mini-tests'. While they might be used as such, the emphasis is generally on discussing, and preparing students thoroughly for, the kinds of task they will meet in the exam.

The cyclical pattern described above is reflected in the Coursebook itself by a colour coding on the first page of each Unit. Thus, Cycle 1 Units (1, 6, 11 and 16) are colour-coded purple, Cycle 2 Units (2, 7, 12 and 17) blue, Cycle 3 Units (3, 8, 13 and 18) green, Cycle 4 Units (4, 9, 14 and 19) red, and Cycle 5 Units (5, 10, 15 and 20) orange.

Outline of a Unit

All Units contain a variety of phases and activities, and all include practice in listening, speaking, reading and writing, as well as in integrated skills. The 'skills bias' in each Unit is thus supported by activities involving other skills.

The Units contain some or all of the following sections:

- Warm-up (with suggestions in this Teacher's Guide)
- Presentation text(s) — written or on tape
- Integrated skills phases ('Listen and write', 'Read and discuss', 'Read, find out, discuss and write', 'Read and interpret', 'Listen, discuss and write', etc.)
- Language focus (with a reference to the Grammar Commentary section)
- 'What's the difference?' — grammar problems to solve
- Vocabulary or Vocabulary study
- Exam Practice
- Units 16-20 each contain a Tip Strip

How to use the course

General

The general approach of *CAE Advantage* stresses teaching and learning rather than simply testing, as might be the case with a book of Practice Exams.

In order to make the course both effective and enjoyable, the aim should always be for maximum student participation. For example,

- students might be involved in reading and making notes in pairs, or listening and discussing in groups;
- they might be involved in 'jigsaw reading' or 'jigsaw listening' in which different partners in pairs or different groups in the class read or listen for one thing while a partner or another group reads or listens for something else in order to exchange information later.

It is commonly recognised that, because at this level in particular students come to the class with varying degrees of knowledge and skills, pair and groupwork can be invaluable. The value of peer-teaching therefore, whereby students help each other as much as possible, cannot be stressed enough.

The course is designed so that lessons can be conducted with a good variety of pace. Homework and reviews of previous Units will allow you and your students to check how well language and skills have been acquired.

1 Warm-up

Units begin with a separate 'Warm-up' or 'lead-in' phase, except where it is appropriate to go straight into the material on the page (as in Unit 17, for example). This Teacher's Guide provides a number of alternative suggestions for each Unit.

This phase is important. After all, a warm-up activity is rather like limbering up before a sporting activity, practising scales and arpeggios before playing an instrument, or doing breathing exercises before singing. It helps the participant — athlete, singer, instrumentalist or, as here, learner — to get into a 'set'. And in terms of language learning, that means leading students gently into the topic of the Unit and beginning to introduce, or draw from the students themselves, just some of the language that is likely to arise in the next few lessons.

Ideally, while never taking longer than 10-15 minutes of classroom time, this phase should involve all students in pairs, groups or teams so that there is maximum student participation right from the start.

2 Text presentation

In addition to the instructions in the Coursebook and the Unit-by-Unit Teaching Notes in this Teacher's Guide, the following points are worth noting:

1 The initial 'text' in the Unit deserves special study and practice. Following the Warm-up phase, it not only launches students into the topic of the Unit, but it also gives practice in the 'exam paper bias skill'. For example, if the Exam Practice phase at the end of the Unit is practice for Paper 5 Speaking, the presentation phase will also give students practice in speaking (see Unit 5).

2 Time should not be spent unduly on grammar or vocabulary explanation early in the Unit since there are specific Language focus and Vocabulary sections in all Units.

3 Many texts need some explanation of background information, cultural references and vocabulary. These are provided in the Teaching notes in this Teacher's Guide. Cultural references in particular might best be explained before students work on the text.

A word of warning, however: some cultural references and vocabulary explanation should be left in some cases until students have done any exercises designed to promote predicting and skimming, or

any exercises involving using dictionaries to check unknown vocabulary. This applies to presentation and other texts in a Unit with a Reading or Listening bias.

4 When you have explained the procedure and/or students have read the instructions for a task, always check quickly that they know exactly what they have to do before they embark on that task.

5 Encourage students, especially when directed to work in pairs or groups to do exercises related to a text, to pool their resources and knowledge to help each other understand. You might regard your role at this level as more that of guide or mentor, going round checking and questioning pairs or groups, rather than that of information-giver.

6 Always bring the class back together to check what they have done. This will minimise misunderstandings and iron out common problems.

7 Just occasionally, both to save classroom time and to encourage reading outside the classroom, you might want to set a text to be read *before* the lesson. Another word of warning, however: while this can be valuable, check that 'advance' reading will not invalidate any of the skills exercises!

3 Integrated skills phases

The Units in this course contain a host of 'integrated skills' phases from a simple 'Look and speak' to 'Read, discuss and write', 'Think and write, then read and discuss', and so on.

Instructions in the Coursebook and the Unit-by-Unit Teaching Notes provide guidance on the individual procedure and strategies to adopt with such phases.

4 Language focus

All Units in the course contain a phase labelled 'Language focus'. The course combines a variety of approaches: some phases or exercises are described functionally (e.g. 'Comparing people', 'Regrets', 'Narrating past events', and so on) , some grammatically (e.g. *had done/had been doing*, 'defining relatives — and omission', and so on), and some are inductive.

Whether the grammar is assembled under functions, explicitly stated, or to be deduced, the aim is always to present (or revise) and practise English which will ultimately feed into an activity such as a debate, discussion, writing a report, etc. In other words, students are generally required to use the grammar in some communicative task later on.

Many activities draw on students' own knowledge and encourage them to discuss differences between structures and patterns. Many are what might be termed 'language awareness' activities in which students themselves attempt to formulate rules after a) discussing examples or 'what's the difference?' problems, or b) after applying the language to a situation (or situations).

5 Grammar Commentary

The Grammar Commentary section at the end of the book is there for reference before, during or after practice in the Unit. It aims to provide reasonably brief explanations of the language areas under study.

Note that actual answers to exercises in 'Language focus' phases are given in the Teaching Notes in this Teacher's Guide.

For comprehensive grammar information, students should be advised to consult a grammar reference work such as the *Longman English Grammar* (L.G. Alexander, Longman 1988).

6 Vocabulary or Vocabulary study

The 'Vocabulary' or 'Vocabulary study' phases which appear in most Units also, like 'Language focus', vary considerably in format and activities. The Coursebook and this Teacher's Guide give individual instructions for these.

7 Style and register

This is an important area for students at this level, particularly for Papers 2 and 3 in the exam. Many Units contain practice in style, register and appropriacy, often subsumed under some other task.

However, some Units do contain a separate phase labelled 'Style and Register'. Where these phases appear, the Coursebook and this Teacher's Guide will give individual instructions.

8 Listening

All Units contain at least one listening activity. Sometimes it will be a phase on its own, sometimes an activity within another phase, such as 'Language focus'.

There is a wide variety in form and content, from short dialogues to a collection of extracts (people giving views on the same subject), to interviews and speeches of greater length — and many are authentic recordings. All provide invaluable practice for Paper 4 in the exam.

The Coursebook and this Teacher's Guide provide instructions for all listening phases.

9 Speaking

The course contains a wide variety of tasks and activities in which students are involved in speaking. While the Coursebook and this Teacher's Guide provide instructions for all speaking phases, the following are worth noting:

- Before embarking on a discussion or debate, for example, it can be valuable to get students to pool ideas about some of the language (functions and exponents) that they might need. They might jot down such language, or you might write many of their suggestions on the board/OHP for reference during the speaking activity.
- After a task has been performed, a debriefing activity ('Now let's look at what you said ...') can also be valuable. You might, for example, make notes on students' performance (structure, pronunciation, vocabulary, intonation, appropriacy, etc.) and bring the good and bad points to students' attention.
- Recording students' speaking activities so that they can listen later and assess their own strengths and weaknesses can also be very helpful.

10 Reading

All Units will involve students in reading, and the variety of text types and activities will prepare them for the different reading tasks that they will meet in all Papers in the exam. While the Coursebook and this Teacher's Guide provide instructions for all reading activities, the following are worth noting:

- Make students aware that we do not always read, or always need to read, something in great detail. This is particularly important for some of the reading tasks in the CAE exam which require the reader to scan a text or collection of short texts.
- Students are required to work in pairs on many reading tasks throughout the course. This is to encourage them at this level to share their 'lexical knowledge' so that they are not constantly consulting a dictionary for words which a partner might well know and be able to explain.

- Some reading tasks involve unscrambling a jumbled text. Again, students are encouraged to work in pairs, to discuss, to argue and to explain why they think paragraphs should be in a certain order. Although such a task would have to be done individually in the exam, this is invaluable classroom preparation.

11 Writing

Students can usefully learn a lot about the process of writing through various activities in the classroom and it is recommended that a version of the following procedure be adopted for as many of the writing activities in the course as you think appropriate. There are many possible variations on this activity so that students do not always feel they are doing exactly the same thing — for example, changes can be rung by doing the different stages of the activity individually, in pairs, in small groups or as a whole class activity. The important thing is that students should get into the habit of following the basic four stages of writing — planning, writing, reading critically, re-writing.

- **Planning**

  1 Give/Tell the students the subject of the writing activity.

  2 As a class or in small groups students then pool ideas about the sorts of things that they might write about.

  3 It might also be appropriate, then, to consider the kind of language that students would like to use in treating this subject and to deal with any structures or vocabulary ideas that are felt to be required, but about which the students do not feel totally confident.

- **Writing**

  4 It will often be appropriate for the writing stage to be done as homework by the students individually, but you may occasionally wish to make it a paired or individual activity in the classroom where the students can ask you for help and where they have easy access to dictionaries and other reference materials. For exam purposes, it can also be useful for students to do a timed essay in school so that they get used to working within the constraints of the exam structure.

- **Reading critically**

  5 It is usually easier to read someone else's work critically than one's own. Students should be given copies of the work of some other students and they should discuss this work in pairs or in small groups. If possible, photocopy students' work so that each student's work can be looked at by more than one pair of students. Students looking at a piece of writing should be instructed to think about (a) the content in general and (b) the language used. They should be asked to find three things that they like about each piece of work and to make three suggestions for improvement. They should also be asked to mark any language use that they feel is incorrect and to add a correct version.

  The first time this activity is undertaken, it may be appropriate for you to make the comments, suggestions and corrections before the students do the re-writing. Unless the class is very small, this will be quite a time-consuming activity, but it should pay dividends in terms of the development of the class's writing skills.

  6 Students look at the criticisms, suggestions and corrections made to their own work and discuss any points with their 'critics'.

- **Re-writing**

  7 Students write a new version of their work for submission to you. They do not need to take every criticism and suggestion on board and they may well need to check who is correct over some of the 'corrections' made regarding language use. Encourage them to use grammar reference materials and good dictionaries in this process.

  NOTE: For students with word-processors, this writing activity becomes much easier in many ways. It is simple to make multiple copies, it is easier for the students to read typed work, and corrections can be made without too much difficulty.

  Finally, never forget that there are students who do not like working with others on tasks such as writing a piece of English. And further, students cannot plan and write work with a partner in the exam itself. So from time to time it is advisable to assign writing tasks for students to do completely on their own.

12 Exam Practice

The Exam Practice phases at the end of the Units do two things:

1 They provide clear examples of the different tasks students will meet in the different exam Papers.

2 They provide an opportunity to discuss how to tackle those different tasks.

While you might want to use these phases as 'mini-tests' from time to time, the Coursebook provides brief guided discussion on different approaches to the tasks and encourages students to pool ideas.

If you do decide to use the Exam Practice phases as tests (after the discussion phase), you might use the results to produce student profiles, which can then be used as a starting point to negotiate short-term goals and against which to measure progress.

13 Rounding off the Unit

While all Units in the Coursebook close with an Exam Practice phase, this Teacher's Guide also provides a number of alternative suggestions for rounding off Units.

The aim of this 'rounding-off' phase is to revise and consolidate what students have learned and practised. As with the Warm-up, this phase should involve all students and should provide an opportunity to give students a sense of achievement and progress.

14 Homework

Homework suggestions are incorporated into the Teaching Notes, which frequently suggest when particular tasks should be done or completed at home.

When a task is set as a homework assignment, always ensure

a) that it is given the necessary preparation in class, and
b) that students know exactly what they have to do.

Always check and discuss any homework assignments before beginning a new Unit.

The Cambridge Certificate in Advanced English

The page opposite the Contents page of this Teacher's Guide contains an overview of the CAE examination.

It should be read in conjunction with the GENERAL SPECIFICATIONS quoted on pages 4-10 of the Teacher's Guide to the *Longman Practice Exams for the CAE* (Longman 1991).

(For a much more detailed description of the examination, we would refer you to the SPECIFICATIONS SUMMARY and other relevant documentation published by the Cambridge Syndicate.)

CAE Advantage — Skills and Language Content/Syllabus

Pages 12-19 provide a detailed description of the skills and language content/ syllabus of the *CAE Advantage* course. Each double-page spread is devoted to five Units.

The following are supplied for each Unit:

- a statement of the CAE Paper 'bias', and a definition of the specific kind of task to be found in the Exam Practice (EP) section.
- under 'Language and Exam Skills', a list or inventory of the language skills and/or exam skills practised in the Unit. These again are often closely related to the 'bias' of the Unit.
- a breakdown of the language content of the Unit into 'Grammar' and 'Vocabulary', the grammar here corresponding largely and in most Units to the language practised in 'Language focus' sections.

CAE Advantage : Skills and Language Content/Syllabus

Unit and CAE Paper 'bias' and Exam Practice section (EP)	Language and Exam Skills
1 It's a small world Paper 1 Reading EP: Matching statements with text paragraphs	• Predicting • Skimming for gist • Scanning for specific information • Reading for more detailed understanding • Inferring meanings • Reading to summarise with section headings
2 What's in a word? Paper 2 Writing EP: Typical Section A task — writing a letter from input (letter and notes)	Writing a letter to a magazine: • Planning the letter • Co-writing (or drafting) a first version in pairs • Reading, correcting and discussing letters with others Writing a report: • Checking precise meaning and use in a dictionary
3 It's a fact! Paper 3 English in Use EP: Text with gaps followed by multiple-choice items (vocabulary)	• Filling in blanks in a text — importance of clues for structural or lexical completions • Expanding notes into a piece of extended writing, concentrating on past tense sequencing, modal forms and reporting • Proofreading
4 News of the world Paper 4 Listening EP: Listen to a lecture and correct or add to old lecture notes	• Predicting what answers a speaker might give to questions put by an interviewer • Listening specifically to check predictions • Listening and matching • Listening to discover from context the meaning of words and expressions
5 Out of this world Paper 5 Speaking EP: Phase B activity — students describe pictures to each other in order to identify them	• Describing a picture to someone who can't see it • Presenting and organising information • Summarising a written text verbally • Expressing a choice or preference, and giving reasons

Language content	
Grammar	**Vocabulary**
<ul><li>Adverbs and adverbial phrases of frequency</li><li>*Tend to do, have a tendency to do,* etc.</li><li>Commenting and criticising: *will do, is/are always doing, insist on doing,* etc.</li><li>*would do, used to do, be/get used to doing*</li><li>*be + rare/common (for ...) to do/to be done*</li></ul>	<ul><li>A brief revision of collocation</li><li>Revision of some aspects of style and register, especially the effect of vocabulary</li></ul>
<ul><li>Constructions with *wish* : *I wish I did/was, I wish I had done, I wish he would [do]*</li><li>*Can* and *be able* , all tenses: *could, was able to, will be able to, could have done,* etc.</li><li>Criticising with: *not (adj.) enough to do, suffers from a lack of ..., needs a lot more ...,* etc.</li></ul>	Some suggested ways of learning vocabulary:<ul><li>learning words in groups</li><li>using visual aids to memory</li><li>learning words in context (with collocation)</li></ul>Vocabulary connected with success and failure
<ul><li>Past simple (*did*) and continuous (*was/were doing*)</li><li>Past perfect simple (*had done*) and continuous (*had been doing*)</li><li>*Before/On/After/While + doing, ...*</li><li>Modals *may/could have done,* etc. and *may/might have been doing,* etc.</li><li>Reporting</li></ul>	Some common verb-noun collocations, for example: *make an appointment, go for a drive, reach* (or *come to*) *a conclusion, take an interest in, follow a procedure,* etc.
Reported speech:<ul><li>sequence of tenses</li><li>*that* -clauses</li><li>gerund and infinitive constructions</li><li>Passive structures: *It is believed that he is ... / He is believed to be ... / He is reputed to have won,* etc.</li><li>The 'grammar' of headlines</li></ul>	<ul><li>'Reporting' verbs: *mumble, groan, whisper, snap,* etc.</li><li>Adverbs to add to 'reporting' verbs, for example: *grudgingly admitted, apologised profusely,* etc.</li><li>Ordinary conversational English vs 'journalese', for example: *a mistake* vs *a blunder/a clanger/a howler*</li></ul>
<ul><li>*sound, look, seem* + adj.</li><li>*sound, look,* etc. + *as if/as though*</li><li>*seem + to-* infinitive</li><li>Modals (present and past): *can, could, may,* etc. *do, could/might have done* vs *could/might have been doing*</li><li>*fairly, rather, quite* + adj.</li></ul>	<ul><li>Adjectives with suffixes: *-y (sticky), -tight (airtight), -proof (waterproof), - sick (seasick)*</li><li>Adjectives with prefixes: *one- (one-day), sur- (surcharge), non- (non-speaking)*</li><li>Word families, for example: *compete, competition, competitor, competitive*</li></ul>

Unit and CAE Paper bias and Exam Practice section (EP)	Language and Exam Skills
6 We're all in the same boat Paper 1 Reading EP: Match eight possible headings or titles to the six paragraphs in a text	• Predicting • Skimming for gist • Scanning for specific information • Reading for more detailed understanding • Understanding author's attitude • Reading to summarise with section headings, and then a shorter version
7 Just a phase they're going through Paper 2 Writing EP: Section B — open-ended composition in the form of a letter to a newspaper	• Writing parts of letters based on extracts of replies from an 'agony aunt' • Writing a diary extract after literary text input • Writing a letter to a newspaper in response to an article: Planning — paragraphs and language

8 Rich man, poor man
 	
Paper 3 English in Use
 	
EP: Proofreading a text and correcting spelling and preposition/particle errors
	• Filling blanks in a text
	• Proofreading — concentrating on
	  a) spelling
	  b) commonly confused pairs of words e.g. *rob/steal*
	  c) correct preposition or particle in phrasal verbs

9 A rare and exceptional gift Paper 4 Listening EP: Listen to an authentic interview and tick points the speaker makes	• Listening specifically to check predictions • Listening to answer factual questions • Listening for opinions • Listening for structure • Listening and matching statements with what a speaker says
10 Relative values Paper 5 Speaking EP: Phase C — students describe and comment on two photographs	• Explaining and summarising a written text verbally • Reading a 'jumbled' text and discussing the correct order for the paragraphs • Discussing a trend in modern life and expressing opinions

Language content	
Grammar	**Vocabulary**
• *What /The thing we should be concerned with is ... / It's ... that we should be concerned with.* • Passives: *Something needs/will have to be done* (and *need/want doing*) • Modals: *What we have to/must/ought to/should do .../There ought to be ...* • Conditionals: *It would be better if we did ... /If we were to do ..., ... /It might have been wiser if we had done ... /Had we done ... , ... wouldn't have happened*	• The vocabulary related to world problems today: *destruction, rain forests, environmentalists, increase/ decrease, Friends of the Earth, endangered species, population explosion, global warming,* etc. • and vocabulary used when discussing such problems: *a grave danger of ..., run the risk of doing, the problem wouldn't have arisen, a ban on ...,*
• Memories with: *remember/never forget/recall doing* • Regrets with: *regret (not) doing, wish ... had done, should(n't) have done, feel bad about doing,* etc. • Habits with: *used to do, would do, was always* and *was in the habit of doing*	• The vocabulary related to adolescence: *suffer from spots, heartthrob, posters, bully, tease, grow out of,* etc. • and vocabulary used when reminiscing: *(clearly) recall, (always) remember, never forget, stick in my memory*
• Sequencing expressions of time: *As time went by/In next to no time/Eventually,* etc. • Expressing cause and effect: *to result from/in, to cause/to be caused by, to stem from, to lead to,* etc.	• Words easily confused: *rob/steal, value/price, spend/ waste; invaluable/ valueless,* etc. • Phrasal verbs with *do, make, go* and *put* : *make out a cheque, put up with someone, do up a house or flat,* etc.
• Comparisons with: *is far/considerably/a lot/much smaller than ... /* • Superlatives with: *is easily/by far/one of the best, finest, most beautiful,* etc. • Comparing with: *(almost/hardly) as ... as* • *similar to/identical to/different from; have little/a lot in common with*	• Expressions for generalising: *Generally speaking, ... / Broadly speaking, ... /By and large, ... /In the main ...* • Expressions of degree or extent: *to a degree, to a certain extent, in some respects, up to a certain point* • Adverb-adjective collections: *absolutely brilliant, extremely gifted, patently obvious, pleasantly surprised,* etc.
Tense revision, with emphasis on tense sequences (active and passive): • *does/is done; is doing/is being done; has done/has been done; has been doing; will do/will be done; will be doing* • *did/was done; was doing/was being done; had done/ had been done; had been doing; would do/would be done; would be doing* • *will have done/will have been done; will have been doing*	• Set pairs of words (adjectives, adverbs and nouns): *pros and cons, dead and buried, black and blue, time and again, flesh and blood,* etc. • Phrasal verbs (4 types): *take after, look after,* etc. *split up, fall out, break up,* etc. *live up to, look up to, get on with,* etc. *let down, bring up, lock out,* etc.

Unit and CAE Paper bias and Exam Practice section (EP)	Language and Exam Skills
11 All in a day's work Paper 1 Reading EP: Read a text with gaps and choose the correct clauses or sentences from a number of options to fill the gaps	• Predicting • Skimming for gist • Reading and looking for clues to fill in gaps • Reading to summarise each paragraph in one sentence
12 The persuaders Paper 2 Writing EP: Section A — write a letter in response to a friend's request, from letter extract and old lecture notes	• Writing and rewriting advertisements for a variety of goods and services • Rewriting sentences in a pleasanter style — to sound less blunt or rude • Changing and/or correcting advertising copy according to instructions (largely countable/uncountable nouns and expressions of quantity) • Writing a script for a 30-second radio ad
13 Travel broadens the mind Paper 3 English in Use EP: Write a handout for holidaymakers from notes provided	• Rewriting part of a brochure to include other words and expressions provided • Writing a brochure extract on the basis of visual stimulus
14 A chapter of accidents Paper 4 Listening EP: Listen and match a number of speakers with lists of topics, contexts and moods	• Listening to check predictions • Listening for a speaker's attitude • Listening to note how a speaker makes a speech effective • Listening to a number of speakers and matching what they say to pictures
15 All work and no play … Paper 5 Speaking EP: Phase C — discuss whether a particular kind of holiday (cartoon visual) is the best way to get away from it all	• Conducting a questionnaire verbally with a partner, then discussing the results • Talking about activities illustrated — which you do, can do or used to do, or would like to do • Persuading a partner/partners to go on an unusual weekend break • Describing verbally an unusual hobby and how to start an activity/hobby you know well

Language content	
Grammar	**Vocabulary**
• *to*- inf. vs *-ing* form, as in: *afraid to do/afraid of doing, frightened to do/frightened of doing, mean to do/mean doing,* etc. • Infinitive or gerund? *hope to do, aim to do, mean to do, fancy doing, dread doing, consider doing* • Purpose expressed with: *to, in order to, so as (not) to, with a view to, so that,* etc.	• Topic vocabulary related to work and workplaces: *profession, fee, part-time, salary, promote, perks,* etc. • Prefixes: *over-, re-, sub-, self-, under-, anti-,* etc., as in *overpaid, re-apply, sub-committee, self-employed, under-staffed, anti-social,* etc. • Positive and pejorative words
• Definite article, indefinite article and Ø-article: *life* vs *the life of the poor; a cinema* vs *the cinema* • Words usually singular in English: *news, public, politics, luggage,* etc. • *few/a few, little/a little, a small number of … /a vast amount of …* • Qualifying numbers/percentages with: *just over, roughly, something like, in the order of, far less than,* etc. • Revision of defining relatives: *who, that, which* (and deletion)	• Positive and negative words: *terrorist/freedom fighter, thrifty/mean, perspire/sweat, stomach/belly, (news)paper/rag,* etc. • Transitive verbs used intransitively, as in: *This machine washes marvellously.*
• Prepositions and adverbs/adverbial phrases to do with location and direction: *across, down through, in and around, away from, along,* etc. • Giving directions	• Some commonly confused words: *travel, travels, excursion, trip, journey, voyage, flight; to broaden, to widen; mind, brain, head*
• Tense revision • Active vs passive verb forms: revision of basic concept between, for example, *has done* and *has been done* • Causative *have/get something done* • Sequencing adverbs/expressions: *at first, then afterwards, in the end, at the end, on time, in time, eventually,* etc.	• Partitive 'of' with groups or numbers of things: *a flock of sheep, a block of flats, a range of mountains, a bunch of keys,* etc. • Vocabulary of natural disasters: *tidal wave, earthquake, flood, hurricane,* etc.
• Modals: *ought to/should/must do* and *you can't afford not to do* to persuade • *it + be +* adj./noun *(for you)to do / that you should do/ if you can do* • Gerund constructions: *It's no use/no good doing, It's not worth doing, There's no point in doing,* etc. • Gerund and infinitive constructions: *manage to do, succeed in doing, have no difficulty in doing, fail to do,* etc.	• Verbs with the same form as nouns: *a boot/to boot, an eye/to eye, a mirror/to mirror, a hammer/to hammer,* etc. • Phrasal verbs with the particle *off: warn sby off, ring off, knock off (work), bring sthg off, hit it off, pay off, strain off,* etc.

Unit and CAE Paper bias and Exam Practice section (EP)	Language and Exam Skills
16 Body matters Paper 1 Reading EP: Read and match suggested headings or titles with paragraphs in the text	• Reading a 'jumbled' text in order to reconstruct it • Reading paragraphs and suggesting what might have preceded each • Tackling the Reading Paper in the exam
17 Love makes the world go round Paper 2 Writing EP: Section B — choose one from two open-ended compositions, one a letter, the other a brochure	• Writing an entry for a competition • Writing a statement of opinion • Writing an assessment of candidates' potential and suitability for a post • Writing a rejection letter • Tackling the Writing Paper in the exam
18 There's no accounting for taste Paper 3 English in Use EP: Text completion in a suitable register	• Writing a description of your own worst (holiday) souvenir • Proofreading a magazine arts review page in order to check spellings — and then match the headings with the correct paragraphs. • Proofreading a newspaper article to correct errors with prepositions • Tackling the English in Use Paper in the exam
19 I didn't read what it said! Paper 4 Listening EP: Listen and match a number of speakers with listed topics and contexts	• Listening to check predictions • Listening to match products/articles with verbal descriptions • Listening for specific information — things that someone did wrong • Listening to match actions with tools/implements listed • Tackling the Listening Paper in the exam
20 Into the future! Paper 5 Speaking EP: Phase C — students discuss a topic with reference to visual material	• Discussing a photo and caption to predict the contents of an article • Discussing the advantages and disadvantages of living in a particular place • Explaining processes and procedures • Discussing the future • Tackling the Speaking Paper in the exam

Language content	
Grammar	**Vocabulary**
• Possibility and potential expressed through modals, adjectives, adverbs and nouns • Ellipsis: *People suffering* (= People who suffer), *babies born* (= babies who are/were born), etc. • Giving advice with: *one thing you should(n't) do is ...*, *it might be an idea to do, the important thing to remember is ...*, etc.	• Vocabulary connected with body matters, accidents and illness: *earache, a twisted ankle, a nosebleed, a rash, blisters, a stiff neck,* etc.
• *someone, anyone, no one* • *some good champagne* vs *a good champagne* vs *some good champagnes* • *a/an, the, some, any* • Relative pronouns: *who, that, which* and ellipsis: *the boy sitting on the left,* etc.	• Compound nouns: *a lawn mower, a tin opener, an exercise bike, a food mixer,* etc. • Compound nouns formed from phrasal verbs: *an outcast, a showdown, upkeep, downfall, output,* etc. • Some exclamations: *Well, I never (did)! Not on your life! Bless you!* etc.
• Likes and dislikes: *quite/rather/really/absolutely + adore/hate/loathe + doing* • *What I like/dislike most about ... /The thing I think is good about ...* • Preferences with: *I'd rather do* and *I prefer to do* • Regrets: *I wish I hadn't done* or *I regret doing/having done* • Suggestions: *Why not do ...?, Why don't you do ...?, If I were you, I'd ...*	• 'Beautiful' words (*attractive, appealing, exquisite,* etc.) and 'ugly' words (*awful, grotesque, repulsive,* etc.) • Expressions in which the preposition makes the difference: *make a fuss of* vs *make a fuss about*
• Use of participles and noun/adjective phrases to add information • Revision of past tenses: *I'd no sooner done .. than ... ; I was just going to do ... when ... ; When I'd finally done ..., I did ...* • Passives, esp. with modals: *it should be checked, this can be obtained,* etc.	• 'Action' verbs in groups: *rub, scrub, wipe, graze,* etc.; *dip, soak, rinse,* etc. • Cooking verbs: *whisk, stir, pour, scald, cool, remove from heat,* etc. • Tools and implements: *hammer, screwdriver, electric drill, paper clips,* etc.
• Future forms: *will/might do/be doing, will/might have done/have been doing* • Impersonal/anticipatory *it*: *it's only natural (that) such things should happen* • Making compound sentences using: *Whereas, on the other hand, while, apart from, not to mention, let alone*	• Three-word phrasal verbs: *let sby in on, prise sby away from,* etc.; *boil down to, come up with, shy away from,* etc. • Partitive structures: *a pinch of salt, a column of smoke, a herd of cows,* etc.; *a grain of truth, a shred of evidence, a hint of irony,* etc.

Teaching notes

The following pages contain Teaching Notes on a Unit-by-Unit, page-by-page basis. For each Unit we have provided the following where applicable:

- Suggestions for **Warm-up** activities. Very few of these appear in the Coursebook itself. Just occasionally we suggest beginning a lesson immediately with the first phase of the Unit, since we feel the material itself will serve as both presentation and warm-up.

- **Relevance to the CAE exam** of all major phases in a Unit.

- **Background notes and/or vocabulary** for texts (written and spoken).

- **Tapescript** references to the Coursebook, with an indication of authentic recordings.

- **Tapescripts** for Paper 4 (Listening) Exam Practice phases.

- **Classroom treatment** notes for each major phase in a Unit, whether it be 'Read and discuss', 'Language focus', 'Listen, discuss and write', 'Exam Practice', etc.

- Occasional **alternative treatment** for a phase, other than that suggested in the Coursebook.

- Extra questions and points to highlight when dealing with reading and listening texts.

- **Answers** or **Expected/Possible/Suggested answers** for all exercises.

- Suggestions for **Rounding off the Unit**.

IMPORTANT: You are strongly advised to read the notes for a Unit thoroughly before teaching it so that you need only refer to them when, for example, giving further prompts or quickly checking answers, examples or expected responses for certain exercises.

As well as suggesting which tasks might be set as homework assignments, the Teaching notes also suggest pre-Unit home study from time to time.

Symbols and abbreviations used in the Teaching notes:

▷▣	=	recorded on cassette
adj.	=	adjective
adv.	=	adverb
AmE	=	American English
coll.	=	colloquial
CB	=	Coursebook
e.g.	=	for example
esp.	=	especially
etc.	=	etcetera
ex(s).	=	exercise(s)
fml.	=	formal
i.e.	=	that is
p(p).	=	page(s)
para(s).	=	paragraph(s)
S(s)	=	student(s)
sby	=	somebody
sthg	=	something
tech.	=	technical
usu.	=	usually
v.	=	versus, compared with

NOTE: The majority of vocabulary definitions in these notes are taken from the *Longman Dictionary of Contemporary English*.

1 It's a small world

(The expression *It's a small world* is often said when we meet someone that we know well or meet every day at work, college or whatever — but this time perhaps while we are miles from home and not expecting to see them. In everyday conversation, we would often add the tag and say *It's a small world, isn't it?*)

Coursebook pp.6-7

Warm-up

Here are four **alternative suggestions**, all with books closed:

1 Ask the class: 'When do we use the expression in English 'It's a small world (isn't it?)'? What do you say in *your* language in the same situation? If you say something like it, do you say 'small world', 'close world', or what? In English it's always a 'small world': what's this an example of? [Looking forward to collocation on CB p.8.]

2 Ask the class: 'Do you think it's a 'smaller' world than our grandparents lived in? If so, how, and why?' Discuss in groups, then back to the class.

3 If a multi-national class in the UK or elsewhere, ask Ss to find five shops, companies or restaurants that are to be found in all their countries and/or five things that they could all read/watch in their countries in their own language (Walt Disney films/cartoons, Dallas, Agatha Christie, etc). Through discussion, Ss try to create a 'Top Five'.

4 Give a situation you have been in where you could have said 'It's a small world!'. (e.g. Once when I was a student at university, the same university my father taught at, I was on holiday with my parents in Italy. We were staying at a hotel in Florence. On the first day we went down to breakfast and who should we see at the next table but a girl from my history class at university and one of my father's fellow lecturers. We hadn't known that they even knew each other, but it turned out that they were on their honeymoon! I'm afraid the last people they wanted to see were colleagues from home — but it's a small world, isn't it!) Then ask for Ss' own anecdotes.

Read and discuss

CAE Relevance: Papers 1 and 5 (Reading and Speaking)

Background notes and vocabulary

'Food fraud down under' by Peter Ustinov
This article appeared in the newspaper *The European*, which is sold all over Europe and in many other places in the world. In 1991 the actor and writer Peter Ustinov contributed a regular weeekly column in which he commented on matters and events of the week. This piece is written in a slightly ironic style with some gentle humour. One particular feature is the use of metaphor and unusual collocations. (See Vocabulary CB p.8.)
at large: free, uncontrolled: here, Ustinov is free to discuss any topic
down under: common expression to mean Australia and New Zealand
cohesive: tending to stick together; producing cohesion
cliché: an unchanging idea or expression used so commonly that it has lost much of its expressive force
Auckland: the capital, largest city and chief port of New Zealand
neo-Gothic: of or relating to the revival of Gothic art and architecture in the 18th and 19th centuries, esp. in Europe and North America
tucked among the skyscrapers: built and almost hidden among the skyscrapers
a distant hint: a small sign or suggestion in the distance
a slight condiment: a condiment is a powder or liquid used for giving a special taste to food — pepper and salt are condiments — but here the word is used unusually to mean a slight taste or feeling of San Francisco
Tonga: (or Friendly Islands) an independent sovereign state in the South Pacific, consisting of some 150 volcanic and coral islands
a meticulous lass: a girl who is very careful and shows attention to detail in her work
folksy artefact: an article having the character of folk art ['folksy' here is derogatory]

vaunted (a menu): boasted (a menu) — a slightly unusual use of 'vaunt'

precipitate: wildly hasty, done without care or thought

Hollywood films of the Thirties: films made in Hollywood in the 1930s in which an actor would play an Italian restaurateur in an extravagant style

trattoria: an Italian restaurant, pronounced 'tratto'ria', NOT 'tra'ttoria' to rhyme with 'Vic'toria'

The cat was out of the bag: 'To let the cat out of the bag' means to tell a secret, often unintentionally

launch into a tarantella: to begin a tarantella, a rapid Italian dance for two people

'Continental': here, describing food you might find anywhere on the Continent of Europe

spread like wildfire: spread very quickly

'nouvelle cuisine': the French expression (literally 'new cooking') used to describe a method of preparing food in which appearance is more important than taste or quantity

Halifax / warm Yorkshire accent: Halifax is a town in the county of Yorkshire in the north of England: a Yorkshire English accent is quite distinctive and the writer clearly felt it was warm or homely

Exs. 1-6

Classroom treatment

Before Ss undertake the different tasks or exercises (1-6), it is worth explaining the different reading skills in this sequence of activities, as they are all important and they will need all of them when they come to do Paper 1 in the exam. They are:

1 Predicting

2 Skimming

3 Scanning for specific information

4 Checking comprehension

5 Dealing with unfamiliar words/expressions

6 Summarising by giving headings to sections or groups of paragraphs

Ss might best work in pairs throughout these exercises, though you should pause frequently to check answers i.e. when you think the majority have completed a task.

In ex. 4, we suggest S1 reads from the beginning to the word 'Victoria', and S2 from 'The cat was out of the bag' to the end.

Ex. 5 could be done as homework. The reason why this vocabulary task follows 1-4 is essentially to discourage Ss from reading and trying to understand *every* word

right from the start. They do not even need to understand *every* word in order to do ex. 6.

Possible answers

1 Something to do with food in Australia/New Zealand — but there's something wrong with the food — it's a 'fraud'. And, looking at the photo and caption, he might be going to argue that all cities in the world look the same?

3 Countries and nationalities: New Zealand, English, Italian, the Middle East, Lebanese, Japanese, England, Singapore, Tonga. And other countries (Zimbabwe, Canada, the USA and Germany) are implied.

4 S1, first half: What's quite striking? Where was the writer when he wrote the article? What kind of country did the view from his room suggest? etc.

S2, second half: Why was 'the cat out of the bag'? How was the restaurant owner dressed? What was the food like? etc.

5 See Background notes and vocabulary above.

6 Possible section headings:

a) Where in the world am I? b) 'Continental' — certainly not Italian! c) Earrings and Japanese design d) A sound of home

Look, discuss and write

CAE Relevance: Papers 2 and 5 (Writing and Speaking)

Exs. 1 and 2

Classroom treatment

The aim of the activities here is to prepare and write a letter to *The European* in response to the Ustinov article. Begin by asking the whole class about the photo. What does it show? What does it demonstrate? — The fact that you'll find a McDonald's (fast-food restaurant) in most countries in the world.

Then ask for suggestions for other things that you might expect to find almost anywhere in the world, e.g. Levi jeans, Coke, 'Space Invaders' machines, etc. Ss then work in pairs to write a list of perhaps ten such 'universal' things. Give five minutes, then split the pairs so that each S works with another to try to add to his/her list. See how many the whole class can agree on.

Ss then work in different pairs again, this time planning and beginning to write the paragraphs for their letter in ex. 2. Go round helping, questioning and suggesting. A clean version should be written for homework.

(See this TG Introduction p.9 for a description of phases of writing.)

Sample paragraph

This is a sample of the paragraphs students might aim to write.

Sir (*or* Dear Sir),

I refer to Peter Ustinov's entertaining article in which he argues that it's a small world nowadays. I entirely/heartily agree. Like him, it seems to me that one large city in the world is just like any other. And if you were just dropped into a hotel room in any of them, you might have to ask where you were!

Recently I was lucky enough to visit a city in the Far East. On the drive from the airport into the centre I was struck by how different things were — people, villages, buildings, even noises ... But on reaching my hotel, I found myself back in an 'international world' again. The receptionist was a fellow countryman/woman who even greeted me in my own language!

Coursebook pp.8-9

Vocabulary: a brief revision of collocation

CAE Relevance: Papers 2 and 3 (Writing and English in Use)

Ex. 1

Classroom treatment

Write the phrases a) *the world has shrunk* and b) *hammered discreetly* on the board/OHP and ask: 'Which is a common collocation, and which is not?' Point out that authors and journalists sometimes use unusual collocations to create a special effect: here, for example, *hammer discreetly* is in fact a paradox.

(If Ss do not understand the concept of 'collocation', explain by giving examples of words that naturally go together in English and those that do not, for example 'to earn a living', NOT 'to keep *or* have a living'.)

Answers

the world has shrunk — common collocation;
hammered discreetly — unusual collocation.

Ex. 2

Classroom treatment

Ss work in pairs reading the article on pages 6-7 and noting common and unusual collocations. Check with the whole class before going on to ex. 3.

Answers

Common collocations: the world has shrunk; tucked among the skyscrapers; press the button; answer a call; temporarily replaced; visit a restaurant; proclaim itself to be; confirm one's doubts; kiss someone on both cheeks; the cat was out of the bag; a thick accent; wear one's hair long; spread like wildfire; pierced ears; do (= tidy/clean) a room

Unusual collocations: prove something elegantly; a distant hint of the sea; add a slight condiment; vaunt a menu; awaken suspicions (normally arouse suspicions); hammer discreetly; warm accent

Ex. 3

Classroom treatment

Ss should supply common collocations here. They must be able to defend any unusual and/or humorous ones they produce, i.e. tell you where they might say or write them, and why!

Possible answers

to move house; a sore throat; physically/severely/mentally handicapped; a jar of jam/handcream/honey; to take sby/sthg for granted; a can/bottle of Coke; to take/heed/ignore someone's advice; big/small/enormous/dainty/pointed ears; to go for/take a walk; to go on/set out on a long journey

Language focus

CAE Relevance: All Papers

Exs. 1-5

Classroom treatment

1 Do all the exercises (except ex.3) in pairs or groups.

2 Tell Ss to read the Grammar Commentary at home, either as preparation for the lesson, or as revision at the end of the lesson and before the debate.

3 Explain that all the exercises here will give practice in language that Ss might well want to use in the Debate (p.9). They may want to do the following:

Ex. 1 Say how often people do things ...

Most of the temporal adverbs here should be known and to that extent the activity is revision. However, certain words such as *invariably* or *habitually* may be new to some Ss and they can either help each other or use a dictionary — preferably an English-English dictionary.

Ss work in pairs to order the adverbs. Check with the whole class by writing up the concensus on the board/OHP before proceeding to the second activity.

Again Ss work in pairs to deduce some of the 'rules' about the position of temporal adverbs by trying them out in different positions in the sentences. Check with the whole class.

Answers

Possible order:

NEVER, almost never, hardly ever/scarcely ever, very rarely, seldom, occasionally, quite often, often, frequently, commonly, generally, usually, regularly, repeatedly, nearly always, habitually, invariably, ALWAYS

Deduced 'rules':

Words like this come after the verb *be* in 'I am always/often/ frequently, etc. surprised ...'.

They come before the main verb in questions like 'Do you always/invariably know ...?' (although not all of the adverbs would fit in this sentence and have meaning).

They come after the first auxiliary verb or modal in a sentence like 'People will often/generally/ occasionally try to ...'.

They come before the verb in a sentence like 'They seldom dress like that ...'.

Ex. 2 Talking about tendencies and frequency of actions ...

1 Give Ss (or try to draw from them) some questions they might use in a survey about how often their classmates or colleagues tend to do things.

2 Give them time to write perhaps five-ten questions.

3 They then go round asking other Ss within a certain time (say five minutes) and noting their answers.

4 When they have carried out their brief 'survey', they should at least begin to write a report to read to the rest of the class, a report in which they use some of the language suggested. (The final or clean writing of this report might be given as a homework task.) They should try to use the following in their report. Point out the way they are used: *to tend to do; to have a tendency to do; to be inclined to do; to admit to doing*

Possible answers

Some possible survey questions:

How often do you go to the cinema? Occasionally? Frequently? Never?

Do you ever go swimming? If so, how often?

Do you tend to buy clothes once a week? once a month? whenever you can? only when you really have to?

Possible sentences in the report:

Every now and again, a student admitted to never doing any homework.

As a rule, students (in the class) tend to go to the cinema about once a month.

More often than not, students (in this class) are inclined to

do their homework as quickly as they can when they get home.

Ex. 3 Comment and criticise ...

▷ 📼 *Tapescript* (See Coursebook p.147.)
Play the cassette once for Ss to answer the question 'How well do they get on?'. The answer must be 'Not very well'(!) — but ask Ss to say briefly why. (The language they use, the tone of their voices, their intonation, etc.)

Then play it again, pausing frequently for Ss to write down the different ways the man and woman comment on or criticise each other's actions. When they have done this, get Ss to tell you or others in a group what they don't like about other people, e.g. 'I can't stand X. He's always telling lies.' / 'I'm getting a bit fed up with my supervisor at work. She *will* keep on asking me what I'm doing. She can *see* what I'm doing!' etc.

Expected answers

You're always telling me about people you've met.

You *will* keep interrupting all the time! (Note that the word *will* is stressed.)

You just can't stop complaining, can you?

You just can't get out of the habit of making up these stories about famous people.

You're so used to making up stories that you just can't stop!

Ex. 4 Compare past and present habits with *would do, used to do* and *be/get used to doing* ...

Make sure Ss know what each of these structures means and how each is used. Refer them to the Grammar Commentary or explain briefly using the examples given.

Ss work in pairs or small groups discussing some of the differences between life today and life, say, seventy years ago. After five minutes or so, a pair or group spokesperson should briefly report to the class as a whole some of the ideas they came up with, as far as possible using sentences like this: *Seventy years ago people would nearly always grow all their own vegetables and things, but nowadays most people have got used to buying what they need at the market or supermarket.*

Ex. 5 Comment on how rare or common things are ...

Ask Ss to read the paragraph at the top of page 9 quickly and to pick out the sentences which use the words *rare, unusual, common* and *unheard of.* They should then read the text again, cover it and tell you what it said — including the sentences or phrases they have written down. Then give five minutes or so for Ss to write a short paragraph about their own country in the same way. Go round, looking at what Ss are writing. Spot-check some at the end of the writing phase.

If time is short in class, set this whole exercise for homework, but check it carefully at the beginning of the next lesson.

Answers

It was common ... to come across ... / It is rare to find ... / it will be unheard of for men to come home ... / [it will be] most unusual for the evening meal to be prepared on an open fire ...

NOTE: Additionally, students might also find that they will need to use the words *whatever, whoever, wherever, whichever, whenever, however*. Quickly write up the six words on the board/OHP and say: 'Some people think it's terrible that everything's the same everywhere. But there are advantages. What are some of them?' Discuss the question and use phrases or sentences like this. You can replace the verb *find* by verbs of your own. —

Whatever you do, you('ll) [find ...]

Wherever you go, you're (quite) likely to [find ...]

However far you travel, you're bound/ (almost) sure to [find ...]

Debate: 'This house believes that the world is now so small there's no point in travelling.'

CAE Relevance: Paper 5 (Speaking)

Classroom treatment

We suggest that this should be a whole (45/50-minute) lesson. Home study preparation — Ss revise the Language focus material practised on pp.8-9 together with the Grammar Commentary and make notes on whether they think it's worth travelling to different countries now or not, perhaps prompted by the pictures on p.9.

Explain the rules of a formal debate and how it works. They are as follows:

- The discussion point (or statement to be discussed) is called 'The Motion'.
- There is a Chairperson.
- There are two speakers for each side of the motion — a Proposer *for* the motion, and a Main Speaker *against* : each has a Seconder. Speakers should be asked to prepare their speeches at home. Ss must

understand that they are expected to argue strongly either for or against the motion, regardless of their own personal feelings.

- The Chairperson, the Main Speakers and the Seconders sit at a table in front of the audience/ class, the Proposer and Seconder *for* the motion to the Chairperson's right, the Main Speaker and Seconder *against* the motion to the Chairperson's left.
- The Chairperson begins the proceedings by announcing 'The motion before us today is "This house believes that the world ..., etc.". I'd like to introduce our speakers. On my right, and speaking for or in favour of the motion are ... and ..., and on my left, speaking against the motion, ... and ... . I call upon ... to propose the motion.'
- The Proposer *for* the motion then stands and talks for one, two or three minutes. [Set a sensible time limit for each speaker.]
- The Chairperson then calls on the Main Speaker *against* the motion and he or she likewise speaks for one, two or three minutes.
- The Chairperson then asks each of the 'Seconders' to speak in turn.
- The discussion is then 'thrown open to the floor'. This means that anyone in the audience may put up his or her hand to attract the attention of the Chairperson and then speak on the subject (for or against). This part of the debate might take anything up to 15-20 minutes and as many students as possible should be encouraged to participate and say something.
- The Chairperson then invites each of the main speakers to speak briefly again and to sum up their main arguments.
- Finally a vote is taken. The Chairperson stands, thanks the speakers for their contributions, and then says: 'We will now take a vote. The motion is: "This house believes that the world is now so small there's no point in travelling". All those in favour of the motion, (raise your hands). [He/She counts.] All those against, (raise your hands). [He/She counts.] The motion is carried. *or* The motion has been defeated.'
Ss should vote on how well they think the case has been presented (for or against).

Either appoint yourself Chairperson, or suggest that the class elect a Chairperson. Since this is an idea that might be used again from time to time throughout the course with other topics, it might be best if you were to act as Chairperson this first time to give a clear example of the Chairperson's role in directing a debate.

As a follow-up, you might ask Ss to write a short report of the debate (some 200-250 words) as if for a local newspaper. If so, the report should state where the debate took place and when, what the motion was, who the speakers were, some of their arguments, some points made from 'the floor', and whether the motion was carried or defeated.

(A simpler approach, of course, is to discuss the motion or topic in pairs, then in small groups, and then as a class (a 'pyramid' discussion). But we suggest that the set format of a formal debate is one that will appeal to students at this level and one which they will relate to and enjoy taking part in on a number of future occasions.)

Coursebook pp.10-11

Style and register: It's not only *what* you write — it's *how* you write it

CAE Relevance: Papers 2 and 3 (Writing and English in Use)

Exs. 1 and 2

Classroom treatment

Students at this level must begin to appreciate differences in style, particularly formal and informal, and this is reflected in CAE Papers 2 and 3. The aim of this phase is to check what students already know and to begin to build on it.

1 To introduce the phase, give this pair of sentences (orally and on the board/OHP) and ask Ss how and why they are different — to get the ideas of formal and informal, written and spoken.

   a) *In my youth, we rarely paid a visit to my grandfather.*

   b) *When I was young, we didn't often go and see Grandpa.*

   Ask questions such as: Do they both give the same information? Do you think one would be spoken and one written? If both could be spoken, what sort of person might say one, and what sort of person the other? Do you think one is formal and one informal? If so, what makes the difference?

   Try to get as much from the class by discussion before confirming:

a) is somewhat formal and might be found written in a novel or autobiography, or spoken by a very well educated and perhaps elderly person. b) is much more informal and would almost certainly be spoken, or written in a personal letter.

The expressions and words *in my youth, rarely, pay a visit to* and *grandfather* are more formal than *when I was young, not often, go and see* and *Grandpa*.

Ss then work in pairs studying and discussing the four pairs of sentences in the same way. Check their conclusions when they have all finished.

Possible answers

1a is formal and would be seen on a written document. 1b is fairly informal, and almost certainly spoken.

2a is informal and almost certainly spoken. 2b is formal and probably written, or in a formal conversation, for example, an interview.

3a is very informal, almost slangy ('keep his mouth shut'). 3b is reasonably formal, written or spoken.

4a is reasonably formal, with the use of the passive, and the words *similar, invariably* and *prior to*. It would probably be written. 4b on the other hand is quite informal and sounds as if it might be spoken — especially with the use of *are always saying, things like that* and *just before*.

2 Ss work again in pairs to do this exercise. Before they begin, however, ask all to read the first two sentences and to tell you whether they think it is formal or informal in tone, and why. When they have established that it is reasonably formal, they should then do the exercise. NOTE: This is not an exercise in literary writing and there are no right or wrong answers. The aim is merely to help students begin to appreciate what sounds pretty informal and to try to replace such phrases or sentences with more formal-sounding English!

Possible version (rewritten parts underlined)

... they are much alike in so many other ways. <u>When you enter through the front door, the interior is grand and luxurious. A considerable amount of time and money has (clearly) been spent/lavished on it.</u> The staff, too, I find, are invariably and extremely polite, without being obsequious. <u>They certainly give the impression that they have</u> been well trained. And <u>further,</u> of course, <u>absolutely everything is spotlessly clean. The furnishings too, from the style of furniture to the massive chandeliers, invariably give an impression of familiarity.</u>

Exam Practice: Paper 1 Reading

CAE Relevance: Paper 1 (Reading)

Exs. a and b

Classroom treatment

a Explain carefully that this is one of the kinds of reading test that Ss will meet in Paper 1. It employs a testing technique they may not have seen before. Read the rubric with them and ask them to work in pairs to discuss the questions. They should make a list of problems for 1, and a list of ways of tackling the task for 2. In some ways, discussion of the problems and then ways of tackling a task like this is more important than actually doing it, so if necessary use classroom time for discussion and set the actual reading 'test' as homework.

1 Possible problems

Can't understand some of the questions.

Can't understand some of the text.

Do we read the text first, then look at the questions and try to remember where the information was?

Or do we read the questions (all or one by one), then go to the text and scan it to find the relevant information?

Do the number of questions match the number of paragraphs? Or are perhaps some of the paragraphs not even referred to in the questions? (This is actually sometimes the case.)

How can we do the exercise *quickly*?

2 Possible approaches (or ways of tackling the task)

Read all the questions once, then read the text to try and match the information.

Read the first question, then scan the text looking for the matching information.

Read all the questions to understand the range *and* to get an idea of what the whole text might be about — then go back to the first question and scan the text for that information.

Read the whole article first, then read the first question and try to remember where the information was.

etc.

Above all, practise looking for clues in texts, rather than always reading every word in a text from beginning to end.

Ex. b

Background notes and vocabulary

> 'Spin-offs from Space'
> This slightly edited article appeared in *The Times* newspaper.
> *Foiling the cold:* This is a pun on the word 'foil'. As a noun, it is metal beaten or rolled into very thin paperlike sheets: as a verb, it means to prevent (someone) from succeeding. Thus, using foil to foil the cold.
> *spin-off:* a usually useful product or result other than the main thing
> *domestic gadgetry:* all kinds of gadgets or tools that can be used in the home
> *catalyst:* a substance which, without itself changing, causes chemical activity to quicken
> *impetus:* here, a push forward
> *anecdotal:* containing or full of anecdotes — short interesting or amusing stories
> *Apollo Moon programme:* One of the American programmes to send astronauts to the moon
> *Nasa:* [pronounced as a word, not individual letters] National Aeronautics and Space Administration (USA), the organisation responsible for American space exploration

Answers

1 Paragraph 4; 2 Paragraph 1; 3 Paragraph 3; 4 Paragraph 5; 5 Paragraph 10; 6 Paragraph 2; 7 Paragraph 8; 8 Paragraph 6; 9 Paragraph 12; 10 Paragraph 11

Rounding off the Unit

Why not round off this Unit by asking Ss in groups to think of and list other things that might become common all over the world in the next few years — things that have not been mentioned or discussed in the Unit?

OR Ask Ss to tell each other, again in groups, what different customs in their own country/countries they think a foreign visitor would need to understand before, for example, trying to do business there.

2 *What's in a word?*

```
| Coursebook pp.12-13 |
```

Warm-up

Here are three **alternative suggestions**, all with books closed:

1 Ask students to note down (a) how many words they think there are in English (490,000 + another 300,000 technical words according to the *Guinness Book of Records*), and (b) how many words they think make up 90% of any text (about 2,000).

Note: UK residents who have undergone a full 16 years of education use perhaps 5,000 in speech and another 10,000 words in written communication. English has the largest vocabulary of any language in the world.

Compare the students' answers: what were the highest and lowest suggestions in each case?

This will ideally lead into some discussion of what a word is — how many words are *word, words, wordy, wordiness, to reword, to word*, etc? And how many words is *to get rid of*? And how many words is *row*?

2 Ask Ss to write down three languages they wish they could speak and then to read them out to the class giving a reason for each language chosen.

3 Tell Ss: 'You are filling in an application form for a job and this is the last part of the form. Write what you would put on the form.

Which languages do you speak?
How well do you speak each of them?
Do you think you have a flair for learning languages? Why?/Why not?
As far as languages are concerned, what do you think you are good at?
Where do your weaknesses lie?

Now compare your answers with those written by a partner. Do you think your partner has given an accurate assessment of his/her ability?'

Read and discuss

CAE Relevance: Papers 1 and 5 (Reading and Speaking)

Classroom treatment

Ask Ss to read and prepare answers to the quiz in small groups.

When all have finished, check the answers.

Give a mark for each correct answer; one for each correct country or language named in questions 1, 2 and 3; one mark for the students who were nearest with the questions which involved guessing numbers (i.e. questions 8 and 9).

Answers

1 a Swedish; b Spanish; c Turkish; d Japanese; e Greek; f Arabic; g Russian; h Pidgin

2 English, and Scots and Irish Gaelic, Welsh and Cornish, which are all native Gaelic languages still spoken in areas of the British Isles.

There are also, of course, large immigrant communities speaking Urdu, Bengali, Gujurati, Polish, Italian, etc..

3 The British Isles, USA, Canada, Australia, New Zealand, South Africa, Caribbean islands, India, Nigeria, etc.

4 Mandarin Chinese (825 million); English (431 million); Hindi (325 million). Next comes Spanish (320 million) and Russian (289 million) — according to *The Top Ten of Everything*.

5 He spoke German to his horse and Spanish to God.

6 He spoke Italian to women — and French to men.

7 Kangaroo.

8 The word *set,* which is said to have 56 noun uses, 126 verbal uses and ten adjectival uses (*Guinness Book of Records*).

9 The Ubykh language in the Caucasus has 80-85 distinct consonant sounds and the Rotokas language in central Bougainville Island has only 6 (b, g, k, p, r and t).

10 The earliest known example of alphabetic writing was found at Ugarit (now Ras Sharma) in Syria. It was a tablet of 72 cuneiform letters and has been dated to 1450 B.C., so it is nearly three and a half thousand years old.

Students' own quiz questions

Suggestion for working with the students' own quiz questions:

- Have each group ask a question in turn.
- Give the group a point if their question is in perfect English.
- The groups are allowed to confer on each question and to write down their answers. Only one answer is allowed for each question.

- When all the questions have been answered, the answers are then checked and the groups can total their scores.

Read, discuss and write

CAE Relevance: All Papers

Background notes and vocabulary

> *census form:* the form people have to fill in when a country's population is being counted
> *Hispanics:* Spanish-speaking people in the USA, either native-born or immigrants from Mexico, Cuba, etc.
> *substantial:* large
> *funds:* money

Exs. 1 and 2

Classroom treatment

1 Point out to Ss that, in the CAE, they have to be able to read fast and to get the gist of an article from a quick reading. Allow them no more than two minutes to read as outlined in question 1.

2 Question 2 may be dealt with in pairs or as a full class as appropriate.

Suggested answers

The important points about each letter are:

a The writer is clearly an American who is angry about the proposal to produce US census forms in Spanish. We know he/she is angry because of the reference to the proposal as 'absolutely ridiculous'. Although there is a large Spanish-speaking population in the US, the writer feels that they have to learn English.

b The writer is sad: *it grieves me* = it makes me sad. He/She has been listening to BBC radio broadcasts and has heard a number of things which he/she considers incorrect about the language. All the points objected to are 'mistakes' which are now so commonly made by native speakers that it is perhaps wrong to call them mistakes any more. The letter was, therefore, probably written by an older person or by someone rather pedantic in their views — a language teacher, perhaps. A split infinitive occurs when the speaker or writer separates the 'to' part of the infinitive from the other part by some other word — 'to quietly talk', for instance. 'Between you and I' should be 'between you and me' The word 'hopefully' used with the meaning of 'it is hoped that' is considered by some to be very American and bad style. According to such people, 'hopefully' has the perfectly good meaning of 'full of hope' as in 'to travel hopefully is better than to arrive', and it should not be used in any other way.

c This letter is about Esperanto, an artificial language created with the idea of having one very simple language which everyone could learn to speak in order to communicate with people of all different nationalities.

The writer is arguing against Esperanto and for English as a language for worldwide communication, suggesting that everyone should be encouraged to learn English whatever their mother tongue may be. This writer is not angry in the same way as those of all the other letters but the suggestion he/she is making might well make some other people angry. It seems certain that the writer is a native English speaker.

d The writer is a teacher in an area where many of the children are from immigrant families. However, these children are being taught, not in their own language, but that of the country where they are living. The writer of the letter speaks the children's own language but is the only teacher to do so. He/She feels that this is wrong. He/She uses the strong word 'disgrace' to describe the situation and so we know that he/she is angry about it. He/She feels that children should be helped to learn about their own language and culture and should not have an alien culture imposed on them. (*alien* means much the same as foreign but it is a rather colder, sadder word suggesting the loneliness and unhappiness of being in a foreign place). The person who wrote letter **a** would almost certainly disagree with this writer.

e Again the writer is angry and this writer is almost certainly a woman with feminist views (although it could, perhaps, be a 'new man'). She is objecting to the use of *man* when referring to someone who may be a man or a woman or when talking about people in general. This used to be done a great deal in English. Churchill said, however, that when talking about mankind he always thought of 'man as embracing woman'. The use of the words given in the letter is now considered sexist and most writers will try to avoid them where possible.

Alternatives for each could be: *bravely* (= manfully); *chairperson* (= chairman); *humankind, the human species* (= mankind); *sporting* (= sportsmanlike); *the typical citizen* (= the man in the street); *staffing the switchboard* (= manning the switchboard); *courageous* (= manly); *tastes differ* (= one man's meat is another man's poison).

Exs. 3 and 4

Classroom treatment

3 Ss should discuss in pairs which letters they agree with and which they disagree with. They should then form a foursome with another pair and compare their feelings.

4 Ss write letters in pairs: they can either work with their original partner or a new partner. Draw attention to the fact that Ss have to add some new points of their own as well as comment on some or all of the letters in the Coursebook. Make sure that plenty of time is spent planning the letter and writing a plan before any full-scale writing is done. (See Introduction p.9.)

Either stick up the letters on the wall for everyone to walk round and read

or read out some or all of the letters to the other students asking for comments from the class as a whole both on the language and the content of each letter.

Model answer

Here is an example of the kind of letter which good students at this level might be expected to produce:

Dear Sir,

The recent letters which you printed on various aspects of the subject of language were of considerable interest to me as I am currently studying the connections between language and politics.

In their way, all of the points made are political points. Language is defined as our major means of communication and yet so often it seems to cause problems between different groups of people. People of all language backgrounds naturally wish to ensure that their own native language is preserved and respected. They wish to make certain that no language used fuels prejudice with regard to their own particular race, sex or class.

For this reason I strongly favour the more widespread use of the neutral international language, Esperanto. The use of Esperanto in multilingual situations would free native languages to develop naturally within their own cultures. Moreover, Esperanto does not carry with it the nationalist, sexist and class-ridden prejudices present, albeit on a subconscious level, in all the main world languages. It is simple to learn and can be used to carry out all the functions that would be required of it.

Indeed, might I suggest that your magazine could make an invaluable contribution in this area by carrying a series of

teach-yourself-Esperanto articles over the next few months? Yours faithfully,

---

Coursebook pp.14-15

Learning vocabulary

CAE Relevance: Paper 4 (Listening)

▷ ▣ **Tapescript** (See Coursebook pp.147-148.)

Ex. 1

Classroom treatment

The aim of this listening activity is to improve Ss' ways of learning vocabulary.

Spend some time with the class as a whole talking about question 1. Ask the students how they themselves learn vocabulary: How do they write it down? Do they write down every new word they come across? Do they try to learn lists of vocabulary? Have they any special techniques of their own or have they read about any special techniques perhaps?

Exs. 2-6

Suggested answers

2 Subject of composition: Ways of learning vocabulary

　1 Grouping words that have something grammatical in common

　2 Grouping words by meaning

3 Possible examples:

　1 *information, advice, furniture, weather* (all uncountable nouns); or *cut, put, split, cast* (all irregular verbs with the three basic forms the same)

　2 *to flow, a torrent, stagnant* (all words connected with water)

4

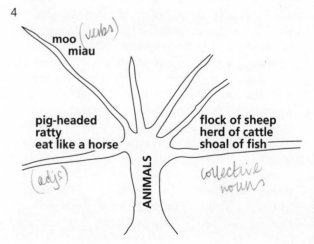

5 To illustrate the point that different words have different associations.

There are, of course, thousands of different examples that could have been used to illustrate the point. Some others might be *ripe apples, fresh fish, new potatoes.*

6 INCREASE

Exs. 7-8

Classroom treatment

7 Open discussion of the pictures. Make sure that students know what all the words mean and why their illustrations are apt.

8 The approach will vary if working with a monolingual or a multilingual group.

If the group is **monolingual**, ask the students in pairs to find a new English word to teach the class using the method illustrated by *carte* and *bashmak* on the tape. They should choose a word and think of an appropriate association from their own language. When every pair is ready they should teach their words to the rest of the class. They should ask the class to close their eyes and think of the picture based on the meaning of the word and its association — giving the English word and its meaning at the same time, of course. After all the words have been presented in this way, the teacher can then test the class to see how many of the words have been remembered. This test could be repeated in a few days' time too.

If the class is **multilingual**, ask students to work in pairs with a partner who speaks a different language. They should then teach each other a word from their own language making a pictorial association based on an English word that sounds like the word being taught (as is the case with *carte* and *bashmak* on the tape).

Exs. 8-10

Answers

8 *carte* = map; *bashmak* = shoe

9

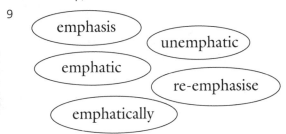

to emphasise	the importance of
	a point
	an opinion
	her best features
	the first syllable

10 a It's got a visual element.
  b It's learning words in a context.
  c It's learning words with a structural association together.

In other words it sums up all the points they have been talking about.

Exs. 11-12

Classroom treatment

11 How Ss choose to do this exercise will, of course, depend on the words they choose but it is something that they should certainly be encouraged to do as a way of reinforcing the important points raised by the listening text, not to mention the vocabulary covered in the course so far.

12 Remind Ss of the points they suggested in question 1, particularly if they thought of ideas that were not suggested on the tape. If this is the case, ask them how the man could also slot their ideas into his composition.

After listening to the tape students could be asked finally to write a plan for the composition the man will eventually hand in. They could also write the composition for homework.

Using a dictionary

CAE Relevance: All Papers

Exs. 1-5

Classroom treatment

We recommend that you spend an entire lesson on this important point.

Ask Ss first what dictionaries they use — bilingual and/ or monolingual, and the names of them. You should be ready to recommend a suitable bilingual and monolingual dictionary for your students. *The Longman Dictionary of Contemporary English* is ideal for students at this level, for example. It could be worth pointing out how much more information a monolingual dictionary will give than a bilingual one, although a bilingual one can be useful to check the exact meaning of a word (particularly when it is a matter of a word having one concrete meaning e.g. *sparrow, cherry, cement*).

1 Spend a reasonable amount of time on this activity, making sure that all the following points are given due attention: meaning, basic grammatical information, pronunciation, and how a word is used.

If possible look at some monolingual dictionaries with Ss in order to see what grammatical information is provided — parts of irregular verbs, whether a noun is countable or uncountable, what prepositions are associated with a word and so on.

Look also at how the pronunciation of a word is indicated, the IPA. Draw Ss' attention also to how stress is indicated in the dictionary.

Look at some words recently studied to see how the way they are used is illustrated by the dictionary. You could perhaps use some of the words illustrated on these pages for this exercise – *abstract* and *angle* , perhaps.

2 Ss should not attempt to answer the question at this stage. Simply read it through and make sure that the Ss are clear what the task actually involves.

3 Check on the meaning, pronunciation and usage of each of the words listed. Make sure that the Ss come up with or find out these phrases: *cope with, have difficulty in* or *with, have little trouble with, to fail to do, to succeed in doing, to have a flair for, to be hopeless at, to have an aptitude for, could do with something* (e.g. *more experience), to need more practice in, to suffer from, to be brilliant at* . (Remind students how *good, bad, terrible, fantastic, dreadful,* etc. are all like *hopeless* and *brilliant* and are followed by *at* .)

4 You might suggest, if the Ss do not do so themselves, that the words should be grouped according to which preposition they go with — thus *having an aptitude* and *having a flair* would go together as they both take *for*, and so on. You might also suggest that the words are written down in a slightly fuller context e.g. *He has difficulty with English verbs.* or *I have difficulty in remembering irregular verbs.*

5 If there is time, work on this in class. Suggest that students write 12 sentences using each of the phrases discussed in 3 and 4. Encourage them to write their sentences in a logical way — perhaps grouping all the strengths together first and then dealing with the weaknesses. If there is no time to complete this in class, discuss how to approach it and then ask Ss to write their reports for homework. (See Introduction p.9.)

Coursebook pp.16-17

Language focus: I wish I could, but I'm not good enough — yet

CAE Relevance: All Papers

Exs. 1-5

Classroom treatment

Ideally the Ss will have looked at the Grammar Commentary at home before the lesson and so they should be able to deal with questions 1-5 fairly quickly in order to leave time for question 6.

Ex. 1

Check that Ss understand all the questions in the 'appraisal box'. The kind of English that Ss will need in order to answer these questions include expressions like those practised in the 'Using a Dictionary' section on p.15, *can* and *be able to* , possibly conditionals, possibly wishes, and so on.

Ex. 2 Criticising

Ss work with different partners. Instead of asking Ss always to work with the person sitting next to them, why not mix them up in one of the following ways:

- Ask Ss to arrange themselves in a circle by birthdates and then to work with the person whom they land up next to.
- Write pairs of associated words onto separate slips of paper — 'fish and chips', 'here and there', 'now and again', and so on. Then ask Ss to mill around until they find their partner.
- Ask Ss to choose one word each that they have learnt in the last day or two. They should then arrange themselves in alphabetical order and work with the person they end up next to.

Suggest to Ss people they could criticise, but let them make other choices if they prefer. Possible choices might be unpopular political figures known to the students, singers/musicians who are not to their taste, sportsmen or women who don't quite come up to the mark, actors and actresses whom they dislike.

Ex. 3 Ability

Ss work individually on the exercise before the answers are checked as a class.

Answers

1 *can;* 2 *has been able;* 3 *was able;* 4 *could;* 5 *was able;* 6 *could have;* 7 *would be able;* 8 *will be able*

Can is a defective verb i.e it does not have all the forms that most verbs have. A variation of *be able to* has to be used for the forms that *can* does not have itself. Refer Ss to the Grammar Commentary (and perhaps a grammar reference book for more information if required.)

Ex. 4 Wishes and regrets

Classroom treatment
Answer the first two parts of the question as a class.

Ask Ss to complete the girls' wishes in pairs. Then have each pair read out their wishes for the others to correct if necessary. Write all (or the best of) the possible wishes suggested on the board/OHP.

Each pair of Ss should write down their sets of wishes and should then hand them to the teacher. The teacher reads out some of the sets of wishes and the Ss have to guess who those wishes originated from.

Possible completions
I wish my teacher had more patience.
I wish English was/were easier.
I wish I had more time to do this.

Ex. 5 What's the difference?

Classroom treatment
It may help Ss to write meaningful sentences if you give them a situation e.g. 'Imagine yourself as an Australian of the opposite sex: how would or might your life have been different?' Ss complete their sentence and then each reads out to the rest of the class.

Answers
would have spoken is referring to something that would certainly have been true under the circumstances stated.

might have spoken could mean 'I didn't, but it's possible I would have done, given different circumstances', *or* 'I can't remember if I did or not' — depending on the context.

could have spoken could mean 'It would have been possible for me, but I didn't, or I didn't feel like it' *or* (as with *might*) 'I can't remember now if I did or not' — again depending on the context.

Ex. 6

Classroom treatment
Make sure that students appreciate what an appraisal interview is: i.e. a yearly meeting between a boss and an employee in which they discuss the employee's work and how each feels about it; the aim is for both sides to

discuss how each can help the other to work better and more happily. Tell students that their appraisal interview can relate either to their job or to their English learning situation as they prefer. Divide Ss into manager/employee (or teacher/student) pairs. Allow Ss five-ten minutes for their first interview and then tell them to change roles.

Coursebook pp.17-18

Exam Practice: Paper 2 Writing

CAE Relevance: Paper 2 (Writing)

Classroom treatment
1 Follow the instructions in the Coursebook and spend about 20 minutes on the preparation phase outlined in point 1.

a Ss should be clear that they are going to write a formal and informative letter to a publishing company informing them about tastes in learning materials. They have to answer the four questions asked by the publisher and to base their answers on the two sets of notes under the letter. They do not have to add any ideas of their own — although they may if they have space and what they say does not contradict any of the information provided. They have to write about 200 words which is a little shorter than what they will be expected to write in the exam itself (250 words).

b Ask the students the questions in the publisher's letter to check their comprehension. Then compare their personal answers with those given in the notes at the foot of the page.

c The important bits of information to mark are (from introduction to letter) full answers, own opinions typical, other students; (from the questions) books, stories, spare time, how often, recorded material, buy, what kind; bought or consider buying computer software, video; grammar materials, language exercises. Everything in the notes is important.

If the Ss feel that other points are also important, that doesn't matter, but everything mentioned above should be highlighted.

d A typical way of organising the letter would be to have a brief introductory paragraph giving the reason for writing and then to have a paragraph dealing with each of the four questions. A sentence should be enough for the concluding paragraph saying, perhaps, 'I hope these answers will be of some use to you and look forward to using some of your new materials in the future.'

Within each of the basic four paragraphs it would be appropriate first to give the writer's 'own' opinion as outlined in the first set of notes and then to indicate how far this is typical for the rest of the class, adding in any appropriate points from the second set of notes.

2 It is probably most sensible to write individual answers at home although this could, of course, be done in class if preferred. Ask students to write their homework as neatly as possible and to use a black pen so that work can be easily photocopied and read by others.

3 Divide students into groups with about four people in each. As students are going to be reading each other's work, group the students appropriately avoiding having the three best students together with the weakest one. If possible make photocopies of people's work so that each student has a copy of everyone's work in their group. (At this stage have a look at the work students have produced and make a note of any glaring problems that you notice.) Encourage them to read each piece of work at least twice thinking first about question 3a and then about 3b. Remind them that they should be on the lookout for good points as well as weaknesses. They should write notes on their photocopies for the writer of the original.

4 The groups then discuss each of the pieces of work in turn. Monitor the groups carefully to ensure that each student is getting some helpful feedback on their work. Make sure that any glaring problems that you noticed yourself when you had the work for photocopying have been dealt with.

5 Students then re-write their work. It is probably a good idea to do this in class as students can then ask each other about points they were not clear about and can also call on you to deal with any disagreements on the spot.

Collect the work and mark it, making sure that you also think about overall content as well as accuracy.

Possible model answer

Here is an example of the kind of writing good students at this level might be expected to produce:

Dear Mr Roseberry,

Thank you for your letter enquiring about students' tastes in language learning materials. Our class carried out a survey on the questions you asked and we felt you might be interested in the results.

It may be useful to know that we are a class of twenty-five students studying in Britain. We come from a variety of national and professional backgrounds and our ages range from 17 to 29.

Our class was split with regard to the first question. Over half the class like reading fiction, in particular love or adventure stories. A third of the group enjoy biographies. The rest of us prefer non-fiction, especially books on medical or scientific topics or travel. Humour is also very popular.

Only ten of us have actually bought language cassettes because they are too expensive. The cassettes which those ten people bought all dealt with pronunciation. We all do, however, often buy song cassettes in English.

Only two of us have ever bought computer disks to help us learn English. Although most of us have computers at home, language disks cost so much. Could we put in a plea for the prices to be brought down?

We were in total agreement about what we like in grammar materials and language exercises. It is important that all explanations should be clear, that books should include a key and that there should be plenty of space in the margins for adding our own notes.

We hope these comments may be of some use to you.

Yours sincerely,

Rounding off the Unit

Why not round off this Unit in class by asking Ss to make a study plan for the next month or three months as appropriate. They should make resolutions about:

• What they are going to read in English.
• How they are going to increase their vocabulary.
• How they are going to improve in the areas they feel most necessary for them.

A copy of these resolutions should be kept by the Ss and a copy given to you. In a week or so, there should be a discussion (and, if appropriate, modification) of these resolutions.

3 It's a fact!

<table><tr><td>Coursebook p.19</td></tr></table>

Warm-up

Here are four **alternative suggestions**, all with books closed:

1 Ask Ss to read the 'Read It Quick!' text and get reactions. Prompt with questions like: 'Do facts like this worry you? Can you work out how much the human population will increase in an hour/in a day/ in a year?' etc.

2 Ask Ss to think of ways in which facts are used e.g. in ads to make them sound more convincing, or by politicians to make their arguments more convincing. Ss discuss in pairs/small groups to write lists. Then check with the whole class.

3 Which exams in particular do you need facts for? (Chemistry, History, Physics, etc.) Are they really important? Group or class discussion.

4 Read out the beginnings of some factual statements and ask Ss to complete them. They may try to think of what the real answers or facts might be, or make up humorous ones. Here are some with correct completions:

a) If all the Chinese people in China were to jump up and down at the same time ... [it would cause a tidal wave that would swamp the UK]!

b) Calchas, an ancient soothsayer, died laughing when he heard ... [that he had outlived the predicted hour of his death]!

c) The author Ray Bradbury wrote the science fiction novel *Fahrenheit 451* in the basement of the University of California on a pay-typewriter which ... [cost 10 cents for every half hour of use]!

d) In the 19th century two Frenchmen called De Grandpré and Le Pique fought a duel with pistols while they were ... [riding in hot-air balloons half a mile above Paris]!

e) Patent No. 889,928 was filed at the US Patent Office in 1907. It was for an alarm clock that ... [sprayed water onto the face of the sleeping person when the alarm went off]!

f) What killed 20 million people in 1918 was not the Great War: it was ... [influenza/flu]!

Read, fill in and report

CAE Relevance: Papers 1 and 3 (Reading and English in Use)

Background notes and vocabulary

> Both texts are taken from a book of amazing and humorous facts.
> 'Allow Us, Sir'
> **to staff:** to supply with staff (= a group of workers)
> **to do his rounds:** to visit a number of different places (rooms, offices, etc.) on a regular basis (here, to check the security of the hotel)
> **to stumble:** to catch your foot on the ground while moving along and start to fall
> **the (hotel) lobby:** the hall or passage which leads from the entrance to the rooms inside a building
> **to hail a cab:** to call a taxi
> **gems:** jewels
> 'Prisoner X'
> **Alexandre Dumas:** (1802-70) French dramatist and novelist, best known for his historical romances such as *The Three Musketeers* and *The Count of Monte Cristo*
> **to sentence:** to give a punishment e.g. to sentence to death/life imprisonment, etc.
> **velvet:** a type of fine closely-woven cloth made esp. of silk but also of nylon, cotton, etc., having a short soft thick raised surface of cut threads on one side only

Classroom treatment

The purpose of this exercise is to begin to raise Ss' awareness of strategies to apply when doing a blank-filling task in the English in Use Paper in the exam. Unlike similar tasks in the exam, however, the blanks to be completed in these texts may be structural or lexical.

Tell Ss to work in pairs and to decide who is going to read which text. Ss then read their texts, using English-English dictionaries to help with new or difficult words if necessary, and try to complete each blank with one appropriate word. When they are both ready, they take it in turns to tell each other the story of what they have read and explain to each other why they filled in the blanks as they did.

Alternatively, split the class into two halves (e.g. left and right of the class). Ask one half to read and try to fill in the blanks in one text while the other half read the other text and fill in their blanks. In this way, it might be easier for you to monitor reading comprehension and explain (surreptitiously!) to a whole group any words or phrases they are having problems with. You can also check completions (again surreptitiously!) with each whole group before they find a partner to work with from the other group to tell their stories to.

It would be valuable to close the lesson with a brief class discussion of ways of tackling this kind of 'blank completion' task. For example, Ss should read the whole text first. Then read more carefully, thinking of meaning and grammar, and ask themselves: What part of speech is missing from the blank? Is a word really 'necessary' in the blank? If not, it'll probably be an adjective or an adverb. etc.

Answers or possible answers

NOTE: When blanks have to be completed structurally or grammatically (e.g. 'was falling'), there is usually one clear correct answer (although occasionally there may be two or more alternative completions). When blanks have to be filled with vocabulary items, there may be any number of possible correct solutions, depending of course on the context and surrounding language (e.g. a preposition may force the use of a particular verb).

'Allow Us, Sir': came/walked/(ran?); was; dropped; called/found/grabbed; held; had; informed/ told; stolen

'Prisoner X': may/might/will/must; was; had; given/wearing; was; had; had; has; found/discovered

> ## Coursebook pp.20-21

Language focus

CAE Relevance: All Papers, but particularly Paper 3 English in Use

Background notes and vocabulary

> '£6,000 for Nelson's Column!'
> The text is written in a personal, but fairly typical note form. It therefore includes abbreviations (recognised and personalised) and misses out many words such as *a/an, the, in, and, were, so,* etc.
> *Trafalgar Square* and *Nelson's Column:* Trafalgar Square is one of the best-known of London's many squares, within a few yards of Charing Cross. On the south side stands Nelson's Column, 168.5 ft high and surmounted by a statue of Admiral Nelson.
> *Iowa:* a state on the Middle West plains of the USA
> *Admiral Lord Nelson:* Horatio Nelson (1758-1805), British admiral and national hero. He was killed at his greatest victory, Trafalgar (1805), having saved Britain from the threat of Napoleonic invasion.
> *entrusted with sale:* given the charge of the sale with complete trust
> *to jump queue:* 'to jump the queue' = to obtain an unfair advantage over others who have been waiting longer
> *got no joy from …:* here, didn't get any satisfaction from, didn't manage to get any work done by …
> *swindled:* cheated
> *Big Ben:* although many seem to refer to the whole clock tower of the Houses of Parliament in London as 'Big Ben', it is really the bell which strikes the hours
> *down-payment:* part of the full price paid at the time of buying or delivery, with the rest to be paid later
> *Buckingham Palace:* the London home of the British sovereign (king or queen), constructed by Nash (1821-36) and partly redesigned early in the 20th century
> *gullible:* easily deceived or cheated
> *leased:* rented or hired
> *the White House:* the official residence of the US president, in Washington, built in the late 18th century
> *the Statue of Liberty:* a bronze figure (almost 46 m. high) of a woman holding up a torch, on Liberty Island in New York harbour, designed by Bartholdi
> *Gov:* abbreviation for the Government
> *Aussie:* slang term for an Australian

Exs. 1-6

Classroom treatment

NOTE: The final objective of all the work here on past tenses, tense sequences, modals and reporting is the writing of the article or story of the conman in one of the forms in ex. 6. And this involves expanding notes into a piece of extended writing, one of the test types in the English in Use Paper. The Grammar Commentary can be referred to before work on these pages (as preparatory homework), during the work, or as homework study while writing the article/story.

You might begin by introducing some of the vocabulary students will need here. Ask the class as a whole:

'What do we call a man who cheats someone by, for example, selling them a famous building?' — A conman, a confidence trickster, or a swindler.

'And what does a conman do?' — He 'cons' people, 'swindles' them, or 'dupes' them.

'And what adjective could you use to describe someone who falls for a 'con trick' like this?' — Gullible, or easily taken in.

Then Ss work in pairs. Before they work on the exercises, ask them first to read carefully and understand the handwritten notes on p.21. They should ask for your help to explain anything they don't understand. Point out that these are typical personal notes, with lots of words missed out (*in, a/an, the, who was, were, but,* etc.), abbreviations (*F* for Furguson, *A* for the American), and dashes (—) to indicate new ideas.

To give Ss a start here, you might read out the whole message for the first two lines, thus: 'One morning in the summer of 1923, a Scotsman (named/called) Arthur Furguson saw/spotted an American in Trafalgar Square. The American, who was rich and from Iowa, was gazing/staring at Nelson's Column.'

Alternative classroom treatment
Perhaps for weaker groups it might be advisable to let them follow the notes while you tell the whole 'story' in completed form. However, they should not be given the opportunity to write it out now, since all the Language focus exercises are intended to help with the language they will need in order to expand the notes themselves in ex.6.

Ex. 1 Narrating past events
Classroom treatment
Emphasis here should be placed a) on the correct question forms *was he doing ...?, had he been doing ...?* and *did he do ...?* together with b) an understanding of the clear distinction between the tenses. Ask the class as a whole one or two of the questions before getting Ss to work in pairs.

As further practice, get them to quiz each other about other parts of the story using the same tenses.

Expected questions and answers
1 What was the American doing when Furguson approached him in Trafalgar Square? — (He was) gazing/ looking/staring at Nelson's Column.

2 How long had the American probably been gazing at the Column before Furguson approached him? — He'd probably been gazing at it for some time/quite a while.

3 What did the American do when Furguson told him Britain wanted to sell Nelson's Column? — He asked him the price./He wanted to know how much it was.

4 What did Furguson do when the American gave him the cheque? — He gave him a receipt and left.

5 What did Furguson do when he came out of prison? — He retired and lived in luxury in Los Angeles.

6 Where was Furguson living when he died? — (He was living) in Los Angeles.

Ex. 2 *had done/had been doing*
Classroom treatment
The aim of this phase is to revise the distinction between *had done* and *had been doing*. Write this on the board/OHP —

She had been watching TV for 2 hours when I arrived.

She had watched 3 programmes   when I arrived.

Then ask 'What had she been doing when I arrived? And for how long?' and 'How many programmes had she watched when I arrived?'

Ss then work in pairs to read the text in order to complete the sentences.

Suggested answers
1 Furguson had been conning people for only two years when he went to the States/he decided to cross the Atlantic.

2 Furguson had no sooner told the American about Nelson's Column than he wanted to buy it/he wanted to know the price.

3 He had hardly arrived in the States before he leased the White House to a cattle rancher.

4 Once he had sold one national monument, he found it easy/it was easy/he didn't find it difficult to sell another one.

5 Almost as soon as he had 'sold' Nelson's Column, Furguson sold Big Ben.

Ex. 3 *before doing, on doing,* etc.
Classroom treatment
Write these sentences on the board/OHP and ask which Ss think would be written more often than spoken, and why:

a After she'd finished work, she went home.

b After finishing work, she went home.

'b' would probably appear more in writing than speech because it's more formal, although you will hear it spoken on occasion.

Ss then work in pairs on the exercise.

Answers

1 *Before he began* work on his symphony, the composer went on a long holiday.

2 *After they had finished* their exams, the students all went out to celebrate.

3 *When she heard* the news, she went straight out to tell her friends.

4 *While he was walking* into town, he had time to think about the problem.

More possible sentences

1 *Before selling* Nelson's Column to the American, Furguson went away to phone his 'superiors'.

2 *After giving* the American a receipt, Furguson left.

3 *On arriving* in America, almost the first thing he did was to lease the White House to a cattle rancher.

4 *While living* in America, Furguson swindled a cattle rancher out of $100,000.

Ex. 4 *must have done, might have been doing,* etc.

Classroom treatment

Try to get Ss to explain these sentences so that the import of the different modals here becomes clear, for example:

He may have sold ... = It's possible that he sold ...

He could have gone to prison ... = Perhaps he would have gone to prison for a lot longer if he hadn't been so lucky ...

All his victims must have been stupid = I assume all his victims were stupid

The American might have been having a holiday = It's possible the American was having a holiday

Again, stress the distinction between the simple and continous forms: *might have done/might have been doing, could have done/could have been doing,* etc.

Again, Ss work in pairs on this task.

Possible statements

1 When Furguson saw him, the American may have been wondering who built Nelson's Column.

2 The American must have thought Furguson was honest.

3 The Australian might (well) have been working with the police!

4 When Furguson came out of prison, he could have gone back to being a conman!

Ex. 5 Reporting

Classroom treatment

The aim of this brief phase is to revise some of the basics of reported speech in English: *tell someone that .../explain to someone that ...* ; changes of tense *has done* to *had done*, etc; reporting questions with *want to know, wonder, + if/whether ...*, etc.

Ss might do these verbally in groups, then as a whole class suggest different ways of reporting what was said. If there are errors at this point, remind them of some of the basics above. But don't go into a full revision of reported speech at this stage: Ss will do that in Unit 4.

Answers

1 Furguson told the American (that) he had been entrusted with the sale of Nelson's Column and told him/said (that) the price was £6,000. He told him/added that he could accept a cheque and that he could give him the name and address of a reliable company to do the job.

2 Furguson told the Australian/explained to the Australian that New York Harbour had to be widened and that the Government was prepared to sell the Statue. He wanted to know/wondered if/whether he was interested.

Ex. 6

Classroom treatment

Allow Ss to decide which form of the article or story they want to write. Each will involve expanding the notes, and each will mean using the language they have been practising. Depending on the time available, they might begin writing in class (in pairs or on their own) or write the whole piece as a homework assignment. (See Introduction p.9.)

If you want Ss to concentrate on clarity and correctness, you might suggest they write just half the story.

They should give the piece a title, either the one given ('£6,000 for Nelson's Column!') or one of their own (e.g. 'Aussie finally cons conman' or 'The Greatest Conman Of All Time?').

Draw Ss' attention to the extra phrases and expressions provided, particularly those beginning with an adjective:

Strange/Odd/Incredible as it might sound,/though it may seem, almost everyone was taken in by Furguson!

Possible version of the story (in form (b))

'I was the Greatest Conman of all time!'

I am now retired and living in luxury in Los Angeles. The year is 1934 and I am writing this to tell the story of my career.

It all started one morning in the summer of 1923 when I saw an American gazing at Nelson's Column. I later learned that he was rich, and from Iowa. I went up and spoke to him and explained what the statue was and who Lord Nelson was. Then I told him that the Square wouldn't be the same without it, but that Britain was going to sell it, the Column, the statue, the lions and the fountains. The American immediately asked the price and I told him that the Government would accept £6,000, but of course it had to be the right buyer.

I told him I had been entrusted with the sale, but that it was secret. The American wanted to jump the queue, so I went off to phone my superiors for instructions. (Of course I did no such thing: I just walked round the corner and waited.) When I returned, I told him all was well and said that I could accept his cheque there and then. I even supplied the name and address of a 'reliable' firm to take the Column to the States!

The American gave me a cheque, I gave him a receipt and we parted. And of course I cashed the cheque as fast as I could.

That summer I also 'sold' Big Ben, and *almost* 'sold' Buckingham Palace — both to gullible Americans.

Obviously they seemed to be my best 'clients', so I decided to cross the Atlantic, and sailed to the States in 1925. There the first thing I did was to lease the White House to a cattle rancher for 99 years at $100,000 a year. He paid the first year in advance!

My ideal victim was an Australian from Sydney — or I *thought* he was my ideal victim! I told him that New York Harbour had to be widened but that the Statue of Liberty was in the way, so the American Government was prepared to sell it. He went away and spent the next few days trying to raise the necessary $100,000 deposit from Sydney. He was very keen, and it was then that I made a terrible mistake. I allowed myself to be photographed with the Australian in front of the Statue. For some reason, he became suspicious and took the photo to the police. To cut a long story short, that led them to me and I was sent to prison for five years.

I came out four years ago and have been living in luxury ever since.

<hr>

Coursebook pp.22-23

Read and discuss

CAE Relevance: Papers 1 and 5 (Reading and Speaking)

Preparation

As preparation homework for this part of the Unit, ask Ss to consult books and encyclopædias to find some amazing facts and figures that they must bring with them to put into a 'Did you know ...?' quiz of their own in ex. 2. (They might also think up some amazing 'false facts and figures' for the quiz.)

Exs. 1 and 2

Classroom treatment

1 Ss either do the quiz as suggested i.e. individually, then check with a partner, etc., OR you read out the items one by one, pausing for Ss to mark whether they think they are true or false.

2 Ss construct their own quizzes in pairs or small groups. Unlike the one in the Coursebook, their 'facts' should definitely include some that are false. Then, when all are ready, organise opposing pairs or opposing groups for them to read out their 'facts' to each other in turn as a competition.

Answers

1 Believe it or not, they are *all true* — at least according to Michael Caine's *File of Facts: Not Many People Know This 1988* (Guild Publishing 1987).

Listen, make notes and speak

CAE Relevance: Papers 4 and 5 (Listening and Speaking)

▷ 📼 **Tapescript** (See Coursebook p.148.)
Exs. 1 and 2

Classroom treatment

The aim of this phase is to introduce some more 'facts', this time to give practice in listening for gist, then listening for detail and then note-taking. (A similar task may occur in exam Paper 4 Listening, although in the exam candidates will probably have to complete sentences already started.)

1 Introduce the listening piece and give Ss a minute or so to read the three questions. Play the tape and get answers from the class as a whole.

2 Play the tape again, this time for Ss to make notes as suggested. Their notes should be as brief as possible (see suggestions below). Play the tape again if necessary to give Ss a chance to compare again what they hear with their notes. They then tell each other what they heard, working from their notes.

As a follow-up, you might ask Ss to write up the items as if for a short 'On This Day' column for a newspaper.

Answers

1 a 9th March; b 4 (events); c open-ended

2 Possible notes:

Item 1: Bobby Fisher — chess master — born in Chicago (or b. Chicago) 1943

Item 2: Yuri Gagarin — born/b. 1934 — Smolensk — world famous after space flight — April 1961: hero of Soviet Union — travelled round world — even lunch with Queen in London. Died in air crash.

Item 3: French Foreign Legion — founded 1831 — by King Louis Philippe. Very hard discipline — still 3 applicants for each place.

Item 4: Napoleon married Josephine — 1896. Nap. arrived 2 hours late for wedding — too tied up in plans. Both said 28: Nap was 27, Jo 33 and widow.

Vocabulary: You're the Editor

CAE Relevance: Paper 3 English in Use

Background notes and vocabulary

This text was adapted from an English magazine article about Agatha Christie.
Agatha Christie: (1891-1976) author, most famous for her murder mysteries and her two detectives, the Belgian Hercule Poirot, and the English spinster Miss Marple
Guildford: a town in the southern English county of Surrey
Harrogate: a town in the county of North Yorkshire in the north of England

Exs. 1 and 2

Classroom treatment

Explain that one of the tasks in the Engish in Use Paper will be a proofreading and/or editing task. This means Ss will have to read a passage, look for particular kinds of mistakes and correct them: these may be spelling mistakes, punctuation errors, mistakes in verb forms, vocabulary mistakes, and so on. This phase is to help with proofreading to find vocabulary mistakes, in particular wrong verbs.

1 Remind Ss briefly of the Vocabulary section in Unit 1 (CB p.8). This follows on from that and is an essential exercise because these collocations (or mistakes with them!) occur in the passage below.

Give Ss some 5-10 minutes working in pairs to match the verbs with the nouns. There will often be more than one collocation. Then check with the whole class.

2 Tell Ss that there are 22 mistakes to look for so they have to read the whole text rather carefully. This is an exercise in intensive reading. They may work in pairs or individually for some 15-20 minutes. When checking with other Ss and then with the class as a whole, they should explain *why* the verbs they have picked out are wrong.

Answers

1 In English, we can 'make an appointment', 'arrange an appointment', 'keep an appointment', 'have an appointment with somebody', 'set up an appointment', 'postpone an appointment', 'cancel an appointment' and 'break an appointment'.

Collocations:

catch a chill; **commit** murder, commit suicide; **do** one's best, do an interview (= conduct an interview with someone), do oneself an injury; **find** a solution, find an explanation; **follow** [someone's] progress, follow a procedure; **give** a reward, give poison (to someone), give the appearance (of being stupid, for example), give an interview (to an interviewer), give an explanation; **go for** an interview (for example, in a radio studio), go for a drive; **grant** (someone) an interview (= give an interview); **lose** interest in, lose one's memory; **make** progress, make an exception, make an effort, make a search (of a place), make an appearance (= to appear in person); **offer** a solution, offer a reward, offer an explanation; **put** (something) on record; **reach** a conclusion; **suffer from** a loss of memory; **take** poison, take a drive (NOTE: We *can't* 'take an exception' in English, but we *can* 'take exception to (something)'.)

2 Paragraph 1: ~~made~~ a drive = gone for a drive or taken a drive

Paragraph 2: ~~written~~ on record = put on record

Paragraph 4: ~~put~~ some injury to herself = done some injury to herself

~~taken~~ a chill = caught a chill

~~done~~ suicide = committed suicide

~~given~~ poison of some kind = taken poison of some kind

~~followed~~ murder = committed murder

Paragraph 5: ~~paid~~ great interest in the case = took great interest in the case

~~putting~~ a reward = offering a reward

Paragraph 6: ~~followed~~ their best = did their best

~~to do~~ every effort = to make every effort

~~took~~ their usual procedure = followed their usual procedure

~~went for~~ another search of the area = made another search of the area

~~done~~ no progress = made no progress

~~catching~~ a solution = finding a solution

~~took~~ the conclusion = reached the conclusion

Paragraph 7: ~~did~~ a re-appearance = made a re-appearance

~~taken~~ the most complete loss of memory = suffered from the most complete loss of memory

Paragraph 8: ~~awarded~~ interviews = gave/granted interviews

~~took~~ no exception = made no exception

The only explanation she ~~put~~ = The only explanation she offered/ gave

~~mislaid~~ her memory = lost her memory

Coursebook p.24

Exam Practice: Paper 3 English in Use

CAE Relevance: Paper 3 English in Use
Exs. a and b
Classroom treatment
a With the class as a whole, discuss the questions about how best to tackle this kind of task. Follow up each question with the class doing what is suggested: for example, ask Ss to read the text very quickly and to say very briefly what it is about. Then perhaps ask for suggested completions for items 1 and 2. (Ss should of course cover the items at the bottom of the page if you do this.)

b If time allows, let Ss do the exercise in pairs or individually in class, or set this as a homework assignment. When checking in the next lesson, Ss should be prepared to *explain* not only why one option is correct but also why the others are wrong.

Key
1 C; 2 D; 3 A; 4 B; 5 D; 6 B; 7 B; 8 C; 9 C; 10 A.

Rounding off the Unit

Why not round off the last lesson here by asking how many of the strange facts Ss can remember from the Unit (and perhaps also from previous Units — for example, facts about language from Unit 2)?

4 News of the world

(The title of this Unit is also the name, when spelt with a capital 'W', of one of Britain's best-selling Sunday newspapers, a popular, sensational, often rather salacious tabloid.)

Coursebook p.25

Warm-up

Books closed. To interest students in the idea of the media (and they will have treated the subject several times in other classrooms, other courses), get them to discuss these questions in small groups and then give a quick summary of their discussion to the class. Of course they should be encouraged to give reasons for their choices throughout.

1 You can take one of the following to the desert island you've been banished to, to help keep you sane for the rest of your life. Which of each category will you take? (Your choice can be British or otherwise!)

   Which daily newspaper?
   Which Sunday paper?
   Which weekly, fortnightly or monthly magazine?
   Which TV comedy programme?
   Which famous radio or TV 'voice' on cassette, record or CD?

2 Given that you could have one — and only one! — of these on your desert island, which would you choose to have?

   A daily newspaper of your choice delivered every day?
   Unlimited use of a TV with programmes from all over the world?
   A video camera with playback facilities?
   A radio that will pick up any station in the world?

Listen and discuss

CAE Relevance: Papers 4 and 5 (Listening and Speaking)

Background notes and vocabulary

> **Referred to on tape**
> **The BBC World Service:** set up, as stated on the tape, in 1932, it produces and transmits radio programmes, in English and 36 other languages, to all parts of the globe
> **The Empire:** here, the British Empire
> **The Cold War:** a term describing the post-1945 tensions between the USSR and Eastern Europe on the one hand and the USA and Western Europe on the other
> **de-colonisation:** the process of mainly African countries taking or being granted independence from Britain (and other countries)
> **The Indian sub-continent:** the vast area of South Asia that includes Pakistan, India, Bangladesh and Nepal
> **vernacular services:** here, the meaning is programmes transmitted in the native language (not English) of the intended audience
> **Mandarin:** the major language of North China, now promoted as the national spoken and written language
> **Cantonese:** a variant spoken in South China
> **Ukrainian:** a Slavonic language spoken (in 1991) by 75% of the inhabitants of the Ukraine, a country in Eastern Europe
> **Zulu:** a language spoken in Southern Africa
> **Tamil:** a language spoken in South East India and in North Sri Lanka
> **Singhala:** (or Singhalese) official language of Sri Lanka
> **Baltic languages of the Soviet Union:** Mr Tusa was interviewed before the dramatic events of 1991; it appears likely at this time that 'Baltic languages of the Soviet Union' may soon be an outdated term. He was thinking of Lithuanian, Latvian and Estonian.
> **Mentioned in the exercises**
> **Arthur Miller:** American playwright (*A View from the Bridge, The Crucible, Death of a Salesman*), one-time husband of Marilyn Monroe, born 1915
> **Cubism:** an abstract art movement — 'a work of art exists in its own right rather than as a representation of the real world' — developed by Georges Braque and Pablo Picasso in about 1908

▷🔲 **Tapescript** (See Coursebook pp.148-149.)
This authentic interview with Mr Tusa was totally unscripted.

Exs. 1 and 2

Classroom treatment

1 The first activity gives practice in the important skill of predicting and getting mentally prepared for the sort of language to be listened to. You might broaden things by asking questions such as: What sort of accent do you think Mr Tusa will have? Will his language be chatty or formal, do you think?

After the first play of the tape, allow feedback on how accurate Ss' predictions were. Did they think he answered the questions well? Was he clear and concise, or did he ramble? Was he humorous or dry? etc.

2 The suggestion for the split listening task is a) to reduce the load of information students have to search for and process, and b) to provide the possibility for real exchange of information. (Although groups A and B will have heard the same piece, they will have to concentrate hard to get their own required information, let alone the other group's.)

Before a second play of the tape, you might continue the predicting practice by asking students (from Groups A and B) to guess at some of the answers to the questions. Students of twentieth century history, for example, might already be able to predict the answers to Group A's first exercise.

As an additional exercise, Group A could be given one similar to the contextualisation of phrases that Group B have. Write these on the board/OHP:

an international voice for Britain
binding the Empire together
the new needs of the Cold War
the period of de-colonisation
the world at large
the broad outlines

After a second listening, Group A students have to relate these phrases to context and say how/why they were used.

Answers to listening exercises

Group A

The matching of decades with the World Service aims should be:

A '40s;   B '50s;   C '70s/'80s;   D '30s;   E '60s;

'Cooking for One' (D) is the programme not suggested by Mr Tusa's list.

Group B

BBC programmes are received in:

Africa — most of the continent
the Indian sub-continent — most of it
China — the greater part
Latin America — rather weak
North America — rather weak, too

Contextualising and explaining phrases:

1 He says the World Service really is 'a global broadcaster', meaning that it broadcasts pretty well throughout the world (to all four corners of the earth and to all parts of the globe).

2 He says their 'core activity', meaning the most important aspect of their broadcasts, is news and current affairs.

3 He says the World Service broadcasts to countries with news about themselves and about the world, and that getting 'the right balance' between the two types of broadcasting is an interesting challenge.

4 'To establish our credibility' here means to prove ourselves efficient and effective broadcasters with the listeners. He says to do this they have to report accurately and well to any particular country about what is going on in that country.

5 Their 'own domestic sources' here means a particular country's own radio stations and other communications media. He says the World Service doesn't just want to duplicate information provided by them.

The World Service broadcasts in: Cantonese, Mandarin, Portuguese, Tamil, Hungarian, Nepali and Japanese

It does not as yet (or did not at the time of the interview), according to Mr Tusa, broadcast in: Singhala, Ukrainian or Zulu

---

Coursebook pp.26-27

Language focus

CAE Relevance: All Papers

NOTE: These two pages contain some demanding and time-consuming exercises. You might like to intersperse the sections with other parts of the Unit rather than do all this work in one 'chunk'.

Ex. 1

Classroom treatment

This phase can be used as a diagnostic test of how well Ss remember the 'rules' of tense change in reported speech. Exs. 3 and 4 assume a good knowledge of them, as does the final writing task in ex. 8. If necessary, do some remedial work. Ask Ss, for example, each to give a word that normally 'changes' in reports. (This could be a group team 'game'!)

These will include auxiliaries and modals: do > did, am/is > was, are > were, has > had, can > could, will > would, may > might

Also determiners, adjectives, pronouns, adverbs, even main verbs: this > that/the, these > those/the, here > there, now > then, today > that day, yesterday > the day before/the previous day, tomorrow > the next day/the following day, ago > before/previously, come > go, bring > take, etc.

If you want further 'free' practice, you might remind Ss of the people they heard talking about learning vocabulary in Unit 2 and see if they can recall some of the main points made (using reported speech, of course). For example:

I remember her saying that one way to learn vocabulary was to ...

Expected answers

1 He said the face of the service had changed in every decade since the 1930s. Then it had been its aim to keep the Empire together. He said that in the 1940s ... etc.

2 He said it was quite difficult to get the right balance when they were reporting to a particular country in that country's language about their own situation as well as about international affairs.

3 He said that recently in Burma, during a student uprising, the BBC World Service had been the people's main source of news.

4 He said he thought there were certain languages the BBC should broadcast in and that they got a lot of requests to start new services.

Ex. 2

Classroom treatment

This exercise is basically a lead-in to exs. 3 and 4, but also, we hope, a little fun as students check their knowledge of the 'speaking' verbs found in the ten sentences and then act them out. Exaggeration is welcome here and an 'I can do better than that!' element welcome. Lead into it by making a few comments to the class and asking them to describe

how you spoke: Did you snap/bark/mumble/whisper etc?

(The quotations in this exercise are in most cases genuine, but it is obviously not important that Ss should be able to identify the speakers. However, you and they might recognise, among others, the words of Ronald Reagan, Ben Johnson, Oliver North and Margaret Thatcher.)

Exs. 3 and 4

Classroom treatment

Initially best done in pairs, after as much input and classwork as you think necessary. Check with your class that they know the constructions that follow the verbs in ex. 3. You might suggest that Ss study the Grammar Commentary on page 130 the previous evening for homework — or perhaps suggest they refer to the Commentary while doing ex. 3.

There may well be a word order problem for students in ex. 4. Adverb order is neglected too much at intermediate level and consequently students may now be surprised that depending on such things as the adverb they choose, its length, commonness of collocation, the length of following object, it will come more naturally before or after the verb it relates to. Generally, if the adverb is describing the manner of speaking (*loudly, quietly,* etc.) it will be safer after the verb, sometimes breaking that 'rule' of not putting anything between verb and direct object; if it is a comment on the fact or a very common collocation like *strenuously/categorically deny* , it will normally come before.

If students are unable to find a single adverb for some of the sentences, allow — even encourage — an adverbial phrase like 'at the top of her voice' or 'under his breath' as alternatives.

Answers to exs. 3 and 4

Matching the verbs in ex. 3 with the sentences in ex. 2:

1	confess / confirm	Sentence 8
2	deny / stress	Sentence 4
3	warn / point out	Sentence 7
4	admit / claim	Sentence 1 (example given)
5	demand to know / suspect	Sentence 6
6	accuse / maintain	Sentence 3
7	compliment / regret	Sentence 10
8	object / threaten	Sentence 2
9	apologise / emphasise	Sentence 9
10	agree / insist	Sentence 5

In the example on p. 26, students are shown   ... , *but claimed that* ... and also ... , *claiming at the same time that* ... to link the two parts of the sentence. In the model sentences below we have chosen one or the other — conjunction or present participle — at random. The other would normally, of course, be acceptable. Ss should certainly be encouraged to try out the participle as linker — often an attractive stylistic device.

1   He confessed (tearfully) that the baby was his and confirmed that he intended to resign.
2   He (categorically) denied having known about it/that he had known about it and stressed (forcefully) that he hadn't been involved.
3   He warned them (vociferously/vehemently) not to forget what had happened in Vietnam, pointing out that the same thing could happen again.
4   Example in CB.
5   He demanded to know who was running the economy, (sarcastically) adding that he suspected neither of them knew.
6   They accused her (unanimously/heatedly) of being a bad European, maintaining that she had never believed in their principles.
7   She complimented him (warmly/cordially) on having been a great minister and (sincerely) regretted him/his going/(or the fact that he was going).
8   He objected (bitterly) to being made a scapegoat and threatened to tell/that he would tell the whole story if they did.
9   He apologised (abruptly/briefly) for what had happened, emphasising that they had not been informed.
10 He (reluctantly) agreed to let her be/to her being/becoming Prime Minister, but insisted (unconvincingly) on being Defence Minster himself.

Point out the two patterns with the verb *agree* :

*He agreed **to do** it (himself).*
*He agreed **to me/my doing** it.*

Ex. 5

Classroom treatment

This invention exercise perhaps demands more inventiveness of students than may appear to be the case at first sight. It is certainly an exercise which would bear most fruit with students working in pairs, threes or even fours, pooling ideas. They will need to produce a mini short story for each of the six situations. Point out that the first verb indicates how the utterance is/was spoken and that the second and third verbs reflect the content of what is/was said.

Model answers

(As with the model sentences for exs. 3 and 4, we have mixed the use of conjunction and present participle to link the two parts of the sentences.)

Possible target language would be:

1   'Thanks a lot!' he shouted. 'I'll do the same for you one day!'

    He thanked her at the top of his voice and promised to do the same for her one day.

2   'Congratulations on your win!' he called. 'Remember, it was my money you bet with!'

    He congratulated her loudly and mentioned (,almost as an afterthought,) that it had been his money she had bet with.

3   'Why isn't there any air-conditioning in this office?' she moaned. 'At least they could put a fan in here.'

    She complained that there was no/about there being no air-conditioning in the office and suggested that they could at least put a fan in.

4   'P-please f-forgive me,' he stammered. 'I'll p-pay for everything m- myself.'

    He urged her desperately to forgive him, offering to pay for everything himself.

5   'Please come with me' he pleaded. 'You won't regret it.'

    He implored her to go with him, assuring her that she wouldn't regret it.

6   'What's gone on is all your fault!' she screamed. 'You might have known something like this would happen!'

    She blamed him unreservedly for what had gone on and criticised him openly for not realising something like that would happen.

Ex. 6

Classroom treatment

This could easily be set for homework or might produce some interesting co-operative activity with students working in pairs to produce a mini-article.

Before students write, spend a little time discussing the style of newspaper headlines with the class.

What sorts of words are often omitted? (Articles, conjunctions, the verb *to be*.)

What is the tense of most verbs? (Present simple, although the events described are usually past; *to -* infinitive standard way of expressing future e.g. QUEEN TO VISIT USA.)

Get students to express the headlines on page 27 in full, normal sentences:

Fighting broke out in a college meeting (last night).

(Yesterday) in court, a judge threw out/wouldn't accept the evidence given by the police and dismissed the case.

A recent (or planned) meeting of the (local) council has angered people who live in ... .

A top/famous film star has recently criticised (or perhaps yesterday physically attacked) a person who was interviewing him/her.

An athlete has been banned from competition for life after failing a drugs test.

Model articles

These are examples of the target language to which students should be aspiring:

1 Fighting broke out last night at a meeting of college students who had come together to discuss plans for setting up a new right-wing political group at Brightwell Polytechnic. The incident is believed to have started after a speech by one of the students suggesting a restriction on the number of non-whites attending the college. A spokesperson for the new group claimed that their ideas were shared by up to 60 per cent of the student population and that they intended contacting the Minister of Education with their proposals. Chief Inspector Smythe from Brightwell CID said he thought the violence had been just a bit of fun, adding that students were entitled to let off steam sometimes and that there was nothing so awful in what the new group had been saying.

2 A (Winchester) judge yesterday dismissed the case against Mr Terence Haskins of 39 Cherry Gardens, (Southampton). The defendant had been charged with the assault of a police officer on the night of February 5th, when it was alleged that he repeatedly punched and kicked PC Brian Smith outside the 'White Swan' restaurant in (Southampton). Dismissing the case, Justice Harvey Brown told the court he had no reason to believe that Mr Haskins had been anywhere near the 'White Swan' on the night in question and felt that this was a clear case of mistaken identity. When interviewed later, Mr Haskins said he was glad that justice had been done, adding that it had all been an awful ordeal which he was relieved to see at an end.

Ex. 7

Classroom treatment

This exercise could easily be set for homework. If done in the classroom, it would certainly benefit from another working-in-pairs arrangement.

Model answers

Discuss with the class afterwards which of the two structures used seems more comfortable in each item.

1 He is reported to be planning a takeover of ICI.
   OR It is/has been reported (in *The Times*) that he is planning a takeover of ICI.

2 He is alleged to have killed at least thirteen women.
   OR It is/has been alleged that he killed at least thirteen women.

3 She is known to have had at least five husbands.
   OR It is (a) well-known (fact) that she has had at least five husbands.

4 He is said to be a good friend of the Queen.
   OR It is said that he is a good friend of the Queen.

5 He is believed to have embezzled millions from the company.
   OR It is believed that he embezzled millions from the company.

6 He is thought to have been taking drugs for years.
   OR It is thought that he has been taking drugs for years.

Ex. 8

Classroom treatment

See Introduction p.9 for notes on such extended writing tasks.

Again, best done as a piece of 'Now see what you can do that you couldn't do before' homework, or as a collaborative piece in the classroom, two or three Ss working together to produce the article.

A lead-in to this activity could be a short class discussion of current events in the world. The chances are that your using of this Unit coincides with another independence bid by this or that country, an earthquake, strike, election, major sporting event, scandal. Discuss possible headlines and content for such an article. An alternative idea is to use a local school or workplace event that could be written up as a newspaper article. Just as much fun, and just as valid in terms of language practice.

Coursebook pp.28-29

Vocabulary: Style and register

CAE Relevance: All Papers

Exs. 1 and 2

Classroom treatment

1 Look with the class at the examples of journalese words given. Possibly instigate a short discussion about the effect that words like 'slaughter' and 'massacre' applied to sport might have on the reader.

Do people even notice any more that to 'axe' 100 jobs or workers is a particularly brutal turn of phrase? You might at this point, before doing ex. 2, add (but not too much) to the list of journalistic pet-words: argument > storm; break a record (easily) > smash; reduce by a lot > slash; sunny spell > heatwave; etc.

2 Do the first one or two items together with the class, producing a model version on the board. (This is really quite a difficult exercise.) Then set the other two or three for Ss to write in pairs, before checking with the class. Ss should be encouraged to make use of dictionaries for this exercise, rather than get explanations of any remaining new words from you.

Model answers

CALLS FOR HEAD TO GO OVER EXAM BLUNDER
There have been lots of people saying the headmaster of our local school should resign because of the mistakes that were made with the examinations last summer.

CHAMP TROUNCES YOUNG PRETENDER
Did you hear that last night the champion (Mike Tyson) beat that young chap who was challenging him in the first round?

BATTLE OVER OUSTING OF UNITED BOSS GOES ON
Apparently they're still arguing about the way the manager of (Manchester) United (the football team) was sacked from his job last week.

CLASH OF HEADS AS SCHOOL PLAN HITS SNAG
You know about the plan to merge our two local secondary schools? Well, it seems the two headmasters now can't agree on how it should be done and there are all kinds of problems.

Exs. 3 and 4

Classroom treatment

Students can be asked to do this exercise in pairs, before answers are checked and doubts discussed. Again, use of dictionary should be encouraged to overcome problems.

Answers to ex. 3

Normal	Journalese	Normal	Journalese
anger	fury	to rise	to soar
to restrict	to curb	vital	key
a setback	a blow	a quarrel	a feud
an attempt	a bid	to question	to quiz
to encourage	to boost	to criticise	to slam [Example]
to promise	to vow	a division	a split

Model answer for ex. 4

The version of the passage (in journalistic style) should read like this:

The government's bid to boost the economy suffered a serious blow last night when their long-running feud with the unions flared up again. Union leaders, unable to contain their fury after stormy talks with ministers, vowed to fight the government every inch of the way if they try to curb wage increases. With inflation set to soar again, wages are clearly a key issue and there are signs of a split in the Cabinet as to what should be done. When quizzed on his plans, the Chancellor slammed the unions for their intransigence.

Ex. 5

Background information

> *Chancellor of the Exchequer:* the minister in Britain, known in many countries as the Finance Minister, who is responsible for the budget or the economic aspect of the country
> *the Opposition:* the political party or parties not in power
> *Shadow Chancellor:* the member of the Opposition who would be the Chancellor of the Exchequer if his/her party were in power

Classroom treatment

Go through the headlines on the left carefully with Ss to make sure they understand the 'message'. Elicit from them the basic information: the amount of investment has dropped dramatically, inflation has risen to a very high level, the same with the number of unemployed, the value of shares has dropped dramatically, and manufacturing production figures are as low as they have ever been.

Set this exercise as a group writing task.

Model article

The (very high) target language for students in this exercise would be:

There was bad news for the government from all sides yesterday as news came in of soaring unemployment figures and a fall in investment and the value of shares, a drop in manufacturing output and a dramatic rise in the rate of inflation. The Chancellor of the Exchequer, when questioned, said he thought that this was no more than a temporary setback and was confident that there would be an upturn in the economy very soon. The Shadow

Chancellor felt that this was just further evidence of the government having lost control of affairs, and called for a general election immediately, adding that this government had lost the confidence of industry, business and the people.

Exam Practice: Paper 4 Listening

CAE Relevance: Paper 4 (Listening)

▷ 🖭 **Tapescript**

TUTOR: Unit 4. Look at page 29, Exam Practice **a**, exercise 2. Listen to these extracts from the lecture and decide whether the information you hear is relevant to the questions or not. One.

LECTURER: Er as you can see from what I've written on the board here: four titles in the first category ...

TUTOR: Two.

LECTURER: It only sells about 400,000 copies on a good day.

TUTOR: Three.

LECTURER: *The Daily Telegraph* , the mouthpiece of the Conservative Party, some would say, perhaps unfairly ...

TUTOR: Four.

LECTURER: 1986 was a big year for newspapers.

TUTOR: Five.

LECTURER: And the last two have been having a running battle for readers for some time.

TUTOR: Six.

LECTURER: *The Guardian* would have had 24 pages at most, now it has between 36 and 40 on a normal day.

TUTOR: Seven.

LECTURER: And the fact that there's only 5p between most of the middle-brow papers and the out-and-out popular papers suggests it's not a question of cash.

TUTOR: Unit 4. Exam Practice **b**. Look at page 29. You're going to hear the beginning of a lecture on the British press. The information you see at the bottom of the page is out of date. As you listen, change the notes and add to them.

LECTURER: Let's start with the daily press. Now, most people would divide the dailies up into three groups: the serious papers, sometimes called the quality press, the er midddle-of-the-road group, can't make up their minds whether they're serious or not, and

the er popular press, which decided a long time ago that it's well basically not ... er serious, I mean. Er, as you can see from what I've written on the board here: four titles in the first category: *The Times*, the most famous, I suppose, the oldest — over 200 years old, and the one with the smallest circulation, ha ha, yes, it's ironic, isn't it? It only sells about 400,000 copies on a good day. Then there's *The Guardian*, the paper with the big heart, ha ha, er 550,000 copies a day, *The Daily Telegraph*, the mouthpiece of the Conservative party, some would say, perhaps unfairly, recently fallen to just above a million daily circulation, call it a million, and the baby of the serious papers, *The Independent*, at half a million a day is getting quite near to *The Guardian's* figure.

Now the middle-of-the road group has also had a recent addition in the form of *Today*, the first daily to make extensive use of colour — now of course, all of them use it occasionally. 1986 was a big year for newspapers, what with *Today* and *The Independent* starting up — er *Today* has had a chequered history, now selling roughly 900,000 a day, which is probably the minimum it can sell to survive. But *Today's* in there with the *The Daily Express*, founded in 1900, which at about 1.9 million a day outsells *The Daily Mail*, which I often think is more female than male, ha ha, by 100,000.

And that leaves us with three in the er I shouldn't say bottom group, three representatives of the popular press. There's *The Daily Star* — the most recent of them, as you can see, started in 1978, *The Daily Mirror*, the voice of socialist Britain, and the *Sun*. And the last two have been having a running battle for readers for some time. *The Sun's* been out in front for a few years now with a readership — well, some would say people don't actually read the *Sun*, just look at it ha ha — a circulation of er about 4.2 million, about 400,000 ahead of the *Daily Mirror*.

Lots of changes over the past few years, colour, one or two new weekly or twice-weekly titles, Saturday supplements, and perhaps quite significantly, the papers have got bigger. Incidentally I counted over 200 pages in a recent copy of the *Sunday Times*. But that's another story. I don't know if it's because there's more news about ha or whether it's because papers are technologically speaking easier to produce, but they *have* got bigger. The tabloids have gone from an average of 36 pages five or six years ago to between 42 and 46. *The Guardian* would have had 24 pages at most: now it has between 36 and 40 on a normal day, a two-part newspaper with supplement. And the same's true of *The Times* and *The Independent*, they're normally between 36 and 40 as well. *The Telegraph* has remained at about 36 pages. *Today's* usually 32 and the *Express* and *Mail* generally run to between 44 and 50.

Er there's been a lot said and written about what makes people choose a particular newspaper. Some say it's simple economics and some people choose the cheapest. But you can see there's not much difference in price really: all the pop ones at 25p compared to the middle-of-the-road ones at 30p, except *Today*, which for some reason only asks 25p of us every day, and the qualities 40p. And the fact that there's only 5p between most of the middle-brow papers and the out-and-out popular papers suggests it's not a question of cash. At least, not principally. No, the issue is a much deeper one than that. And that's what I'd like to go on to next.

Ex. a

Classroom treatment

This lecture is an example of a monologue that Ss will only hear once in the examination. If they fail to catch a particular fact or figure, they lose a point. This fact will naturally create greater pressure than with pieces heard twice. In this exam practice we lead Ss into the 'test' by way of warm-up exercises which should serve to reduce this pressure.

1 This activity, giving valuable practice in predicting, may be done with the whole class contributing ideas or initially with Ss working in small groups and subsequently sharing their conclusions with other groups.

Expected conclusions to be reached:

- The columns left to right show i) Circulation figures in millions, ii) Year paper was founded, iii) Number of pages, iv) Price in pence (p.)

- Missing information for *The Independent* and *Today* pure guesswork, but if Ss deduce that they were new, young newspapers in 1986, they may

infer that a) circulation wouldn't have been very high, b) their first year was probably 1986, c) the number of pages similar to the other papers in their 'group', and d) the price likewise.

- Ss must realise that the first group of papers are the 'serious, quality' dailies, the second group 'middle-of-the road' and the third group the 'popular tabloid' press.

- Outdated information could be in any of the columns except the year the paper was founded

- Possible problems: hearing 14 v. 40 etc, dealing with large numbers like 750,000 or 1.6 million, dealing with a lot of numbers coming one after the other, doing quick calculations if the speaker says things like *5p more than before, half what it was in 1986,* etc.

2 Play the first part of the tape, the extracts from the lecture, first asking students to write Y(es) or N(o) for each extract they hear, depending on whether they think it contains useful information.

The exercise gives help to students by way of a preliminary encounter with the voice and style of speaker, and should reinforce the idea that not every piece of information needs to be processed — or even understood! — when they are listening to such passages.

Answers to preliminary exercise

1 No; 2 Yes; 3 No; 4 Yes; 5 No; 6 Yes; 7 Yes.

Ex. b

Classroom treatment

Play the full lecture on tape, warning students that they will only hear the piece once and then will have their answers checked. (Although Ss may only hear such a monologue once in the exam, obviously in the classroom the piece can be played a second and a third time for the checking of answers and discussion of problems encountered.)

Answers

When all changes and additions have been made, the grid on page 29 should look like this. Students score $^1/_2$ point for each piece of information in bold that they have correct. (They lose $^1/_2$ point if they have changed something that did not require changing.) Total points available (29 items) = 14 $^1/_2$

	Circulation (in millions)	Year founded	No. of pages	Price (in p.)
The Daily Telegraph	**1.0**	1855	**36**	**40**
The Guardian	0.55 [Example]	1821	**36-40**	**40**
The Times	0.4	1785	**36-40**	**40**
The Independent	**0.5**	**1986**	**36-40**	**40**
The Daily Express	**1.9**	1900	**44-50**	**30**
The Daily Mail	**1.8**	1896	**44-50**	**30**
Today	**0.9**	**1986**	**32**	**25**
The Sun	**4.2**	1964	**42-46**	**25**
The Daily Mirror	**3.8**	1903	**42-46**	**25**
The Star	1.8	1978	**42-46**	**25**

Rounding off the Unit

Why not round off this Unit by letting Ss discuss in relaxed fashion their favourite newspapers and what they like about them — and what they don't like about papers they choose not to read?

This might lead to the setting up of a survey which they could conduct (in English or L1) with a cross-section of the general public. (What is your favourite newspaper? What is your favourite/least favourite TV programme? How long do you spend each day reading a paper, watching TV, listening to the radio? etc.) Ss would then report back to class with their findings, which could be collated into a statistical document.

5 Out of this world

(The expression *Out of this world* has two distinctly different meanings. It can mean, literally 'out of this world', in space, in the heavens, but it can also mean 'extremely unusual', 'weird', 'strange' *and* 'fantastic' or 'wonderful'.)

Coursebook pp.30-31

Warm-up

Here are three **alternative suggestions**, all with books closed:

1 Ask Ss for any expressions they can think of using the word 'world', hoping first that they'll remember the title of the first Unit ('It's a small world'). They may come up with 'the big wide world', 'go/come up in the world', 'the world of fashion', 'be on top of the world', 'think the world of someone', 'worlds apart', and perhaps 'out of this world'. Ask them to explain and use any expressions they've listed.

2 Ask Ss individually to make a note of three things that they would consider 'out of this world' and then compare their lists with each other.

3 Ask Ss in pairs to agree on (a) a food, (b) a piece of music, and (c) a place which for them is 'out of this world', and then to compare their suggestions with those of others in the class.

Look and speak

CAE Relevance: Paper 5 (Speaking)

Background notes and vocabulary

'Space Station Hotel'
supply modules: sections of the hotel which provide its basic needs
guest modules: sections of the hotel with 'bedrooms', etc.
elevators — lateral/vertical: lifts which go to the side and up and down
recreation area: part of the hotel designed for leisure activities

Classroom treatment
Ss work in pairs. They look at the picture and discuss questions 1 and 2.

Spend a few minutes at the end of this activity pooling the questions prepared by each pair.

Read and discuss

CAE Relevance: Paper 1 (Reading)

Background notes and vocabulary

'Five-star holiday is out of this world'
five-star holiday: in Britain, registered hotels have 'star' ratings; one star is the lowest, five star is the best — luxury
spaceport: a 'port' in space (compare with other 'space' compounds: *spacesuit, spaceman, spacecraft, spacewalk, spaceship, spacerocket,* etc.)
intrepid: brave, courageous (It has echoes of *Star Trek* and boys' adventure stories.)
whirring: here, travelling at great speed
super-fit: here, extra specially fit and healthy (compare with other 'super' compounds: *superstar, superman, supermarket, superhuman*)
may negatively influence: a rather formal or scientific way of saying 'may have a bad effect on'
on the threshold of: on the edge of, on the point of beginning
space package: a holiday in space where the traveller pays for everything in advance and all is organised for him or her (compare *package holiday*)
Star Trek: an American space film and TV series: 'Scottie' is a character in that series.
gravity: the physical force which keeps our feet on the ground. Normally in space people experience 'weightlessness' rather than the pull of the earth or gravity.

Classroom treatment
Ask Ss to read the text, making sure that they understand the task.

Ss first prepare the task individually. They then compare and discuss their answers with a partner. Finally, check the answers with the whole class, asking Ss to explain how they ordered the paragraphs.

When Ss have done the task, refer back to the questions they originally prepared. Discuss whether these were in fact answered by the text. If not, could the Ss perhaps imagine their own answers.

Additional practice

At some point you might draw Ss' attention to certain vocabulary areas, for example:

Which words in the original first paragraph (b 'Forget the golden beaches ...) sound like words from a travel brochure? — *golden beaches, idyllic, ultimate, get-away-from-it-all, holiday of a lifetime, out of this world, best views of the world* (Note: usually in brochures this would be the best views **in** the world: why the change of preposition?)

Note the prefix 'mini' in mini-break. Ask Ss what it means. (small) Ask Ss if they can think of any other words using *mini* in this way? (*mini-skirt, mini-bus, mini-cab*) And the opposite? *(maxi)*

Additional practice

You might also introduce one of the grammar points of this Unit by asking Ss to think about how each of their five senses would be affected by the experience of visiting this hotel.

Make a point of revising here the verbs relating to the five senses: *to look, sound, taste, feel, smell* + adjective or 'like' or 'as if/as though'.

Do a little practice with each in turn. For example, ask the Ss to close their eyes and then make a noise e.g. slam a door and then ask students to make sentences using each of the three constructions e.g. *It sounded as if you were angry, It sounded like a door slamming, It sounded aggressive.*

Similarly, for *feel* , Ss close their eyes and are given something to touch — this could be done in twos or threes with each partner in turn having to close his/her eyes and be offered something to feel by his/her partner.

For *look* , take in an abstract art picture and ask Ss to make sentences with *look* based on the picture.

Taste and *smell* may be difficult sensations to arrange to experience in the classroom (unless you are prepared to cut up pieces of, say, apple, potato, carrot, pear, etc. in advance and ask Ss to identify them (again with eyes closed). It is probably simpler (and more productive of language) to ask Ss to think of a summer picnic in a favourite place and to describe the tastes and smells they think of. Point here to the construction *to taste/ smell of (something else)*, in addition.

Answers

Paragraph **a** follows paragraph 4. This is made clear by the phrase 'another consideration' which can only refer to the reason why holidaymakers will spend such a short time in space. The consideration already referred to is the point that being in space could have a harmful effect on people's health.

Paragraph **b** is the opening paragraph of the text. This is clear because (a) it introduces the topic of the whole article and (b) the writer has taken particular trouble with this paragraph trying to open in a way which is likely to catch the reader's attention.

Paragraph **c** follows paragraph 7. The end of paragraph 7 refers to the 60 guest rooms and paragraph c clearly carries on from this.

Thus the correct order of the paragraphs in the original article was:

b, 1, 2, 3, 4, **a**, 5, 6, 7, **c**, 8, 9

Optional homework

Ask Ss to write a letter to someone from the space hotel, telling him/her about their holiday there. Encourage Ss to remember all their five senses when writing the letter.

Homework

Ask Ss to read and prepare the texts on p. 33 at home.

Coursebook pp.32-33

Vocabulary: 'Non-smoking oxen'?!

CAE Relevance: All Papers

Background notes and vocabulary

'Make your wildest dreams come true!'
'Make your own record'
to cut a disc: to make a record
your Valentine: the person you love — from St Valentine, the patron saint of love, whose day is celebrated on February 14th with the giving of cards and presents to the person you love
Yellow Pages: a telephone directory listing businesses in a particular area according to category (electrical goods, TV repairs, window-cleaners and so on)
sleeve: the cover of a record
the charts: a weekly list of the current most popular records

'Jump out of a plane'

charity: a good cause e.g. medical research, handicapped people, old people. People raise money for charity by doing a parachute jump in the following way: they ask their friends and colleagues to sponsor them — in other words, if they are brave enough to do the jump, their friends agree to pay them a certain amount of money. The jumper then gives that money to a good cause or charity.

'Immortalise your pet'

pooch: slang term for *dog*

moggy: slang term for *cat*

pass on: a euphemistic way of saying *to die*

repro: short for reproduction

'Appear in the movies'

an extra: someone with a non-speaking part in a film, someone in a crowd scene, for instance

your vital statistics: your measurements (height, hips, waist and bust)

Casting: finding actors to fit parts (here, the name of a department)

'Sleep under the sea'

flippers: what divers wear on their feet to help them to move

Exs. 1-5

Classroom treatment

Work through the exercises in class. Most refer to the text on p. 33.

Check any other comprehension points relating to the text.

Suggested answers

1 You could make your own record.

You could do a parachute jump.

You could have an enormous banner saying whatever you wanted towed across the sky.

You could have a sculpture made of your pet.

You could be an extra in a film.

You could throw a custard pie at someone.

You could stay in a villa under the sea.

2 Examples of colloquial style

All the contractions; *pooch* (= dog); *moggy* (= cat); *to go bananas* (= to go crazy); *chuckers* (= throwers);

soggy (= wet and not solid); *squishy* (= wet and not solid); *the tops* (= the best); *mod. con.* (short for modern convenience); *gawping* (= gazing with an open mouth); *drops in* (= pays a spontaneous call on)

Examples of humorous style

The colloquial words listed above are all used in a rather humorous way.

Other examples of humorous style

— *before it's landed*

— *passionate red plastic* (one doesn't normally associate the word plastic with the adjective 'passionate')

— *if you can persuade Fido not to fidget* (Fido is a typical dog's name in England and some humour is added to this sentence thanks to the repetition of the 'f' sound in the words Fido and fidget)

— *or is it the bottom* (this is playing on the two meanings of the word 'top')

3 *one-day* is in the first text; *sticky* is in the pie-throwing text; *surcharge* is in the banner text; *non-speaking* is in the appearing in the movies text; *airtight, waterproof* and *seasick* are all in the text about the underwater villa.

Other examples of words using these suffixes are:

-y   *sandy, dusty, cloudy, windy, sunny, crunchy*
-tight   *watertight*
-proof   *fireproof, dustproof, childproof, foolproof, idiot-proof*
-sick   *airsick, homesick, travel-sick*

Other words using these prefixes are:

one-   *one-off, one-week, one-mile, one-horse, one-eyed, one-legged*
sur-   *surplus, surfeit*
non-   *non-smoking, non-aligned, non-stick*

4 *radii, spacecraft, geese, criteria, bases, people*

Other examples of words with irregular plurals are:

mouse (mice); tooth (teeth); ox (oxen); foot (feet); man (men); woman (women); child (children); sheep (sheep); deer (deer); fish (fish); phenomenon (phenomena); aircraft (aircraft)

The words can either be divided up according to meaning — animals, words describing people, etc. — or according to the way the plural is formed — no change, internal vowel change, end change that is not *s* .

5	operation / operator	operate	**operative** / operational
	passion	[no verb]	passionate / impassioned
	sculpture / **sculptor**	**sculpt**	**sculptured**
	record / recorder / recording	record	**recorded** / record
	(note the change of stress from the first syllable for the noun and adjective, **re**cord, to the second syllable of the verb, re**cord**)		
	guarantee / guarantor	guarantee	**guaranteed**
	luxury	**luxuriate**	**luxurious** / luxuriant
	production **/ product / producer**	**produce**	**productive**

Language focus

CAE Relevance: All Papers

Exs. 1 and 2

Classroom treatment

Ask Ss to work on answers to all the questions except 2d in pairs. Encourage students to write individual answers to 2d and to write at least three sentences.

Go round and check as they are working. Then ask Ss with rather different answers to read their answers to the class — three or four answers for each question, perhaps.

Possible answers

1 a Jumping out of a plane sounds terrifying/like my worst kind of nightmare.

  b Eating in an underwater villa looks (as if it could be) interesting.

  c Even though it's expensive to have your pet sculpted, it's money well spent for people who love their pets.

  d The girl in the picture on the left seems to be enjoying herself.

  e The girl in the picture on the right looks as if she is having a good time.

  f In spite of the expense, I'd love to stay in the undersea villa.

  N.B. **a** and **b** should be followed by adjectives rather than adverbs.
    c and **f** must involve some kind of contrast.

2 a I'd most like to appear in a film because it would be interesting to see what it's like.

  b I would hate to jump out of a parachute because I'd be terrified.

  c I'd like to write a novel.

  d I certainly wouldn't like to visit the space hotel until it had been running safely for some time and I knew that it was not dangerous to stay there. I think I would be a bit nervous of going there and there are plenty of places on earth which I would like to see before I considered a holiday in space.

Coursebook p.34

Language focus (continued)

Ex. 3 Grammar problems to solve — What's the difference?

Classroom treatment

Ss discuss the question in pairs. Check as a class that everyone has understood the difference between the sentences in each pair. Be the oracle if and when necessary.

Expected answers

• In the first sentence the person addressed has been on a journey and it looks as if it was a difficult one. In the second sentence the person hasn't actually just been on a journey, hard or otherwise, but they look as if they had i.e. they look tired and bedraggled.

• *He seems to enjoy painting* is talking about his liking for painting over a long period of time; it is making a very general statement, whereas *He seems to be enjoying painting* implies 'at this moment'; in other words, it is talking about some enjoyment that is temporary, either this afternoon, or perhaps during this (academic) term.

• *They must have done it wrong* focuses on the completed action and means that the task was not completed in the proper way. *They must have been doing it wrong* focuses on the method used and says that they were using the wrong method.

• *She looked good* means that she looked smart, elegant, whereas *She looked well* refers simply to health.

• *Fairly* suggests a little bit warm, not too much (we want it warm here), whereas *rather warm* suggests that the hotel is a bit too warm.

- *I should think* is much more tentative than *I think*. It suggests perhaps that the speaker has not thought too much about the subject and/or that she/he is open to persuasion of a different point of view.

- *It was quite funny* means it was fairly amusing, whereas *it was quite ridiculous* means it was absolutely ridiculous. (*Quite* has the meaning of totally or absolutely before an adjective that is so extreme in meaning itself that it cannot really be modified by a word meaning fairly or a little bit.)

Further classroom treatment
Now practise the points raised a little more as a whole class activity. Ask Ss perhaps to explain the difference between the following pairs of sentences (they illustrate more or less the same points as explained above):

- I feel good. / I feel well.
- She appears to study hard. / She appears to be studying hard.
- The art gallery is fairly modern. / The art gallery is rather modern.
- I don't think you need a coat. / I shouldn't think you need a coat.
- She must have worn her red dress. / She must have been wearing her red dress.
- He looks as if he'd had too much to drink. / He looks as if he's had too much to drink.

Then ask Ss if *quite* would mean 'fairly' or 'absolutely' before the following adjectives:

wonderful (absolutely), warm (fairly), fantastic (absolutely), disgraceful (absolutely), good (fairly), appalling (absolutely), magnificent (absolutely), friendly (fairly)

Ex. 4 Read, listen and discuss

CAE Relevance: All Papers

Background notes and vocabulary

> *droning:* a monotonous sound
> *changing pitch:* becoming higher or lower in sound
> *Morse code:* a code made by using two varieties of sound long and short with a specific combination to match each letter in the alphabet
> *haunted:* inhabited by ghosts or supernatural beings
> *cockpit:* where the pilots sit in a plane
> *hangar:* 'garage' for a plane
> *spooky:* eerie, mysterious, weird

▷ 📼 **Tapescript for ex. 3** (See Coursebook p.149.)

Classroom treatment and Key
Read the text to the students. There are only vocabulary and structural practice questions in the book, so it may be useful to do some quick comprehension check work first before going into the printed questions.

Suggestions for **comprehension check** questions (to be given after the initial reading of the text):

What is a Lincoln? (An old military aeroplane.)

When did it last fly? (30 years ago.)

What did the radio presenter do? (Left a tape recorder on the plane and went away locking the doors, having checked that no one was there.)

What happened? (The recorder picked up all sorts of flying noises.)

How did he feel? (A little frightened.)

What else is strange about the Lincoln? (It's unexpectedly warm inside.)

The questions in the book should be dealt with after Ss have had a chance to look at the text themselves.

1 Ask Ss individually to underline words that answer question 1 before checking their answers.

   aeroplane words: bomber, on the ground, pilots, in flight, engines droning and changing pitch, aircrew, aircraft, cockpit, plane, hangar

   (Remind Ss again that the plural of *aircraft* is aircraft.)

   strange or frightening words: mystified, eerie, haunted, shuddered, spooky, strange

2 Remind students of the difference between *could have happened* and *could have been happening* (the former focuses on the complete result and the latter on the process leading up to the result rather than the result itself).

   In pairs Ss brainstorm as many answers as possible to the three questions. Then compare ideas as a class. Do not spend too long on this as some pairs may find it difficult to come up with more than two or three ideas.

Possible answers
Ss may have much better suggestions:

a Someone could have played a trick on the radio presenter.

b A storm might have been blowing during the recording.

c The plane could be exceptionally well insulated.

3 Play the recording to the whole class and discuss the sounds together.

The sounds on the recording represent the following:

1 Wind howling; 2 Footsteps of two people walking through leaves; 3 Someone shivering; 4 Someone sighing 'We're nearly there, thank goodness'; 5 Someone opening a creaky door; 6 Feet scurrying away; 7 Birds inside a building; 8 Someone howling; 9 Slow plodding footsteps accompanied by clanking chains; 10 Whispers followed by a scream.

If the Ss interpret the sounds in different ways, that does not matter as long as they make appropriate sentences. Note that *It could/might be* and *It sounds like* should be followed by a noun or noun phrase whereas *It sounds as if* must be followed by a clause with a complete verb.

4 In pairs Ss discuss their ideas for a story involving the different sounds. Before they plan their story, remind them of all the vocabulary they have studied in this Unit. Suggest they look through their notebooks and try to use at least some of the new words they have studied.

(See Introduction p.9.)

Homework

Ss write their versions of the story at home. After you have corrected the stories, ask Ss to re-write them without mistakes and then pin up their work on the walls for other Ss to read (and thus remind themselves of new vocabulary etc. dealt with in this Unit).

Possible model answer

Here is an example of the kind of writing that a good student at this level might produce. Notice how use has been made of some of the new vocabulary presented in the Unit.

Jane and Martin had booked up for a 'weekend to remember' at a hotel in the countryside. The brochure had promised them that their stay there would be truly out of this world. However, things were not to turn out exactly as they had anticipated. They were on their way to the hotel in Martin's car. It was a chilly autumn night and the wind was howling in the trees.

Suddenly the car's engine started to drone, then it thudded a couple of times and stopped completely. 'We can only be about ten minutes away from the hotel now', Jane said. 'Let's walk there. We can get the car sorted out in the morning.' So off they went. They found the drive up to the hotel and started trudging up it. It was hard going as it was covered in leaves. 'This is a little strange' said Martin. 'No car

can have been up this drive for a long time. I hope we're going to the right place.' 'I'm freezing', said Jane, shivering. 'It wasn't anything like as cold as this when we left town.'

They rounded a corner and could see a house looming up in front of them with a glimmer of light coming from it. 'We're nearly there, thank goodness,' sighed Jane. As they approached the house, it seemed strangely silent for a hotel. Martin pushed open the door which was heavy and creaked as if it had not been oiled for many years. As they opened the door they could hear feet scurrying away into the distance. There were no other sounds of humans, just birds twittering. 'Those birds are inside the building, not outside it,' said Jane. 'I don't think I like this place.' They both froze as they heard a long sad wailing noise coming from the room to their right. Martin shuddered. A slow plod of footsteps, interspersed with clanking noises, could be heard crossing the room.

'Let's get out of here' whispered Martin. 'I'd rather sleep in the car than in this so-called hotel.' The door on their right opened and Jane screamed as she looked and saw a suit of armour standing in the dimly lit doorway. 'Welcome to the haunted hotel' said the suit of armour. 'Would you like to sleep in the bedroom with the ghost or the one with the bats in it?' 'I'm afraid we've made a mistake,' said Martin, and they turned and ran as fast as they could back down the drive to the safety of their own car.

Coursebook p.35

Exam Practice: Paper 5 Speaking

CAE Relevance: Paper 5 (Speaking)

Exs. a and b

Classroom treatment

a Spend time discussing the questions above the pictures.

The important points to clarify are that in Phase B each partner is given about a minute to talk on something that he/she is given — usually a picture of some kind. The other candidate has another picture which relates to the one being described in some way. As he/she listens, he/she has to compare what he/she hears with what he/she can see. Encourage Ss to think of their approach to describing a picture which the other candidate cannot see. It is much easier, for example, if they give a brief summary of what their picture is about before describing something in one corner. Encourage them also to think about the kind of language needed for describing a picture:

- *there is, there are,* and *there's a .../there are ... doing*
- lots of prepositions
- the present continuous tense
- *it looks as if*
- *it could be*
- *it might be*
- *it's not very clear but...*
- *seem/appear to be doing,* etc.

b Divide Ss into pairs and ask Student A to choose one of the four pictures and describe it to Student B who has to guess which picture is being described. Allow Ss a moment or two to think about what they are going to say and then tell the As to begin talking. Tell them when a minute is up. When A has finished, repeat the same process with B. The idea of timing the Ss is simply to let them feel roughly how long they will be expected to speak.

After they have done exercise **b**, discuss question **a** again. Did they follow their own tips? Were they useful? Would they now add any other ideas/useful language to that discussed before?

Continuation of practice

Useful practice for Section B of the speaking part of the exam is to train Ss in speaking for one minute on topics that may seem quite difficult. Write a different topic on a set of cards (one for each student in the group) — or

ask the Ss each to write a topic on a card. Possible topics: my ideal home, elephants, my ambitions, what I like reading, breakfast, pets, etc.

Ss then choose a card in turn and have to talk on that topic for a minute. Comment at the end on accuracy and content of the talk (try to think of or elicit at least one positive thing and one bit of constructive criticism for each student) but the main point of the exercise is to give students practice in extended talking on a subject where they may initially feel that they have nothing to say.

Rounding off the Unit

The Exam Practice idea can be extended by asking Ss to do this task:

Draw an abstract picture using a range of colours and geometrical shapes. Describe your picture to your partner, who must try to draw an identical picture. When he/she has finished, compare your pictures. What differences do you notice between them?

OR Why not ask Ss individually (in about five minutes) to design an advert for a space hotel? They could then do a 'describe and draw' exercise with a partner, describing their advert to a partner who has to draw it (without looking at the original).

6 We're all in the same boat

(The expression *We're all in the same boat* means 'we are all in the same unpleasant conditions, or we're all facing the same dangers'. Imagine you're out on a walking expedition with some friends, with very little water or food left. One of the party keeps moaning 'I'm hungry, I'm thirsty'. You might say, 'Look, we're all hungry, we're all thirsty. But there's not much we can do about it. We're all in the same boat.')

Coursebook pp.36-37

Warm-up

Here are four **alternative suggestions**, 1-3 with books closed:

1 Ask Ss what the expression 'We're all in the same boat' means. If no one knows, explain it and the relevance of the title to the Unit. It's about problems we're all facing.

2 Ask Ss to give you some world problems — problems which face the world as a whole — and write them up anywhere on the blackboard/OHP e.g. growing population; global warming/the greenhouse effect; famine; pollution, especially in cities; the motor car; endangered species; war; poverty; AIDS; etc.

   Pairwork: Ask Ss to list the problems in order of importance (or urgency) to be solved.

   Groupwork: Through groupwork and then the class as a whole, see if the Ss can come to an agreement about the order.

   Don't go any further at this stage in the Unit with the problems. This will be enough to open the subject. There will be a time and a place later in the Unit for students to discuss and suggest solutions.

3 Conduct a brief classroom discussion on this question: Do you feel optimistic or pessimistic about the future of the world? Why? (This would have to be brief, just to broach the topic, otherwise we're into the whole Unit!)

4 Books open: Ask Ss to look at the cartoon, then to describe and discuss it. Prompt questions might be: Do you think the cartoon illustrates the state of the world today? Why?/ Why not? etc.

Read, find out, discuss and write

CAE Relevance: Papers 1, 2 and 5 (Reading, Writing and Speaking)

Background notes and vocabulary

'The burger that ate a rain forest'
This article appeared in the weekend colour magazine which accompanied *The Sunday Times* newspaper in Britain in February 1989.
burger: beefburger or hamburger: despite the latter's name, a 'hamburger' is often made from beef, not ham or pork
rain forest: a wet tropical forest with tall trees growing thickly together
chainsaw: a saw made up of an endless chain fitted with teeth and driven by a motor
ketchup: a thick red liquid made from tomatoes, used as a sauce for giving pleasant taste to food
US congressional committee: a committee formed as part of Congress, the federal legislature of the United States
fast food (industry): (the industry which produces and/or serves to the public) food which is pre-prepared and quick to serve e.g. beefburgers, frozen chips, etc.
environmentalists: people who try to prevent the environment from being spoilt
a clearance: the act or result of clearing (away)
pasture (land): a piece of land where grass is grown for cattle to feed on
the World Bank: the International Bank for Reconstruction and Development founded at the Bretton Woods Conference (1944) by the Western powers and provided by them with assets (in bullion and currency), on the basis of which member nations may obtain credit for approved development and reconstruction enterprises without drawing upon national reserves. The World Bank is affiliated to the UN Headquarters, Washington.
grazing: here, an area for cattle to feed on: to graze = to feed on grass
one head of cattle: one cow or bull: the word 'head' is often used to count animals e.g. 50 head of cattle
eroded wasteland: useless land worn or rubbed away by wind, floods, etc.

> *fast-food chain:* a number of shops, restaurants, etc. under the same ownership, and selling fast food
> *carcase (or carcass):* the body of a dead animal, esp. one which is ready to be cut up as meat
> *a boycott:* the act of refusing to do business with

Exs. 1-9

Classroom treatment

Exs. 1-7: It is worth repeating here that these exercises give practice once again in the different reading skills that Ss will need to apply in Paper 1 of the exam (see Unit 1, p.22 in this TG). It's important that Ss work through the exercises one by one in pairs, and not read the article as a whole in fine detail until they get to exercise 6.

Check Ss' answers to each question with the whole class before they move on to the next.

Before Ss do ex. 7, remind them of the typical language of headlines or newspaper article section headings

Ex. 8: Ss might work in pairs or groups of three or four here. This discussion should be reasonably free, but here is some language students might find useful in their discussions:

Reactions

I think it's [dreadful]. The Americans should have stopped eating 'forest beef' a long time ago.

I was horrified when I read that ...

What I thought was terrible was the fact that ... etc.

(And) what makes the situation so serious is the fact that ...

Suggesting solutions

Sooner or later something will have to be done about the situation.

I think there ought to be a total ban on beef from Central America.

I think it would be wise if ...

If they were to stop cattle ranching, then ...

Ex. 9 should be prepared in class (see Introduction p.9) and then best set as a homework assignment.

Answers or possible answers

1 It's going to be about beefburgers (or hamburgers), the way we raise beef for them, and some connection with the rain forests in South America (and perhaps other places in the world).

2 Open-ended.

3 He is generally pessimistic about the situation. Although the import of beef into the USA has helped to reduce inflation, the production of beef has had a disastrous effect on the rain forest zone. There is *some* hope e.g. Burger King have stopped buying Central American beef — but a lot of beef still goes into the USA, and the rain forest has become 'eroded wasteland'.

4 Central America (rain forests), the USA (where people eat the burgers), Costa Rica (which used to sell beef to Burger King), San Francisco (where RAN is based).

5 a) Fifties: (the 1950s) that's when the clearance of forests began;

   b) 20: that's the number of years in which the number of beef cattle in Central America has increased by *two-thirds* ;

   c) *1985*: that was the year when *90%* of the output (= beef) was exported to the USA;

   d) 55: that's the number of square feet of rain forest needed to raise enough beef to make one American hamburger;

   e) *20-30*: that's the number of species or kinds of trees and bushes that you would find in a forest;

   f) *2.5*: that's the number of acres one head of cattle eats/ grazes in a year;

   g) *10*: that's the number of years the African grasses survive before weeds take over;

   OR that's the number of years before one head of cattle needs 17.5 acres instead of 2.5;

   h) *1987*: that's when Burger King stopped buying Costa Rican beef;

   i) *17.5*: that's the number of acres one head of cattle needs after 10 years/after a pasture is planted;

   j) *70,000*: that's the number of cattle/carcases Burger King used to buy from Costa Rica;

   k) *8,000*: that's the number of tons of beef the USA still imports from Central America.

6 Some possible questions:

   Para 1: What destruction is the American fast food industry thought to be responsible for?

   Para 2: When did the clearance of the forests begin?

   Para 3: Why don't they use domestically produced beef to make hamburgers or beefburgers in the States?

   Para 4: Why is the production (or raising) of beef so destructive to the rain forest zone?

   Para 5: How long does it take for the forest to become a wasteland?

   Para 6: Where is the Rainforest Action Network based?

   Para 7: How much beef is still imported into the USA?

Para 8: How much beef do local people in Central America eat?

7 Possible paragraph headings or titles:

Para 2: Loans Help Ranchers Clear Forests

Para 3: C. American Beef Imports Cut Inflation

Para 4: 1 Hamburger = 1 Small Kitchen!

Para 5: 10 Years from Forest to Wasteland

Para 6: Boycott Stops Burger King Buying Beef

Para 7: 8,000 Tons of Beef Can't Just Disappear

Para 8: Cats Eat More Beef Than Costa Ricans

9 Possible article for the college students' newspaper:

RAIN FOREST BEEF

Did you know that the American fast food industry is responsible for destroying more than a quarter of Central American rain forests?

The clearance of forests to create pasture for beef that could feed America began in the early Fifties, and the number of beef cattle has increased by two-thirds in the last 20 years. 90% of that beef goes to the USA, much of it to make beefburgers. The reasons is simply that it is cheaper than 'home-grown' beef.

The problem (for Central America) is that the production of beef destroys the forest: it takes an area the size of a small kitchen, for example, to produce enough grazing for just one beefburger! And not only does cattle ranching cause terrible damage, it also creates very few jobs and only short-term profits. In only 10 years, what was once forestland can become a wasteland.

There is some hope. Burger King, one of America's largest fast-food chains, stopped buying Central American beef in 1987, and McDonald's say they have never used 'rain forest beef'. Nevertheless, about 8,000 tons of beef a year are still imported into the USA from Central America.

Coursebook pp.38-39

Language focus

CAE Relevance: All Papers

Background notes and vocabulary

The notes about the mandrill accompanied a photograph which appeared as one in a series in a weekend magazine devoted almost exclusively to world environment problems. The other notes have been written in the same style in order to define the problem. Each therefore uses all or some of the same headings. They are —

Size (how big or small the animal, thing or problem is)

Range (where the animal or problem can be found)

Habitat (what kind of environment the animal or problem thrives best in)

Diet (what the animal or problem eats or feeds on)

Status (this refers to whether the animal or problem is growing in numbers or size, or becoming less)

Threats (the things that are threatening the survival or growth of the species or the problem)

Note that there is clearly a certain amount of irony here, especially when talking about 'threats to the motor car' or 'threats to poverty and famine', for example.

an endangered species: a group of plants or animals that are of the same kind and which are in danger of becoming extinct. The mandrill here is just one example of thousands of endangered species in the world now.

Cameroon: a federal republic in West Africa

Gabon: a republic in West Central Africa

Congo: a republic in West Central Africa

'homo sapiens': Latin name for the human species

omnivorous: eating everything, esp. eating both plant and animal food

brainchild: somebody's idea or invention

to wean: to accustom (a young child, baby or animal) to food instead of mother's milk

unleaded petrol: petrol with little or no lead content

'Siamese' twins: a pair of people joined together from birth at some part of their bodies

vagaries: unusual, purposeless or unexpected ideas, acts or thoughts. We often talk about the 'vagaries of the weather' because the weather is so changeable in the UK.

Exs. 1-6

Classroom treatment

1 Ss read the details about the five world problems individually or in pairs. Check comprehension before they start discussing the problems.

Alternatively, Ss work in groups of five: each of the five Ss reads one of the world problems and describes or explains it to the others in the group. This phase should simply concentrate on exchanging information. The 'listeners' should be encouraged to ask the 'reporter' questions so that any problems with vocabulary etc. are cleared up before they begin discussion.

2 Explain (if you need to) that we use a wide range of structures when we want to discuss world problems like these — which is why there are a number of grammar points to revise or practise.

Run through the language areas (1-6) as quickly or in as much detail as necessary (depending on the general level of the class) so that Ss can draw on any of the language when discussing the problems. Draw Ss' attention particularly to the following in the different areas:

1 Stating the problem

The expressions *We are facing a problem* and *We are faced with a problem* — and sentences which begin with clauses like *What we are faced with ...*, *The reason a solution is so urgent ...*, etc.

2 Discussing what needs to be done

The verbs *need* and *want* followed by the gerund or passive infinitive.

3 Suggesting what people should do

The use of *should do* and *ought to do* — and the use of *Surely* at the beginning of a sentence to mean 'I can't believe it's not true'.

4 Suggesting courses of action, and possible consequences

The use of conditional sentences — and the construction *It's (about/high) time we did something*.

5 Pointing out dangers

The use of *risk doing, run the risk of doing* and *There's a risk of doing* to point out dangers.

6 Looking back and expressing regrets

The use of past conditionals, the inversion construction *Had we done that sooner, ...* — and once again the use of *Surely* at the beginning of a sentence.

Reference to the Grammar Commentary will help with a number of the points.

3 Ss now discuss the problems one by one, using as much of the language from 1-6 as they need. You might begin by discussing one with the class as a whole before they discuss the rest in pairs or small groups. Encourage Ss to state the problem, say what needs to be done, point out dangers, etc.

4 As a final activity, and to draw all the language and ideas together, you might ask Ss to prepare and hold a debate in the next lesson. One suggestion might be: 'This house believes that, if we can solve the problems of poverty and famine, we will have found the solution to all other world problems.'

(See Unit 1 for the conduct of a formal debate.)

Listen, discuss and write

CAE Relevance: Papers 4, 5 and 2 (Listening, Speaking and Writing)

▷ ▭ **Tapescript** (See Coursebook p.150.)
Exs. 1-3

Classroom treatment

1 Ss are going to hear a conversation about a national problem. It could be one of the problems they've already discussed, or something else. Ask them to suggest or predict what other problem the discussion might be about.

Play the tape once to check Ss' predictions and to say what the problem is.

Play the tape again to answer question **b**.

Play the tape once again for Ss to note how the speakers use some of the language they have practised on these pages.

2 Ss now discuss a 'local' problem of their own choosing. During the discussion they should be encouraged to make notes on suggested courses of action, etc.

3 This writing task should be prepared and perhaps begun in class, but might be set as a homework assignment. (See Introduction p.9.)

Answers to ex. 1

1a The problem is an increase in petty crime.

1b The man thinks we should make the punishment fit the crime. The woman thinks we should look at why young people are committing petty crimes.

And here is some of the language they use:

Some countries are facing increases ...; what we're faced with is ...; To be honest, if we don't do something soon, there's a serious risk of the situation getting out of hand; the problem wouldn't have arisen if the courts hadn't been so soft ...; Surely something could have been done a long time ago; it's about time we made the punishment fit the crime; it might be a lot better if we started ...

Coursebook pp.40-41

Read, discuss and write

CAE Relevance: Papers 1, 5 and 2 (Reading, Speaking and Writing)

Background notes and vocabulary

Both letters appeared in *The Times* newspaper. As is often the case in the 'Letters to the Editor' column, the first letter refers to a previously published letter, and the second to the first letter.
captive market: this is a variation on the phrase 'a captive audience' = a group of people who are not able or not allowed to stop listening or watching. In this case, drivers stuck in traffic jams are not only a good 'market' for sellers and the like, but are 'captive' because they can't move.
Lagos: the capital of Nigeria, Africa
Diary: here, the 'Diary' column in the newspaper which reports in brief on happenings and events from around the world
entrepreneurial, adj. from *entrepreneur:* a person who makes the plans for a business or a piece of work and gets it going
Colosseum: famous ancient amphitheatre in Rome, dating back to 80 A.D.
the World Cup: the international soccer/football competition which takes place every four years
Caracas: the capital of Venezuela
similarly immobilised: made unable to move (i.e. stuck) in the same way
windscreen wiper blades: the long rubber parts on wipers that clean the windscreen of a car

Exs. 1-6

Classroom treatment

1 Read the letters with the class, OR Ss read them in pairs, looking up or helping each other to understand any unknown vocabulary.

2 Ask and discuss the questions with the class, OR Ss discuss or answer the questions in pairs, and then check with the whole class.

3 (Q.6) Ask if Ss know about any other cities where people do this kind of thing i.e. try to sell you things or services while you're stuck in a traffic jam.

4 Ss work in pairs to prepare and write a short letter *either* about a city where similar activities go on *or*

suggesting solutions to the problem.
(See Introduction p.9.)

Answers

1 Both letters refer to people selling articles or services to people stuck in traffic jams in cities.

2 They are both Britons living in a foreign city.

3 Rome, Lagos and Caracas. In all three cities 'entrepreneurs' try to sell you things when you're stuck in traffic.

4 You can have your car windows washed, you can buy handkerchiefs, newspapers, flowers, cigarettes and sunglasses — and even buy back your own windscreen wiper blades!

5 They both seem slightly amused by the whole thing. Certainly there's no evidence that they're angry. Even the fact that John Doherty got to work an hour late comes after the fact that he had time to read the whole newspaper and arrived at work 'refreshed and well informed'!

Exam Practice: Paper 1 Reading

CAE Relevance: Paper 1 Reading

Background notes and vocabulary

'British Wildlife In Peril'
This passage, although taken from the 'young readers' section' of a popular magazine, is still adult in style.
hunt ... to extinction: hunt an animal so much that it has died out as a species
hay meadows: fields of grass for animals to eat, esp. hay = grass which is cut and dried for animal food
fens: areas of low wet land esp. in the east of England
field ponds: areas of still water (smaller than lakes) in fields
hedgerow: a row of bushes, esp. along country roads, or separating fields
verges: edges or borders, esp. of a road, path, etc.
marshes: pieces of land that are all or partly soft and wet because of their low position
estuaries: wide lower parts or mouths of rivers, into which the sea enters at high tide
to fell: to cut down
otters: fish-eating animals that can swim, and have beautiful brown fur

barn owls: a species of white-breasted, greyish-brown owl which was endangered until recently, since when many have been raised in owl sanctuaries and released into the wild

dormice: plural of 'dormouse', a very small European forest animal, having a long furry tail and looking a little like a squirrel

fertilisers: chemicals or natural substances put on the land to make crops grow better

pesticides: chemical substances used to kill pests (e.g. insects that harm or destroy crops)

robins: common European birds, quite small, with a brown back and wings, and red breast

hedgehogs: small insect-eating animals which come out only at night. A hedgehog has spines which stand out from its back to protect it.

gamekeepers: men employed to raise and protect game animals and birds on private land

a reserve: a piece of land reserved for a stated or special purpose, here to protect wildlife

the Isle of Rhum: a very small island, one of hundreds, off the north west coast of Scotland (south of the Isle of Skye)

Let's keep our fingers crossed!: Let's hope for the best.

Exs. a and b

Classroom treatment

a Explain carefully that this is one of the kinds of reading test that Ss will meet in Paper 1 of the exam. The aim of this phase is to discuss various ways of tackling the task. There is no one correct way of doing it: some people will use one method, some another. With the class as a whole, or with small groups or pairs, investigate each possible method — not only those suggested (1 and 2) but also any others Ss might suggest. Here are two more possible methods:

1 Read the whole passage once or twice to get a clear idea of what it is about. Then read the headings one by one and try to match them with appropriate paragraphs.

2 Read the first suggested paragraph heading, then begin reading the passage until you reach the paragraph you think it summarises. Then take the second suggested paragraph heading and again begin reading through the passage until you reach the paragraph you think that one summarises, and so on.

b Ss now do the task in class, or as a homework assignment.

Expected answers

A Paragraph 4; D Paragraph 5; E Paragraph 2; F Paragraph 1; G Paragraph 6; H Paragraph 3. (Headings B and C do not fit.)

Rounding off the Unit

Why not round off this Unit by asking Ss to recall all the different problems they have discussed, and perhaps to suggest others that they think are just as important, but which have not been mentioned?

7 Just a phase they're going through

Warm-up

Books closed: To interest Ss in the unit title, invent a mini-story along these lines: I heard someone say to a friend the other day: 'Oh it's just a phase she's going through'.

Ask Ss to write down possible answers to these questions, then compare with a partner, group, class, etc.

- Who do you think the 'she' was or might have been?
- What was the phase she was or might have been going through?
- Are there possibly different answers if it had been 'he' and not 'she'?

Encourage Ss to think of more than one answer for each. It might not have been a teenage daughter after all. Why not an ageing granny? Or a cat? Or a wife?

The ensuing discussion, however, should centre on the 'phases' of teenage life.

Read and write

CAE Relevance: Papers 1 and 2 (Reading and Writing)

Background notes and vocabulary

> 'Halina Swift answers your letters'
> *split ends:* hairs that split into two or three strands at the end
> *split-ups:* (marital or other romantic) separations
> *there are plenty more fish in the sea:* a cliché used to suggest that there are many other people one might meet and perhaps fall in love with

Classroom treatment

This is firstly an exercise in deduction and inference.

See if any of the class knows the term 'agony aunt'. Explain, if necessary, that it's the (usually female) columnist in popular newspapers/magazines who gives advice to readers with problems.

Encourage Ss in pairs to try and work out the 'gist' theme of the four problems before they write paragraphs from the original letters. Discuss with the class what conclusions they have reached and what clues helped them.

You may need to prompt with questions such as these for extract 1:

What, from the context, does 'unsightly' probably mean? (Ugly.)

What things can be ugly in an adolescent (or an adolescent's mind)? (Spots. Inexperienced shaving cuts. Split ends. Birthmarks. Moles. Crooked teeth. Sticking-out ears.)

What advice is given to the reader? (Go out. Have a good time. Don't stay at home and mope.)

What do you think 'mope' means? (Feel depressed and sorry for yourself.)

How do you think the last sentence is going to end? (Join a club. Phone a friend. Find a girl/boyfriend.)

The writing activity is not as 'serious' as some. Ss might enjoy going slightly 'over the top' in their letters. You could get them to work in pairs and halfway through each letter, ask them to exchange letters and complete the one started by their partner. Change partners after each letter.

Possible themes

1 Teenage spots the favourite, but see above
2 Girl's heartbreak after losing boyfriend
3 Parents critical of child's hair
4 Parents in conflict with 16-year-old son about how he spends his free time (or perhaps his money)

Target language for the paragraph-writing exercise might be along these lines — this for the first:

You see, for a couple of years now I've had this problem with spots on my forehead and chin. At first, my mum and dad said that it was just a phase I was going through and that they would soon disappear. But they haven't! If anything, they've got worse. I've tried everything to get rid of them: creams, lotions, changes in my diet. Nothing works. It's got so bad now that I hardly dare go out, and things like parties are a thing of the past.

Vocabulary study and listening

CAE Relevance: all Papers, especially Paper 4 Listening

▷ 📼 **Tapescript for ex. 2** (See Coursebook p.150.)

Background notes and vocabulary

> 'Did You Have A Normal Adolescence?'
> **heartthrob:** a person who makes the hearts of people of the opposite sex beat faster; an innocent version of a sex symbol
> **'latest flame':** the person you have most recently become emotionally involved with

Ex. 1

Classroom treatment

Among other things, the questionnaire gives practice in the structures:

a) *Did you use to ...?*
b) *to get bullied, laughed at,* etc.
c) *to have your hair pulled/your spots laughed at,* etc.

It may be necessary to point out that a) the question form of *used to* drops the *d,* b) *get* is commonly used to replace *be* in passive structures, and c) *to have something done* is not always used to express something we cause to happen but often when something (often unpleasant) is done to us.

First check that Ss know all the words in the questionnaire. Some of the difficult vocabulary has been previewed already. Where inference is not possible, encourage the use of dictionaries or choose to pre-teach/check words you think might cause difficulties.

Give Ss a couple of minutes to find a fourth item for each question.

For the conduct of the questionnaire, allow Ss to move around the room, filling in a grid that they should have prepared, looking like this:

Name *Hans*	a	b	c	d
1	*Yes*	*No*	*No*	*Yes*
2	*No*	*No*	*Yes*	*Yes*
etc.				

The totalling of points after the questionnaire has been conducted is not a key element in the practice, but a quick feedback of results may produce some interesting comment and analysis.

Possible answers

The possibilities here are almost endless, but you could expect some of the following:

1 shyness / an inferiority complex / nosebleeds / dandruff / tooth problems
2 naughty / aggressive to your brothers and sisters / sulky / dishonest
3 smacked / beaten / caned / laughed at / ignored / sent to see the Headmaster/ Headmistress
4 'flu / influenza / a broken arm / a broken leg / bronchitis / food poisoning / chicken pox
5 write love poems or songs / send Valentine cards to him/ her
6 stay in for a whole day / take a cold shower / run a long way as a punishment
7 steal apples from someone's garden / put a pin on the teacher's chair
8 hand slapped / bottom smacked / homework read out as an example of how it should/shouldn't be done

Ex. 2

Classroom treatment

A lot of the difficult vocabulary has been previewed in **1**. However, you might like to pre-teach/check: *pin-up posters, pinching apples, end-of-term reports, detention, juvenile, chickenpox, measles, mumps, whooping cough.*

For the listening exercise, explain carefully what Ss are going to hear; it is not something one hears every day! Make sure Ss are ready to make notes; otherwise the follow-up exercise is rendered invalid. Play the tape, pausing long enough after each extract for students to write notes on the problem, the symptoms, how they would feel and what they would do. Stress that they are making notes, not writing a composition!

It may be best to stop after the first extract, allow time for students to make notes and demonstrate the target language for their subsequent group discussion. If you feel at this point that they have not understood very well, replay the extract and likewise for the next few extracts, allowing a second listen.

If it seems they are unable to control an utterance like this: I w*ould probably ignore it because I think if I interefered and tried to change the way he was behaving he might well feel that his life was not his own* , do some slow build-up work with questions like: *How would you react if your eight-year-old son was asked to be in a Hollywood film / your fifteen-year-old daughter wanted to get married / your ten-year-old wanted to become a* *champion gymnast* ? Show how an extended answer works grammatically with past tense clauses, *would/ might* -clauses. This is conditional grammar practice for real!

After the listening phase, Ss in twos or threes share their views on the six problems and interesting comments are reported back to the class.

Ex. 3

This is an extension of what was happening at the end of **2**, with Ss supplying their own hypothetical situations. Ss should be able to invent at this stage, but you might have ready a few prompts like these:

— boy playing drums till after midnight;
— daughter wanting to become a nun;
— child gifted in sciences wanting to give up science subjects at school;
— child refusing to say please or thank you;
— child doing homework in front of TV;
— child with appalling table manners, etc.

Coursebook pp.44-45

Read, deduce and write

CAE Relevance: Papers 1, 2 and 3 (Reading, Writing and English in Use)

Background notes and vocabulary

> *Penelope Mortimer:* English novelist, whose best known novel to date is *The Pumpkin Eater* (1962)
> *Garbo:* a reference to Greta Garbo, the legendary Swedish beauty who made films and became famous for her desire 'to be alone'
> *Bergner:* Elizabeth Bergner (1900-1986) Austrian actress, well known in German, British and American theatre and cinema
> *hair-slide:* a small, often decorative fastener to keep a girl's hair in place
> *flighty:* unsteady and too influenced by sudden desires or ideas
> *Gary Cooper:* (1901-1962) American actor, perhaps most famous for his role in the film 'High Noon'
> *Good Companions:* a novel written in 1929 by the British author J.B. Priestley (1894-1984)
> *John Gielgud:* an English actor, famous for Shakespearian roles and recent Hollywood movies

> *Conrad Veidt:* (1893-1943) distinguished German character actor who also made films in Britain and Hollywood. Among many other films, he appeared in *Casablanca* (1942) and *The Thief of Baghdad* (1940).
> *Bach:* Johann Sebastian Bach (1685-1750) German composer
> *Vivaldi:* Antonio (Lucio) Vivaldi (1678-1741) Italian Baroque composer
> *Gershwin:* George Gershwin (1898-1937) American composer
> *Toad of Toad Hall:* a character in *The Wind in the Willows* by the British author, Kenneth Grahame (1859-1932). A.A. Milne dramatised the book and entitled it *Toad of Toad Hall.*

Ex. 1

Classroom treatment
As per rubric, Ss read the questions first, so that they know what information they are searching for, then read the text and make notes to answer them.

They then compare notes with a partner and argue over any differences.

Conduct a short feedback session with the whole class.

Possible answers

1 She was almost certainly at boarding school and at the time of writing probably in the sanatorium or sick bay (Miss Grenfell's nurse's uniform).

2 Somewhere between 13 and 15. Her 'boyfriend' was about 15 (though how he had a motorbike at that age, who knows?); she was obviously entering adolescence.

3 Her eyes stopped squinting and were steady; she was able to stop wearing glasses. In celebration she changed her hairstyle, giving herself a fringe.

4 Her mother was probably a very 'correct' kind of woman, somewhat old-fashioned in her attitudes, middle-class trying to be higher or lower-middle trying to be middle.

 Her father's job was probably in some way associated with the church. Perhaps he was the vicar.

 Her brother was certainly 'much' older than 15; Denis at 15 was very junior to him in school terms. He was probably 17 or 18.

5 Denis was 'pretty', handsome in a youthful sort of way, but also clumsy — like the writer — and rather uncoordinated. She was no doubt attracted by his musical talent and appreciated his more modern taste in music. Memory suggests he was rather unreliable — who isn't at that age? — but sweet and caring.

Exs. 2-4

Classroom treatment

Ss do the post-reading exercises in pairs, but change partners between **2** and **3** to guarantee new stimulus and cross-references. Ex. 4 is best set for homework.

Model answers

2 1 a comical reference: she thought the mirror might be playing a game or trick on her and thought if she looked at it cautiously, she might prove her point: she might prove that the mirror had been lying on the previous day.

2 After so many years, her face didn't have that awful wire and steel thing, her glasses. She felt naked, without clothes, because suddenly what had always been there on a part of her body wasn't

3 To be flighty — light-headed, light-hearted, free with one's emotions — was not an easy 'image' for her, 10 stone (over 63 kilos) and more. It was unlikely that she could be 'flighty' looking as plump as she was.

4 All the girls in the school had the same secret dreams and thoughts as the writer.

5 The organ needed the air that she pumped into it to produce sound.

6 My change (from little girl wearing glasses to young woman without glasses).

7 A reference to how adults (especially teachers and educational psychologists perhaps) think of children, categorise, pigeon-hole them, box them up. The phrase suggests that she doesn't approve of certain age-groups being classified as 'children, adolescents' etc.

8 She had an excited, tingling feeling running down her spine.

9 This was how her mother referred to the word 'boyfriend'. She disapproves of the term; *common* can mean *vulgar, crude.*

10 Here, *searching for it* means *trying to remember it or recall it* .

3 a Open-ended.

3 b

1 probably Christmas or any other annual festival which leads to overspending on a massive scale.

2 child going to first school/going to boarding school/ leaving home to get a flat/to get married.

3 spots on the face

4 a love letter

5 examinations

You might read out a few more similar descriptions to those in **3b** and see if Ss can identify them. Some suggestions:

6 Six to eight weeks of endless blue. (= school summer holidays)

7 Red pain running through one's fingers — red-faced with shame and anger. (= the feeling of being smacked by an adult)

8 That terrible realisation that one was no longer the centre of one's parents' world. (= birth of younger brother or sister)

4 An open-ended piece, but Ss should concentrate on an informal, personal style much neglected in the 'let's have a complete, grammatically correct sentence' approach of many classrooms.

> ### Coursebook pp.46-47

Language focus

CAE Relevance: All Papers, especially Paper 5 (Speaking)

Ex. 1

Classroom treatment

a Focus attention on the four lines in the box, pointing out that any combination of phrase left is possible with any phrase right.

The two patterns most likely to need explanation and/or practice occur in the fourth line. Ss at this level should be given a lot of practice in openers like *What sticks in my memory is ... / What I really feel is ... / What I don't like about X is ... / The thing we most enjoyed about the holiday was ...* They should be encouraged to use this pattern in **1a** and **1b**. They should also be reminded of the quite common pattern: *I'll always remember ... / I'll never forget .../ I'll never get used to ... / I'll always find odd the idea of ... my mother doing something.*

To help Ss with the short writing task, elicit some truly memorable events in some Ss' lives: moving house, changing school, a holiday, an accident, a local disaster, etc. This may give the 'slower' Ss a context in which to write.

b This activity gives freer, creative practice in what Ss have manipulated in **1a**. Make sure Ss have enough time to make notes for their short 'speeches' before they are required to 'reminisce' to their partners.

Ex. 2 Regrets

Though the active practice for Ss here is in controlling meaningful (3rd) conditional sentences, attention should also be focussed on the structures given expressing regret or absence of it:

I wish I had done X / I regret (not) doing Y / I'd like to have done Z / I feel bad about doing X / Perhaps I should have done Y / I'm glad I didn't do Z / I wouldn't have liked to do X / I've never regretted doing Y

This exercise could be done as part-writing, part-speaking. You could ask Ss to write one or two items and compare their sentences with a partner's, then ask them to improvise in speech along the same lines.

Sample model sentence

This is the sort of language Ss should be aspiring to in this exercise:

1 I think if I had gone on (with my piano lessons), I could have reached a very high standard; I might have been able to join a professional group. Or, who knows, I might have become a guest soloist with a symphony orchestra.

Ex. 3 Habits

Both **3a** and **3b** are open-ended exercises and should not be regarded as simply mechanical slot-filling. Through class discussion, elicit the sort of phrase that would interestingly fill the gaps before setting the exercise as an individual or paired writing task. Let the class hear some of the most interesting contributions afterwards.

Possible model completion for 3a

She was the sort of person who would do anything for anybody, if she felt it would benefit them. I'll always remember her helping and encouraging the children who had most problems academically. If anyone didn't understand what they had to do, she would always spend time explaining to them for the fourth, fifth or sixth time. She never once shouted at a child, preferring always to do things in a calm and patient way. She used to praise us for the simplest things we did well and she was always putting pupils' work up on the wall to make us feel important. If you had met her, I bet you would have fallen in love with her at first sight. That's the sort of person she was.

Possible model completion for 3b

He was an absolute monster/horror/terror. I can't remember one occasion on which he was genuinely sympathetic towards us. He would never praise us, and if any of us said or did anything wrong, he would punish us very severely. He used to lose his temper five or six times every lesson and I can still see him slamming his books down on the desk in anger

and walking out of the room. He was in the habit of pulling our ears if we didn't do what he wanted us to do and, what's more, he was always slapping the backs of our heads when we weren't concentrating. You could never relax when he was around. That's the sort of person he was.

Ex. 4 Permission and prohibition

Classroom treatment

The poem is not intended for exploitation but as a 'different' mode of presentation of language. If you want to *do* something with it, you might ask Ss to underline the stressed syllables throughout. These would probably be:

As <u>kids</u> we <u>do</u> what we <u>ought</u> to <u>do</u>, what we're <u>forced</u> to <u>do</u>,

what we're <u>taught</u> to <u>do</u>.

We <u>think</u> what we're re<u>quired</u> to <u>think</u>, what we're <u>made</u> to <u>think</u>,

not in<u>spired</u> to <u>think</u>.

We <u>say</u> what we're ex<u>pected</u> to <u>say</u>, con<u>ditioned</u> to <u>say</u>, very <u>rarely</u> <u>what</u> we've e<u>lected</u> to <u>say</u>.

We <u>are</u> what we're sup<u>posed</u> to <u>be</u>, what we're <u>told</u> to <u>be</u>

and <u>seldom</u> <u>what</u> we've <u>chosen</u> to <u>be</u>.

We <u>do</u> what we <u>should</u>, <u>not</u> what we <u>would</u> if we <u>could</u>.

Make sure Ss understand the significance of the four columns. Give due time to make some notes in each of the columns before initiating discussion in groups. This is very near to the speaking activity Ss might encounter in Paper 5.

Have a feedback session with the whole class at the end of the group discussion.

Coursebook p.48

Exam Practice: Paper 2 Writing

CAE Relevance: All Papers, especially Papers 2 and 5 (Writing and Speaking)

All the oral exercises here culminate in the writing task at the bottom of the page.

Exs. 1-5

Classroom treatment

1 Allow free-ranging discussion in groups of four or five around the pictures and questions **a**, **b** and **c**.

The first photo is of a couple in the 1980s, the second a couple in the 1940s, and the third a picture from the 1960s. If necessary, prompt discussion with questions such as these:

Which couple do you think ...

felt most optimistic about the world? ... enjoyed the highest standard of living? ... stayed together longest? ... had most fun? ... were most 'moral'?

2 and 3 These are again activities that really should be done in groups with Ss pooling ideas. Important feedback with the whole class later.

4 Discuss the question ('Which of these openers ...?') with each of the eight 'openers'. Get Ss to suggest ways in which a complete sentence could be composed in each case. For example:

I read Brian Head's article with a great deal of interest, but feel bound to make a few comments on ...

He seems to overlook the fact that millions of young people today are seriously engaged in ...

5 This is a chance for a quick recap before Ss are set the writing task, either as a timed piece of work in class or for homework. Review together all of the points that could be made against the attitudes and behaviour of young people today and all of the points that could be made in their defence. Remind Ss of the importance of making a point, developing and exemplifying it, then moving on with some kind of link to the next point. (See Introduction p.9.)

Rounding off the Unit

Why not round off this Unit with a short class discussion on how short childhood will be in the future? One is already reading regularly of thirteen-year-old drug addicts, fourteen-year-old alcoholics, sixteen-year-old professors, and teenage marriages.

Are Ss students generally optimistic about childhood surviving over the next few decades or do they feel that the age of maturity will become younger and younger?

Do they foresee the lines of a Loving Spoonful song of the 60s becoming reality?

Like 'Hey, Dad, can I go ride my zoom?
It goes five hundred miles an hour, suspended on balloons.
And can I put a droplet of this new stuff on my tongue,
And imagine froth and dragons while you sit and wreck your lungs?'

Like 'Hey, Dad, my girlfriend's only three.
She's got her own videophone and she's taking LSD.
And now that we're best friends, she wants to give a bit to me.
What's the matter, daddy? How come you're turning green?
Could it be that you can't live up to your dream?'

OR How about asking Ss to list all the arguments they can think of a) for, and b) against, the statement 'Schooldays are the happiest days of your life'? In fact, these 'for' and 'against' arguments might then provide the basis for a formal debate with the motion 'This house believes that schooldays are the happiest days of your life'.

8 Rich man, poor man

(The title of this Unit comes from a common rhyme spoken particularly by children when counting out the stones they have left on a plate after they have eaten cherries or prunes, for example. There is a superstition that the number of stones will tell you what your future (profession, or perhaps husband) will be. It goes:

Tinker, tailor, soldier, sailor,
Rich man, poor man, beggarman, thief.

Do Ss have similar rhymes in their own language(s)?)

Coursebook p.49

Warm-up

Here are three **alternative suggestions**, all with books closed:

1 Currency quiz

Ask Ss: 'What currencies are used in the following countries e.g. Russia (rouble); Australia (dollar); India (rupee); Brazil (cruzeiro); South Africa (rand); Japan (yen); and so on.' A coin could be offered as an appropriate prize for the student/team which gets the highest score in this quiz. Additional marks could be given for the students who get nearest to the rate of exchange of the currencies referred to in the quiz. (Check the current rates of exchange from a newspaper.)

2 Sayings

What sayings do Ss know about money either in English or their own language(s) (translate these into English)? What truth do they think there is in the sayings discussed? English sayings about money which you might give or which might be elicited from the students could include:

(The love of) money is the root of all evil.
Money doesn't bring happiness.
Money can't buy you love.
Money talks.
He who pays the piper calls the tune.
Time is money.
A fool and his money are soon parted.
In for a penny, in for a pound.
Money makes money.
When poverty comes in at the door, loves flies out of the window.

There's one law for the rich and another for the poor.
Take care of the pence and the pounds will take care of themselves.
It's better to be born lucky than rich.

3 Discussion questions

Use the following questions as prompts for a brief discussion; they should arouse interest but not take up too much of your lesson time.

How much money do you need to be rich?

How little does a person have to have to be called poor?

How would you rate the following items on a 'luxury-to-necessity' scale where luxury = 10 and necessity = 1: car, washing machine, television, newspapers, music cassettes, pen, raincoat, etc.

How much pocket money do you think teenagers should get from their parents when they are still at school?

When young people start work but are still living with their parents, should they contribute to the family budget? If so, how much?

Listen

CAE Relevance: All Papers, although the treatment of the song is particularly relevant for Paper 3

Background notes and vocabulary

Dr Hook: the name of a very successful American pop group in the 1970s
Elvis Presley: (1935-1977) the most famous 'Rock 'n' Roll' singer of this century, often called 'The King'
Fred Astaire: (1899-1987) famous American dancer/film star
get myself a nose job: have my nose reshaped by plastic surgery
Robert Redford: (1936-) blond, athletic American leading actor, whose films include *Butch Cassidy and the Sundance Kid* (1969), *The Sting* (1973), *The Candidate* (1972), *The Great Gatsby* (1974) and many more

> *Fort Knox:* a military post in Kentucky, USA, site of
> the US gold bullion depository
> *I don't guess I'm a-doin' all that hot:* (Am. coll.) =
> I don't think I'm doing very well

▷📼 **Tapescript of 'The Millionaire' by Dr Hook**
(The words **in bold** are those missing from the version
in the CB. The words and phrases underlined are
examples of non-standard English that Ss are asked to
identify.)

1 I'm not a **bad** person,
   I don't **drink** and I don't kill;
   <u>I got</u> no **evil** habits
   And I probably **never** will.
   I don't **sing** like Elvis Presley,
   I can't **dance** like Fred Astaire,
   But there's one thing in my **favour** —
   I'm **a** millionaire!

CHORUS: Well, <u>I got</u> more money than a horse has
         hairs
         'Cause my rich old uncle **died** and answered
         all my prayers.
         But having all this money is <u>gonna</u> bring me
         down
         If you <u>ain't</u> with me, honey, to help me
         spread it **around**.

2 I could get myself a **nose** job,
   I could **diet** for a year,
   But I'll **never** be Robert Redford
   'Cause I'm much too fond of **beer**.
   Please **don't** misunderstand me,
   It's not **love** I'm trying to buy;
   It's just I've got all <u>this here</u> **money**,
   And I'm a pretty **ugly** guy!

CHORUS: Well, <u>I got</u> more money etc.

REFRAIN: I don't mind if you **love** me for my money
          If you love me for **whatever** else I've got,
          But 'cepting all this stuff I'm **alone** in Fort
          Knox
          <u>I don't guess</u> I'm a-doin' all that **hot**!

CHORUS: Well, I got more money etc.

Classroom treatment
Many songs are about love. What songs can your Ss
think of, either in English or their own languages,
connected with the theme of money? What is the basic
idea of each of these songs?

Ask Ss to look at the words of the song in their book.

They should try the song exercise, first in pairs and
then compare their answers with those of the other
students in the class.

Ss try first to identify *where* words are missing — a
typical English in Use exercise, except that they are
helped here in that a word is missing in *each* line —
and then try to predict *what* words might be missing
before they listen to the song. Some of the words
should be fairly easy to predict, others are much harder,
if not impossible: in this the exercise differs from a true
exam-type exercise, of course.

Do not tell Ss whether they are right or wrong in their
predictions. Play the tape and allow them to correct
their own words.

As it is something that features at various points in this
Unit, point to the fact that there are some examples of
non-standard English in this song, as there are in lots
of pop songs. Ask students to identify them.

Discuss and write

CAE Relevance: All Papers

Classroom treatment
Go through the questions first to make sure everyone
understands them.

Draw attention to the significance of the use of the
passive v the active in *How do you spend your money?*
and *How is your money spent?*

Compare with other examples like these:

How do you check your work? and *How is your work
checked?*

What do the teachers teach in school? and *What is taught
in school?*

Poverty causes crime and *Crime is caused by poverty.*

Ss might also like to consider the following questions:

What are the possible different ways of saving money
and which ones do you use?

Make a list of things that people waste money on.

What would be the consequences of increasing or
decreasing government expenditure on: social benefits
for the unemployed and the disadvantaged, defence,
health care, education, transport, the police, housing,
propaganda, etc.?

What are the different ways in which the government
can raise cash to pay for its expenditure? Which way/
ways do you think is/are best?

Homework

Ask Ss to prepare their own answers (they do not need to write more than notes) to the questionnaire at home. If possible they should try to do a little research into the questions relating to government expenditure (either in a library or by asking other people).

When Ss come back to class with their answers more or less prepared, there are a number of different ways in which this survey could be set up depending on the circumstances in which you are working. Here are some possibilities, although you may, of course, wish to adapt them to fit your own needs better.

1 If you are carrying out the survey within the class, this is one way it can be done. Divide the class by nine and give each group responsibility for one question. They should then decide themselves who is going to interview whom — each person or pair should take responsibility for specific other students in the class so that everyone is asked each question by only one person or pair. When everyone has finished interviewing, the groups get together and collate their results, presenting them first orally and then in writing.

2 Another approach is to have Ss working in groups of, say, four, asking each other all the questions and then preparing an oral and a written report based on the findings in their own small group.

3 If it is possible to work with another class whose English is at a similar or higher level, then each student can interview one other student asking all the questions. The answers are then collated as a whole class activity and then presented both orally and in writing to the Ss in the other class.

Homework: Ss write a report summarising the findings.

Coursebook pp.50-52

Look and discuss

CAE Relevance: Paper 5 (Speaking)

Classroom treatment

Ss should briefly discuss the questions in pairs with a quick full-class feedback session. In the feedback session highlight the difference between *What causes ...* and *What is caused by ...* , and the prepositions used after *reason* and *stem*.

Reading and language focus

CAE Relevance: Paper 1 (Reading)

Background notes and vocabulary

> *the Commonwealth:* countries which were once in the British Empire and now have their own independent government but still acknowledge the Queen as Head of State e.g. Australia, New Zealand, Canada
> *Crown Estates:* term to describe the lands which belong to the monarch (the crown is what a king or queen traditionally wears on his or her head)
> *royal residences:* the Queen's houses e.g. Buckingham Palace, Windsor Castle and so on
> *official transport:* the Queen has her own flight of aeroplanes as well as her own yacht, Brittania, and her royal train
> *stud farm:* farm where horses are bred
> *Leonardo da Vinci:* famous Italian Renaissance artist
> *humble:* here, poor
> *inheritance tax:* often referred to as 'death duty', this is a tax which is paid by heirs on wealth they receive after someone's death
> *hazard a guess:* make a rough guess

Exs. 1-5

Classroom treatment

1-3 Follow the instructions in the CB with Ss working in pairs, A reading one text and B the other. Each makes brief notes on his/her text and then tells his/her partner about it. They each then read the other text.

In pairs they should then answer questions 2 and 3 on page 52.

As a class then compare answers to questions 2 and 3 before discussing question 4.

4 Ask students both to identify what is wrong and to say what would be considered standard English.

5 Deal with any other questions the Ss may have about the two texts, then set this exercise for homework. Also ask Ss to read the Grammar Commentary at home.

Answers to ex. 4

Examples of non-standard English used by Kathy:

I don't hardly go out (= I hardly ever go out); *or nothing like that* (= or anything like that); *me mum* (= my mum/

my mother); *it weren't meant to be* (= it wasn't meant to be); *to fetch up kids* (= to bring up children); *fed up of* (= fed up with); *There's people* (= There are people)

Possible extension

You might extend the language work on these texts by doing the following exercises:

a Ask Ss to find words and expressions in the texts on pp.51 and 52 with the following meanings:
to originate from (= *stem from*), yearly (= *annual*), and so on.

b Ask Ss to write out some of the sentences from one of the texts without any prepositions e.g. 'The State takes part ____ the income ____ these Crown Estates in exchange ____ providing the Queen and other members ... ' They then test each other to see whether they can fill in the gaps with the correct prepositions.

Coursebook pp.52-53

Language focus: Sequences and consequences

CAE Relevance: All Papers

▷ ▣ **Tapescript for ex. 4** (See Coursebook, p.151.)
Exs. 1-3

Classroom treatment

1 Discuss this as a class to make sure that the task is clear to everyone. This could be done by some brief preliminary discussion about which problems could be considered.

2 First with the whole class check comprehension of the text and the sequencing adverbials in particular. Then ask Ss to think of an incident from their own lives to describe using as many of the adverbials as possible. You could suggest they describe one of the things from the following list:

a holiday; first days in a new school, college or job; getting to know a special friend.
Ask Ss to work in pairs telling each other their story and asking each other questions where necessary. Then pair the Ss in a different way and ask them to tell their story again to a new partner. Finish by asking one or two people to tell their story to the whole class.

3 Brainstorm ideas on to the board/OHP. Here are some words which Ss might come up with. If they do not produce them themselves, teach those that seem most appropriate to the level of the group.

cause, be caused by, arouse, prompt, bring about, affect, reason, result in/from, a consequence of, effect (have an effect (on)), end result, side effect, necessitate, be rooted in, stem from, lead to, as a result of, etc.

Ex. 4 Listen and write

Background notes and vocabulary

Amstrad: The name of Alan Sugar's company. The name was formed from his initials and the first syllable of the word 'Trading'.
PCW 8526: a model of word-processor produced by Amstrad
capitalised: given a capital value of
It's amazing how many people have fallen for that one: It's amazing how many people have believed that story.
P/E: In a business context P/E stands for Price/Earnings ratio
press-ups: a kind of keep-fit exercise which involves supporting oneself on the floor by the hands and the balls of the feet (while keeping the body straight) and raising oneself up and down using the muscles in the arms
to go bankrupt: to collapse financially

Classroom treatment

Ask if Ss know who Alan Sugar is. If not, tell them that he is a successful young businessman, the producer of electronic equipment, notably the Amstrad computer, an exceptionally cheap personal computer. Ask Ss what they think the business students listening to his talk would like most to hear about.

Then play the tape. Ss listen to the whole tape first and then listen to the introduction and answer questions **a** and **b**. They then listen to each of the three parts mentioned in question **c** individually and answer questions **c** and **d** about each part. Finish by discussing questions **e** and **f**.

Possible answers

a By giving an outline of the history of his company, Amstrad.

b Can the entrepreneur find multi-national success and happiness?

c 1st part: His answer to the question 'How did you make your fortune?'
2nd part: His first experience of the City.
3rd part: His first business lesson.

d He makes the first two parts interesting by telling jokes. He adds interest to each of the three parts by basing what he says directly on his own personal experience.

e No, because he seems to have been very successful in spite of having no business experience or training.

f He'll probably go on to say that an entrepreneur can find both success and happiness.

Ex. 5

Classroom treatment

Divide the class into groups of four Ss. They must decide what problem they are going to discuss, why and how it happened and the likely future consequences. The group must also choose a person to give a speech presenting their point of view and a chairperson whose job it is to introduce the speaker.

Homework

The speaker must prepare his or her speech, the chairperson must prepare the introduction and the other students in each group should write a composition on the topic chosen. Stress that speakers should simply prepare notes and not compositions, explaining that a read composition usually makes a very poor speech, one that is hard for an audience to follow.

Follow-up lesson

Ask each chairperson in turn to introduce their speaker and then have each speaker give their speech. If time allows, have a brief general discussion of the problems dealt with in each speech.

```
Coursebook pp.53-54
```

Exam Practice: Paper 3 English in Use

CAE Relevance: Paper 3 (English in Use)

a Proofreading and vocabulary study

Classroom treatment

Point out that this work provides practice for the second part of Paper 3 which always involves some kind of error correction.

1 Spelling exercise. Dictate these words to the class:

> grateful; offered; really; received; economically; picnickers; illegal; upsetting; believe; impecunious; overpaid; wealthier

Here are the rules which the words illustrate:

grateful

Adjectives ending in 'ful' e.g. *wonderful, graceful, hopeful*, etc. only have one 'l' — except for the word *full* itself, of course.

offered, upsetting

The consonant doubles if the stress is on the final syllable of the basic word (as in *upset — upsetting*) but remains single if the stress is on an earlier syllable (as in *offer — offered* (no double 'r'). This does not apply when the final letter of the basic verb is 'l' when (in English spelling) the spelling always changes to double 'l' when an additional syllable is added e.g. *travelling*.

really

Adjectives ending in 'l' double that final 'l' when forming an adverb.

received, believe

'i' before 'e' except after 'c'.

economically

Adjectives ending in 'ic' form their adverbs with the ending '-ically'.

picnickers

Words ending in 'c' add a 'k' when an additional syllable is added e.g. *trafficking*.

illegal, impecunious

When the prefix *in* is added to words beginning with 'l' or 'r', the 'n' in the prefix changes to 'l' or 'r' as well e.g. *illiterate, irregular*.

If *in* precedes a word beginning with 'b' or 'p', the 'n' in the prefix usually changes to 'm', e.g. *impossible, impolite, imbalance*.

overpaid

Note that the past form of 'pay' is *paid* (NOT 'payed'). Compare the past form of 'say' — *said*.

wealthier

Note how the 'y' at the end of 'wealthy' becomes 'i' when the comparative is formed. This is often the case whenever an extra syllable is added to a word ending in a consonant plus 'y' e.g. *early — earlier*. It remains as 'y', however, when the letter preceding the 'y' is a vowel rather than a consonant e.g. *toyed*.

You may, of course, wish to add other words which you know your students frequently make mistakes with.

2 Ask Ss to discuss these pairs or groups of words and go round monitoring or dealing with problems. As there are a lot of words, do not spend time at the end dealing with them all as a class unless you feel your class really needs and would like this. Simply pick out the ones that were causing Ss most problems and discuss them with the whole group.

Answers

- A *principle* is a guiding idea whereas *principal* means chief or main.
- You *rob* somebody (of something) but *steal* something from someone.
- You *borrow* something from somebody e.g. books from a library, but you *lend* something to someone e.g. the library lends you books.
- You *buy* something, but you *pay for* something, or you *pay* someone.
- The *value* of something is what it is worth whereas its *price* is how much it costs.
- *economic* means simply relating to the economy e.g. economic history or economic relations, whereas *economical* means not wasteful e.g an economical car
- You *rent* a room from someone and you *hire* (or *rent*) a car from someone, but someone *lets* a room to you.
- To *spend* money (or time) is simply to use it but to *waste* money (or time) is to use it badly.
- You *earn* money by working for it, you *gain* experience or wisdom, and you *win* a prize in a competition or game.
- *invaluable* means so valuable that it cannot be priced whereas *valueless* means without value.
- *unique* means the only example of its kind whereas *single* just means on its own or for one person.
- *policy* means a plan of action or a statement of position and beliefs e.g. foreign policy or Conservative Party policy, whereas *politics* means the science of government or political views e.g. to study politics, What are his politics?
- *tasty* refers to food whereas *tasteful* describes something that is in good artistic taste: note that the opposite of both these words is *tasteless*.
- *insure* is to pay money to an insurance company which guarantees to pay you in the event of some problem arising (e.g. sickness, accident, etc.); to *assure* is to tell someone that what you are saying is true.

This is the corrected text with corrections underlined:

> It is my <u>principle</u> never to <u>lend</u> money because you often don't get it back. Nor would I waste money on such frivolous things as <u>paying for/buying</u> drinks for people. I work hard to <u>earn</u> my money and so I always try to be economical.

3 Ss work in pairs for three or four minutes thinking of all the phrasal verbs they can based on *do, make, go* and *put*. Then have a full-class feedback session pooling ideas.

Try to ensure that before working on the text students are aware of at least the following phrasal verbs with *make, do, go* and *put*:

to make up to someone = to be deliberately charming to someone
to make out a cheque = to write a cheque
to make up a sum = to complete an amount of money
to make over something to someone = to transfer possession of something to someone
to make off with = to take or steal, or abscond with
to do up a room = to decorate a room
to do someone out of something = to cheat someone out of something
to go under = to fail, become bankrupt
to go up/down = to rise/fall
to go up to = to approach
to go towards = to contribute to
to put up (at) = to have overnight accommodation (at)
to put up with = to tolerate

Answers

'doing up' ✓; 'make over' should be *make up*; 'going below' should be *going under*; 'gone on' should be *gone up*; 'made up to' ✓; 'make off' should be *make over*; 'made her down' should be *made her out*; 'made off with' ✓; 'puts up at' should be *puts up with*

b Set this Exam Practice task as a homework assignment.

Answers

Spelling (correct spellings given here): 1 securities, 2 receive, 3 flexibility, 4 actually, 5 cooling-off, 6 rapidly, 7 self-catering, 8 tasteful

Prepositions or particles: 1 *put up with* should be *put up **at***, 2 *do off with* should be *do **away** with*, 3 *call for us ...* should be *call **on** us ...*, 4 *make to* should be *make **for***, 5 *put it on* should be *put it **off***, 6 *done in* should be *done **up*** (or *done **out***), 7 *go out for* should be *go **in** for*, 8 *make over* should be *make **out***

Rounding off the Unit

Why not round off this Unit with a spelling quiz that Ss make up for themselves?

OR The class might hold a formal debate with one of these motions:

'This House believes that it's better to be poor and happy than rich and miserable.'

'... that money is the root of all evil.'

'... that everyone should receive the same salary regardless of their occupation.'

9 A rare and exceptional gift

Warm-up

Here are three **alternative suggestions**, all with books closed:

1 Write these words/phrases up on the blackboard/ OHP: *genius; a whiz kid; a child/infant prodigy; a 'savant'; a superman/superwoman; a genius (or a man/woman of genius); a 'smart aleck'*

Then read out these definitions and ask Ss to say which words they define:

a 'a person who moves ahead in life and (especially) in business very fast, because of clever ideas which succeed' (= a whiz kid)

b 'a French expression (used occasionally in English) to describe a 'wise person', in other words someone who is extremely talented or gifted' (a 'savant')

c 'a person with very high intelligence and original thought, especially in producing works of art' (= a genius)

d 'a young child with the abilities or understanding of a clever grown-up person' (= a child or infant prodigy)

e '(in stories) a man/woman with powers of mind and body much greater than others' (= a superman/superwoman)

f 'great ability, especially in producing works of art' (= genius)

g 'a person who annoys others by claiming to know everything and trying to sound clever' (= a smart aleck)

2 Ask Ss to write a list of people (living or dead) that they would describe as geniuses. Examples might be: Leonardo da Vinci, Einstein, Goethe, Shakespeare, Beethoven, Mozart, Salvador Dali, Picasso, Andy Warhol, etc. They then discuss their lists in pairs or small groups. What agreements and disagreements are there? What is 'genius'? What makes 'a genius'?

3 Read this short anecdote to the class and ask what it says about genius or people's ideas about genius. (A 'drudge' is someone who does hard, humble or uninteresting work.)

> Once when Paderewski, the great Polish pianist, played before Queen Victoria, she exclaimed with enthusiasm, 'Mr Paderewski, you are a genius!' 'Ah, Your Majesty,' he replied, 'perhaps. But before I was a genius, I was a drudge.'

Look and discuss, then listen

CAE Relevance: Papers 4, 5 and 2 (Listening, Speaking and Writing)

▷ ▣ Tapescript for exs 2, 3 and 5 (See Coursebook pp.152-153.)

Background notes and vocabulary

> *Royal Albert Hall:* seating 10,000 people, one of the largest concert halls in London, completed in 1871
> *Leonardo da Vinci:* (1452-1519) Italian painter of the Florentine school, and universal genius: sculptor, architect, military engineer, musician, etc.
> *Steffi Graf:* (b. 1969) one of the world's foremost professional tennis players
> *Picasso:* (Pablo Ruiz y Picasso, 1881-1973) Spanish painter, sculptor and ceramicist
> *Joan Collins:* (1933-) leading British actress who has won parts in a large number of international films (incl. *The Stud* 1978) and famous for her part in the TV series *Dynasty*
> *Albert Einstein:* (1879-1955) mathematical physicist of German birth, naturalised American (1940)
> The following occur in the recordings:
> *autistic:* suffering from autism, an illness of the mind, esp. in children, in which the imagination becomes too important and good personal relationships cannot be formed
> *withdrawn:* habitually quiet and for a time seeming concerned not with other people, but with one's own thoughts
> *mute:* silent, without speech
> *Natural History Museum:* a branch of the British Museum in London, opened in 1881
> *Westminster Abbey:* a famous Abbey in central London in which kings and queens are married, and often buried

St Pancras Station: a London mainline railway station, named after the patron saint of children

Molly Malone: a girl's name, from a traditional Irish song called 'Cockles and Mussels'

to improvise: to make up (a piece of music) as one is playing

nanny: (in Britain, esp. formerly in rich families) a woman employed to take care of children

Somerset Maugham: (1874-1965) English novelist, playwright and writer of short stories in a sophisticated, satirical style

Dr Barnardo: Thomas John (1845-1905), British philanthropist, founder and director of homes for destitute children (commonly called 'Dr Barnardo's')

Maria Aitken: (1945-) well-known British actress

Philharmonia Pops Orchestra: an orchestra (an offshoot of the Philharmonia Orchestra) which plays popular versions of classical music

Royal College of Ophthalmology: College specialising in the diagnosis and treatment of diseases and disorders of the eye

Exs. 1 and 2

Classroom treatment

1 Ask Ss to look at the picture of the Royal Albert Hall and, in pairs, decide who they think did the drawing. Don't give any help with the different people here. To check, call out the names of the people one by one and ask for a show of hands each time (to see how many thought Picasso drew it, Leonardo, etc.). Do not comment, but move straight on to ex. 2.

2 Play the tape here for gist and general comprehension — and for Ss to check their predictions and to tell you what is so special about the artist.

Answer

It was drawn by Stephen Wiltshire. He is or was autistic and had great difficulty in communicating with people.

Ex. 3

Classroom treatment

Ask Ss to read the six questions first. Then play the tape for them to make brief notes in order to answer the questions. *Either* ask for answers to the questions from the class as a whole *or* Ss ask and answer the questions in pairs.

Expected answers

a In 1974. b He drew the Royal Albert Hall when he was about thirteen. c No one taught him to draw. d The TV programmes were *The Foolish Wise Ones* and *The Boy Who Draws Buildings.* e He drew St Pancras Station (in London) from memory. f Yes, they have — in three books, *Cities, Drawings* and *Floating Cities.*

Ex. 4

Classroom treatment

Here Ss are being asked to remember the reactions or attitude of listeners in the discussion to information about Stephen. If necessary, play the tape again and get Ss to express their own impressions or reactions to what they have heard.

Expected or possible answers

Rolf and May were amazed. They thought it was absolutely incredible.

Ex. 5

Classroom treatment

Listening and taking notes. For Ss to compare Derek and Stephen, you might provide (on the board/OHP) a chart with headings like these: Age, Public exposure, Talent, Achievements, etc. OR Ss themselves might suggest headings for information they think the recording will give them.

Before playing the tape, take a few minutes to discuss how to take notes: What are you listening for? What do you write down? etc.

Play the tape for Ss to make their notes. Complete the table on the board/OHP with suggestions from the class before Ss work in pairs to begin pooling ideas for drafting, editing and writing the magazine feature. (See Introduction p.9.)

Possible notes about the other person

Derek Parvicini — a gifted child (a *savant*) — music — blind from birth — mental age of 6 — playing piano since (he was) 2 — can't read music — can play after hearing once — and can improvise. Weighed 1 kilo when born — wasn't expected to live — blindness possibly result of too much oxygen — has a nanny — well-to-do family — great grandfather Somerset Maugham — great great grandfather Dr Barnardo. Age 9 — played with Philharmonia Pops orchestra at a gala concert — jazz classics.

Coursebook pp.56-57

Language focus

CAE Relevance: Papers 4, 5 and 2 (Listening, Speaking and Writing)

▷🖭 **Tapescript for ex. 2** (See Coursebook p.153.)

NOTE: The main aim of the practice in exs. 1-3 here is to prepare Ss to write the piece in ex. 4. They might usefully refer to the Grammar Commentary section while doing these exercises.

Ex. 1 Comparing people

Classroom treatment

Ss write down three or four pairs of famous people such as those suggested. Each pair must be (or must have been) in the same profession or walk of life e.g. two famous artists, two politicians, two army generals, etc. In pairs they then tell each other about the pairs they have written down. Encourage them to use phases like 'As far as I'm concerned, ... / I think ... / If you ask me, ...' etc. (See Possible answers below.) Ask Ss what follows a comparative adjective ('than') and draw their attention to the ways in which we reinforce a comparative adjective or adverb: *far/much/a lot/ considerably better, more intelligent, more elegantly*, etc. Can Ss suggest more?

Ss then tell each other which of the two (if either) they think was or is one of the best, the most talented/ popular/important, etc. in their field. Again, encourage them to use phrases like 'As far as I'm concerned, ... / I think ... / If you ask me, ...' etc. (See Possible answers below.) And again, draw their attention to the ways in which we reinforce superlative adjectives: *by far/easily/far and away/without doubt the best ... .*

Quickly review comparative and superlative adjectives and adverbs through discussion of the questions or through reference to the Grammar Commentary.

Possible answers

a Possible 'comparative' sentences Ss might produce:

I think Pele was a far more skilful player than Maradonna ever was.

As far as I'm concerned, Liz Taylor is a much better actress than Joan Collins.

b Possible 'superlative' sentences Ss might produce:

I think Marilyn Monroe was probably the most popular, if not the greatest, actress of the late 50s.

If you ask me/For me, Marcel Marceaux must be by far the cleverest mime artist of all time.

Ex. 2 Giving an impression of a person

Classroom treatment

Before playing the tape, introduce the situation and ask Ss to try to predict some of the things the woman might say. Then play the tape, check predictions and answer the questions.

Draw attention to these sentence patterns that the woman used:

He wasn't even as tall as you.

He was considerably shorter than I imagined he would be.

He was just as pleasant as I had imagined.

He was nowhere near as outgoing as I thought he would be.

Give Ss time to think of someone they have met (or imagine they have met) before they tell each other about their meeting in the same kind of way, using the same kinds of sentence pattern.

Possible or expected answers

The woman met Telly Savalas ('Kojak'). She thought he was a tall man, but he wasn't. He was very pleasant, and not as outgoing as she thought he would be. In fact, she was surprised.

Ex. 3 Comparing people again

Classroom treatment

The aim of this brief phase is **a** to revise *as* + adjective + *as* and again to look at the words that can reinforce the pattern. And in **b** the aim is to look at four adjective/preposition combinations which we might want to use when comparing people.

Ss should work in pairs or small groups for both of these exercises and check back with the class as a whole. In **b** they must give reasons why they do or do not agree with the statements.

Possible answers

a Other possible reinforcing words: *not, nowhere near, (just) about, nearly, nothing like*

Ex. 4

Classroom treatment

Follow the procedure outlined in the CB. This task should be begun in class, but completed as a homework assignment. (See Introduction p.9.)

Read, discuss and write

CAE Relevance: Papers 1 and 5 (Reading and Speaking)

Background notes and vocabulary

Elizabeth Taylor: (1932-) London-born actress later to become a world famous star. She made her first film at the age of 10, in 1942. Called *There's One Born Every Minute,* it was quickly followed by *Lassie Come Home* the following year, and a string of successful films over the next fifty years.

King George V and Queen Mary: George V (the Fifth) (1865-1936), king of Great Britain (1910-1936), son of Edward VII

Paul Klee: (1879-1940), Swiss painter, famous for abstract works, discovering in forms and lines the suggestion of a face, figure or object

Mozart: [See CB p.59]

clavier: a forerunner of the modern piano

recital: a musical performance given by one person (or a small group)

Shirley Temple: (1928-) The Oscar she won in 1934 was 'In grateful recognition of her outstanding contribution to screen entertainment during the year 1934'. Within a few years she went on to top all the other stars as the number one cinema box-office attraction. By the time she was a teenager, however, her film career was in decline and she eventually turned to politics. In 1974 she was appointed US Ambassador to Ghana.

Hollywood Oscars: awards given annually in Hollywood to actors, actresses, producers, directors, etc. for outstanding achievement in films

José Iturbi: (1896-1980) Spanish concert pianist who became famous through many appearances in Hollywood films

Charlie Chaplin: (1889-1977) English director-writer who has become probably the best-known actor in the history of the cinema. His tramp character in his films made him world famous. He not only starred in films, but also directed them, including classics such as *The Gold Rush* (1924), *Modern Times* and *City Lights* (1931).

Michelangelo, Buonarroti: (1475-1564) Italian painter, architect, sculptor and poet and one of the most important figures of the Renaissance. His most famous work is the ceiling of the Sistine Chapel in the Vatican (1508-12)

Michael Jackson: (1958-) world-famous pop star whose record albums have sold millions

Tatum O'Neal: (1962-) American actress, won an Oscar at the age of 10 as the tough-talking, cigarette-smoking con artist alongside her father, Ryan O'Neal, in the film *Paper Moon*

The aim here, through a fun quiz, is to encourage Ss to talk about geniuses, child prodigies and the like, as they might have to do in Paper 5 of the exam.

Exs. 1 and 2

Classroom treatment

Ss read and do the quiz individually, then check their answers with a partner and with the whole class.

Answers

1 Michael Jackson — True; Shirley Temple — True; Elizabeth Taylor — True; Paul Klee — True; Mozart — True; José Iturbi — True; Michelangelo — False: he left school when he was 13 (1488) to become an apprentice in a painter's studio — not quite such an early start as some of the others in this quiz! ; Albert Einstein — False: when he was 12, he recorded his decision to devote his life to solving the riddle of what he called the 'huge world', and when he was 16 he wrote an essay which contained the beginnings of his theory of relativity; Tatum O'Neal — True; Charlie Chaplin — True.

Ex. 3

Classroom treatment

Ss should sit in groups of three-five to discuss these questions freely. However, before they begin, just point up the phrases (at the bottom of the page) that they might want to use at certain points. Go round the groups, listening, questioning and encouraging discussion.

In c), Ss should try to persuade others in their group that their ideas are the best ways of encouraging 'gifted' children. This can be valuable preparation for Phase C of the Speaking Paper.

Coursebook pp.58-59

Vocabulary: Absolutely brilliant! Exceptionally gifted! Extremely talented!

CAE Relevance: Paper 3 (English in Use)

Ex. 1

Classroom treatment

Ask Ss once again what 'collocation' is — or remind them from Unit 1. Then they discuss the questions quickly in pairs or groups of three. Check with the whole class.

Answers

We can say *exceptionally talented* and *extremely gifted*, but other combinations would sound extremely odd in English.

Ex. 2

Classroom treatment

Ss do the exercise individually or in pairs, using a dictionary if necessary. Then check answers with the whole class.

Answers

1 exceptionally; 2 talented; 3 patently; 4 misunderstood;
5 blissfully; 6 disappointed; 7 totally; 8 hurt; 9 mortally;
10 lost

Ex. 3

Classroom treatment

Before doing this exercise, ask Ss to cover the sentences, and then see if (from their present knowledge) they can already add correctly collocating adjectives to the adverbs listed. For example, they might well come up with *physically exhausted, physically handicapped, happily married, happily ignorant (of ...)*, etc. They then do the exercise and check their completions with a partner, other Ss and the class as a whole.

You might suggest that phrases like these should be learned as one expression in the same way as other collocating phrases in English e.g. *go for a walk*.

As a final check, why not give a number of adjectives and let Ss shout out the adverb which would commonly collocate with it — or shout out the whole collocating phrase.

Answers

1 absolutely; 2 hermetically; 3 critically; 4 fully;
5 physically; 6 closely; 7 happily; 8 terminally; 9 pleasantly;
10 remarkably

Extra activity

To reinforce adverb-adjective collocations and to remind students again of the beginning of the Unit, you might use the following as a dictation or for note-taking practice. Introduce it as though it is part of a short newspaper article the day after the radio programme. (Adverb-adjective collocations are highlighted for reference, but do not stress them when reading the passage out.)

> In the past, young people like Derek Parvicini and Stephen Wiltshire would have been ignored or shut away out of sight. Not now. It is <u>patently obvious</u> that they each possess a rare gift, a gift of which each seems almost to be <u>blissfully unaware</u>.
> There is something about the gifts of such children that seems to be <u>diametrically opposed</u>, for instance, to what we tend to accept as 'intelligence'. In the same way that such gifts will appear in children who are <u>mentally or physically handicapped</u>, so one hears from time to time of someone who is <u>terminally ill</u> suddenly being able to paint, or play an instrument. What *is* sure is that the careers of these two young men will be <u>followed</u> by many people <u>very closely indeed</u>.

Read and write

CAE Relevance: Paper 3 (English in Use)

Classroom treatment

This exercise is very close to the kind of 'expansion of notes' task that Ss will be expected to do in the exam. Working in pairs, Ss should first read the notes about Mozart and then begin to expand them into complete sentences, staying as close to the notes as possible. All the while, however, they should discuss different sentence constructions and what might be best. Here are three ways in which the first few ideas might be joined together:

1 *The Austrian composer Wolfgang Amadeus Mozart is regarded by many as the greatest composer ever and he was the most precocious genius in the history of music.*

2 *The Austrian composer Wolfgang Amadeus Mozart, who is regarded by many as the greatest composer ever, was the most precocious genius in the history of music.*

3 *The Austrian composer Wolfgang Amadeus Mozart, regarded by many as the greatest composer who ever lived, was probably the most precocious genius in the history of music.*

Ss might complete the task as a homework assignment. (See Introduction p.9.)

Possible article

The Austrian composer Wolfgang Amadeus Mozart, regarded by many as the greatest composer ever, was probably the most precocious genius in the history of music.

At the age of three he was already playing the harpsichord and could memorise complete musical passages after listening to them only once. By the age of five he was composing minuets and at the age of six was touring the courts of Europe giving violin and clavier recitals. Amazingly he had written his first opera by the time he was twelve, and wrote his fourteenth symphony at the age of fifteen, a symphony which is still in the repertoire of most modern orchestras.

In all, Mozart wrote about 40 symphonies, 21 piano concertos, 24 string quartets, violin sonatas and a number of operas including *The Marriage of Figaro* in 1786, *Don Giovanni* in 1787, *Cosi fan Tutti* in 1790, and, perhaps most famous of all, his humanistic masterpiece *The Magic Flute* in 1791, the year in which he died.

His final masterpiece, however, was a setting for a Requiem which was unfinished when he died from typhus at the age of 35. Penniless when he died, Mozart was buried in an unmarked pauper's grave in Vienna, leaving huge debts and a widow in a state of nervous collapse.

Exam Practice: Paper 4 Listening

CAE Relevance: Paper 4 (Listening)

Background notes

> Composers mentioned by Sir Yehudi in the interview:
>
> *Schubert, Franz Peter:* (1797-1828) Austrian composer, who wrote over 600 songs ('Lieder'), 9 symphonies, 15 complete string quartets, the 'Trout' piano quintet, piano sonatas and many other orchestral, choral and operatic works.
>
> *Bach, Johann Sebastian:* (1685-1750) German musician and composer, the most famous member of the Bach family of musicians, whose musical output was enormous.
>
> *Mendelssohn, Felix:* (1809-47) German composer, whose works include the incidental music to Shakespeare's *A Midsummer Night's Dream*, five symphonies, the E minor violin concerto and a number of oratorios.

▷ 🎞 **Tapescript**

This authentic interview with Sir Yehudi Menuhin was totally unscripted.

TUTOR: Unit 9. Look at page 59, Exam practice **b**. You're going to hear part of an interview with Sir Yehudi Menuhin, the world-famous violinist and conductor, humanist, philosopher, writer and peace-worker. As you listen, tick the points he makes. If you think he does not make certain points, just leave those boxes blank.

INTERVIEWER: Would you make at all any distinction between a 'genius' and an exceptionally gifted person?

SIR YEHUDI: I hesitate. I'm very wary of this distinction. First of all, I believe there's less distinction than people assume. I believe that every child is capable of er acquiring er an expression in in art or in science or in practical, or in sport, or in whatever it may be. Er that there's a very high achievement. I think most children are capable of that, and by creating an artificial er category of, as it were, geniuses, er to which the majority cannot aspire to, you are cutting off the source of er of achievement, of aspiration, um of ambition, which I think is so important for for a child. Also th you're cutting off the attention you're paying a child. The genius very often grows up er in *spite* of circumstances. Naturally er help is always er important, but the genius is usually the one who has had good heredity, good family er background, whose father or mother have helped them through er in whatever field they specialise, whether it was er philosophy or violin-playing or [Interviewer: Yes] sport ...

INTERVIEWER: Um Getting back to the the student in particular, you wouldn't then set a a a in any way some people as of a different order that their qualities um don't require them to study or be taught in the same sort of way?

SIR YEHUDI: Well, I do believe in stretching a child, um their imagination, their ability, their capacities. Unfortunately there are very few people who can stretch a genius, as it were, and they would be very important, um to give a child who's already very gifted and able to learn — a child, let's say, who has mastered er certain levels of er philosophy or craftsmanship er at an early age — they must also be stretched. They should not be restricted to other levels of of other children. Each child moves at its own pace. But I this idea that they should all be moving at the same pace is I think a mistaken one.

(Interviewer: Mm.) On the other hand, the segregation of the so-called genius is also a bad thing. Um it's, you see, we move again from fixed words — segregation, joining, equality. We are obsessed with words which have, as it were, in the flow of events, no meaning. Er so naturally everyone must have a certain amount of privacy. Everyone must have the opportunity of of segregation, if you wish, and yet everyone must also be thrown into the swim.

INTERVIEWER: Do you have experience over the years of er children, um anyone you can think of, or children in general, who excel in one particular area — piano-playing, composing — and yet at other areas perhaps are really quite average? Um ...

SIR YEHUDI: You're absolutely right. We've had such. They were very gifted in music and totally hopeless in er in other subjects. Um music can go together with many subjects. It can go with mathematics, which is *one* aspect of music, which I call aural mathematics. Because it's automatic. We with our overtones we er we multiply automatically: twice a certain note is its octave, and three times is its fifth, and so on. So it's a kind of automatic aural mathematics. And many scient- scientists are musicians: many musicians are scientists.

INTERVIEWER: Finally, then, um I wonder if you could point to anyone in the past as being — I know you don't like the word — but, a 'musical genius'?

SIR YEHUDI: Well, certainly Mozart.

INTERVIEWER: Why?

SIR YEHUDI: Certainly Mozart. And of course Schubert and Bach — they all were. But Mozart, because he was born to er parents, and particularly the father who lived music and was a very accomplished violinist and composer himself. Er Mozart had the opportunity to make music, listen to it, write music from the earliest possible age. And it fell upon the young mind and heart of such gifts, of such genius, that er by the time he was eight or nine or ten he was like Mendelssohn. Mendessohn was another such. They have to have everything for - going for them, the so-called — I always say so-called, because as I told you, I am wary about the distinction between the child and the genius child — I don't like that distinction. Er but they those who have appeared as geniuses have had to have everything for them — genetics, early earliest possible experience of the subject they were, well in the chess player was

playing chess at the age of one or two, or seeing his father or mother play. And they have to have the best possible encouragement, er inspiration, environment. Also, challenge, which is another factor. Which means that not all the environment should of necessity or can of necessity be er you know er kind, and pliable and furthering. There must be an element of challenge.

Exs. a and b

Classroom treatment

a Here, Ss have an opportunity to listen to a great musician talking about the idea of genius. It's not easy, mainly because there are so many of the features of authentic speech — unfinished expressions and sentences, broken sentences, repetition, and so on. So when they come to do the task (in **b**), play the interview as often as necessary.

But first ask Ss how they can 'prepare to listen' to something like this.

Then ask them to read the statements and try to predict what Sir Yehudi might say, what his opinions might be.

b Now play the interview and get Ss to tick boxes according to what they hear. Even at this level, Ss must be encouraged to listen for the general meaning of what the speaker is saying, and not get bogged down with fine detail e.g. words that they hear but do not understand.

This is not a test (unless you wish to make it so): it is a chance to listen to a great musician of our time being interviewed and, at the same time, to do a typical Paper 4 exam listening task.

Play the tape as often as necessary and discuss answers.

Finally, give Ss the opportunity to say what they thought of Sir Yehudi's views.

Answers
1 —; 2 ✓; 3 ✓; 4 —; 5 ✓; 6 —; 7 ✓

Rounding off the Unit

Why not round off the Unit with a brief discussion of which living artists, musicians, sculptors and so on students think will be regarded as geniuses by future generations?

10 Relative values

(The title of the Unit (and the opening article) is a play on words: *Relative values* could suggest values that are seen in relation to each other, but here the word *relative* means a 'family member'.)

Coursebook pp.60-61

Warm-up

Give these quotations and ask Ss to discuss the truth of them in small groups:

'Only children do better at school than those with brothers or sisters.'
'You can choose your friends, but you can't choose your relatives.'
'Sisters never get on.'
'The second child is always brighter than the first.'
'It's a miracle if two strangers who just happen to be brought up in the same house become friends.'
'Absence makes the heart grow fonder.'

Read and interpret

CAE Relevance: Paper 1 (Reading)

Background notes and vocabulary

'High-flying Foxes'
Mick Jagger: ageless lead singer of the *Rolling Stones* pop group
Fun Times: an unusual title for the euphoria that many people experienced in the sixties
The Navigators: a minority Christian sect
chuck in: literally 'throw in', it means 'give up'
The Minerver Story: a film made in 1950 as a sequel to *Mrs Minerver*, which was a classic wartime film made in 1942
a goody-goody: a colloquial expression for a child who does everything right and is never naughty
Sussex: a county in the south of England; Brighton is its largest town
blackberrying: not many fruits become verbs, but this means to go picking wild blackberries from the bushes in the countryside
baize: a rough woollen material, usually green

push-ha'penny: more often known as shove-ha'penny, a game whose aim is to push coins from the edge of a board into particular marked bands along its length
Harrow: one of the best-known English public schools (an expensive private school which attracts a lot of upper and upper-middle class pupils)
racquets: a game, mainly played at 'public' (private) schools, quite similar to the game of squash

Exs. 1 and 2

Classroom treatment

Read the introductory paragraph of the article with the class. See if any Ss are familiar with any of the films the brothers have made and, if so, what they can tell the class about them.

Divide the class as suggested. We would recommend left and right, so that each group can offer assistance in the reading comprehension phase to other members of the group. When the A/B pairs are formed later, about half the Ss have to move from one side of the room to the other; some, of course, only have to turn a chair!

There is a great deal of work on inference in this activity. Ss have to do a lot of reading between the lines a) to appreciate the passages fully, and b) to answer the questions with any degree of certainty.

Expected answers

1 1 A kind of religious sect, certainly Christian, with rather controversial ideas.

   Clues for this lie in the close association with phrases like 'encountered Christian belief', 'my conversion', 'my commitment to my faith', 'I was saddened by his going off with the Navigators'. Generally his faith had obviously upset the family. The brothers grew apart because of The Navigators.

   2 James not as serious about sport, an extrovert, more sociable, more independent, more relaxed, liked jazz, was naughty.

   Edward more serious, the 'good boy', liked classical music.

   3 James started at a very young age, 10, and had early film success. He dropped out of the film world because of his religion and then returned to it, helped a lot by Edward.

Edward's early career was obviously less successful than James' — 'I wasn't envious of him' — and presumably took off at about the time James was giving up his career for his religion.

4   Though different as boys, they were obviously close, and had a 'blissful upbringing' together. James' early success in films 'coloured their relationship', making their lifestyles different. They had a lot of fun together in the 60s with Edward happily playing 'the older brother'. They drifted apart a bit when Edward got married. Then more seriously they drifted apart when James joined the Navigators. They became closer again — 'Edward's generosity as older brother shone through', 'I'm terribly glad he has resurrected his career' — when James returned to acting.

2 1   Edward, talking about the family's rejection of James' religious conversion.

2   James, describing the less extrovert, less sociable, less ambitious Edward.

3   James, who got the first role, despite his father's preference for Edward.

4   James, who felt he was in the middle of all the fun in the 1960s.

5   Edward, who we know was less extrovert and sociable than James.

6   Edward: only a guess, but James sounds wilder, doesn't he?

Ex. 3

Classroom treatment

You might need to be sensitive here. With most classes, this activity could be a lot of fun and produce interesting results. Set the task, referring back to the way the Fox brothers talked/wrote about themselves, each other and their relationship. Remind Ss of language patterns such as 'I can't stand the way he ...', 'I enjoy seeing her .. ', 'What I like most about him is the way he ...', 'I wish she ...'. Set the task as a fifteen-minute classroom writing phase or as homework. Then, at your discretion, when Ss have read what their partner has written about them, read out part or all of some pieces and see if the class can guess who the subject of the passage is.

Coursebook pp.62-63

Vocabulary: It's all part and parcel of the language

CAE Relevance: All Papers

Ex. 1

Classroom treatment

As a warm-up and a neat introduction to the exercises, give Ss the first of a pair of common words (not included on the page) and ask them to supply the second word of the pair. Examples might be: salt and ... (pepper), fish and ... (chips), Charles and ... (Diana), Saturday and ... (Sunday), life and ... (death), sooner or ... (later). Make it clear that these are 'set' pairs and that they are always in the same order: something will happen 'sooner or later' — never *'later or sooner'*.

Ss in pairs work out the 20 matching pairs. There are obviously one or two tricky pairings: 'now' on the left could go with 'then' or 'again' on the right, and only a process of elimination will give 100% correct answers.

Correct matchings (+ meanings)

pros and cons (advantages and disadvantages); *ins and outs* (all the finest details); *dead and buried* (finished, once and for all); *hit and/or miss* (a lottery, just chance); *tooth and nail* (bitterly, to the death!); *time and again* (repeatedly); *upside down* (top where the bottom should be and vice versa); *black and blue* (severely bruised); *(take) the rough with the smooth* (accept the ups and downs of life); *inside out* (the wrong way round, e.g. socks); *(in) black and white* (in writing, on paper); *(the) whys and wherefores* (all the reasons why); *board and lodging* (accommodation); *(my) flesh and blood* (alive, real or of the same family); *part and parcel* (an integral, fundamental part); *ups and downs* (good and bad times); *open and shut (case)* (clearly soluble (crime), no dispute); *now and then* (occasionally); *this and that* (various things, perhaps not very important); *once and for all* (finally, definitively)

Ex. 2

Classroom treatment

Quite a tricky gap-fill exercise this; a lot of options are given and one or two pairs will fit in more than one space. Ask Ss to read the four extracts first before doing the exercise and then (after they have covered the extracts) see if they can already summarise the opinions of the four writers. Then let them do the exercise in pairs before checking with the whole class.

You might, as consolidation, ask them to use the phrases they have studied in what they consider commonly spoken sentences between husband and wife:

'We've got to learn to take the rough with the smooth, darling', 'Such arguments are all part and parcel of living in the same house together', 'I've told you time and again not to leave your socks there!'

To complete this section, Ss might brainstorm (as a team game perhaps) other common expressions involving pairs of words, for example: *Heaven and Hell, bread and butter, gin and tonic, now or never, at sixes and sevens,* etc.

Expected answers

Intro: pros and cons

Letter 1: hit or miss; ups and downs; rough with the smooth; black and white

Letter 2: Time and again; open and shut; board and lodging; black and blue (bruised); upside down; tooth and nail; flesh and blood

Letter 3: now and then (*or* now and again); this and that

Letter 4: whys and wherefores; part and parcel; ins and outs; dead and buried; inside out; once and for all

Language focus

Ex. 1 Two- and three-word verbs

CAE Relevance: All Papers

1

Classroom treatment

As per Coursebook, let Ss discuss why the phrasal verbs have been put into four columns. Get spokespeople from each group then to say what they think. Once the answers have been established, get Ss to suggest other phrasal verbs they know for each of the four columns.

Expected answers

Though they may come up with some interesting alternative theories, the intended answer is that:

go on and *shine through* (as used here) are examples of intransitive phrasal verbs;

chuck in and *take up* are examples of separable phrasal verbs, where the particle can come before or after a noun object but only after a pronoun;

come back to is an example of a phrasal prepositional verb, a three-word verb;

go through (here) is a prepositional verb, where the preposition is never 'separable' i.e. never comes after the object

2

Classroom treatment

Give Ss a few minutes to think about and write down some questions to ask their partner using the listed phrasal verbs. If you like, you could ask half the class to make up questions for verbs in the first two columns and the other half for those in the third and fourth columns — to avoid duplication. Make sure then that the paired Ss come from different 'groups'.

Once prepared, Ss should be given five minutes or so to ask and answer the questions. Though personal questions, the fact that improvisation is being asked for will avoid embarrassment. More examples of the sort of target questions:

Why did you break up with your first boy/girlfriend?

Did you ever stay out longer than you were supposed to?

In what ways do you think you have let down your parents?

Are you happy with the way your parents brought you up?

Who in your family did you most look up to?

Did you ever really stand up to your parents?

Who used to look after you when your parents went out?

Who was the first girl/boy you ever fell for?

Ex. 2 Tense revision

CAE Relevance: All Papers

Classroom treatment

1 This section is a relatively brief revision of basic tenses. If at any point during the exercises Ss' grasp of them is shown to be shaky, refer them to the Grammar Commentary.

Initiate a short class discussion on changes in family life and relationships during the Ss' lifetime. What have been the most significant changes and what has caused them?

Organise pairs in the class and give one of each pair a minute to read the passage. The 'readers' then, with books closed, summarise the piece for their partners. Ask the 'listeners' if they agree with the opinions expressed in the passage.

Go through the piece with the whole class, focussing attention on the tenses used. Ask if it would be possible to substitute another tense like this:

> *have been shaken — were shaken* (No, not in British English)
>
> *are being born — are born* (Yes, but continuous is more vivid)
>
> *are starting — start* (Not really — we are talking about current trend)
>
> *are born — are being born* (Absolutely not)
>
> etc.

2 Remind Ss that the piece was written in 1980 and make sure they understand the rubric for 2. Perhaps reinforce with time lines on the board. Make sure they are aware of what tense changes (and changes of adjective/adverb) will be necessary in their rewrite. The given first line will help. Set the writing task as pairwork.

3 Study the rubric with the class carefully and briefly discuss the tense changes that will be necessary in this rewrite. Change pair groupings for this task.

Alternative treatment

Half the class work together to do ex. 2, while the other half work on ex. 3. Then pairs or groups of four are formed from the two halves of the class and the written pieces are studied, possibly criticised and/or corrected by members of the other group.

Briefly check and give model versions at the end.

Model answers

2 (In the previous thirty years the foundations of family life had been profoundly shaken.) Babies were being born (then/at that time) with little hope of what had once been considered a normal family life. There were ever more frequent stories of child abuse, couples were starting to split up even before their babies were born and teenage crime had multiplied almost beyond the statistician's abilities to calculate.

Figures revealed that in those days only one in two children grew up with their own two parents at home with them and suggested that very soon a two-parent family would be the exception rather than the norm. No-one could say for sure what effect that was likely to have on the broader spectrum of social life.

This/That state of affairs had been getting much worse for some time. Had things sunk as low as they could go? Or would the family 30 years from then be a thing of the past?

3 (Thirty years from now the foundations of family life will have been profoundly shaken.) Babies will be being born (will be born) (then/at that time) with little hope of what is (generally) considered a normal family life. There will be ever more frequent stories of child abuse, couples will be starting (will start) to split up even before their babies are born and teenage crime will have multiplied almost beyond the statistician's abilities to calculate.

Figures will reveal that (at that time/by then) only one in two children will grow/will be growing up with their own two parents at home with them and (will) suggest that very soon (in a very short time) a two-parent family will be the exception rather than the norm. No one can say (No one will know) for sure what effect that is likely to have on the broader spectrum of social life.

This/That state of affairs will have been getting much worse for some time. Will things have sunk as low as they can go? Or will the family 30 years from then be (have become) a thing of the past?

Coursebook pp.64-65

Read, edit and discuss

CAE Relevance: Papers 1, 3 and 4 (Reading, English in Use and Listening)

▷ 📼 Tapescript for ex.2 (See Coursebook p.153.)

Background notes and vocabulary

> *strapping:* big and strong
>
> *filch:* steal something (normally of small value) secretly
>
> *Eastern bloc:* in 1991 the group of countries that belong(ed) to the Warsaw pact: the USSR and its satellites
>
> *25lb:* 11.34 kilograms
>
> *junk food:* bad quality, unhealthy food
>
> *line backer:* a playing position in American (gridiron) football
>
> *nose jobs:* plastic surgery to change the shape of one's nose (see Dr Hook song *The Millionaire* in Unit 8)
>
> *laid-back:* cheerfully informal, relaxed, casual, unworried
>
> *hamstrings:* tendons at the back of the leg, joining bone to muscle
>
> *Robo Quarterback: Robo* is becoming used informally as an adjectival form of robot; compare the American film *Robocop*

Ex. 1

Classroom treatment

The two preliminary questions are designed to give Ss strategies for dealing with the unscrambling type of exercise.

Discuss question 1 with the class and elicit other words and phrases that might serve as 'clues'. Some examples: *then, this, that, moreover, what is more, for example, firstly, in conclusion, finally, be that as it may*.

Ask Ss to discuss question 2 in pairs or threes for a couple of minutes, then check their answers with the class as a whole. (They should NOT attempt to read all the paragraphs yet!) The answers should be along these lines:

h before **i**: Mikhail is introduced in **h**; Marinovich's 'other son' is mentioned in **i**

f before **b**: 'supertots' with quotation marks are clearly being introduced in **f**; 'this trend' is clearly referring to something already mentioned (and the quotation marks have gone)

i before **g**: Todd is introduced in **i** — Marinovich's 'other son'; **g** begins 'his ability', so he must have been introduced previously. It goes on 'Todd, studying ...' with no explanation of who Todd is.

h before **c**: **h** describes Mikhail as a baby, **c** picks things up age 2; in **h** the information begins with a full name to identify the subject; in **c**, 'he' almost certainly refers to a person already introduced by name.

f before **e**: **f** introduces us to Mikhail's father, we are told his first name by way of introduction; in **e** the use of his surname only suggests we have been introduced to him earlier

e before **j**: the clinic is introduced by name in **e**; in **j** 'one source at the clinic' tells us that the clinic has already been mentioned

Set the task as a timed piece. With the preliminary help already given and considering the preview Ss have already had through work on question **2**, 15 minutes would be a fair target. With a strong class, and to encourage real speed work, you might reduce that to 10 minutes.

Answers

The original order of the paragraphs was: h; c; d; f; a; i; g; b; e; j.

Possible headline: 'US parents push 'supertots' to be sporting champs'

Ex. 2

Classroom treatment

Tell Ss they're going to hear some friends arguing about the pros and cons of bringing up children as 'supertots'. Ask if they can predict the arguments that might be put forward in favour of or against such an upbringing.

Play the tape once and ask whether the argument is:

— a woman against two men?

— one woman and one man against a man?

— one woman and one man against another woman and a man?

Play the tape again. Ss make notes of any key phrases used by the speakers. Afterwards they reconstruct the argument with the help of the phrases noted.

Possible key phrases:

'supermen or supergirls' / 'an Einstein or whatever' / 'watching the box' / 'doing him or her a disservice' / 'robbing them of a natural childhood' / 'outsize muscles' / 'flowers out there' / 'they know what they'll take and what they'll refuse to do'

In groups, Ss then discuss the issue, putting forward their own views. A short summary of their discussion is then given to the rest of the class.

Exam Practice: Paper 5 Speaking

CAE Relevance: Paper 5 (Speaking)
Ex. 1

Classroom treatment

Books closed. To introduce this phase, use two or three large photos of your own. Give a picture to, say, five or six Ss and get them to describe it in as much detail as possible to the rest of the class, who are encouraged to ask for more detail or clarification: Where exactly is she standing? What do you mean by 'plain'? How big would you say it is? etc. Do the same with other groups of five or six, until all Ss have had a 'go'. This will provide a chance to check on Ss' use of 'locating phrases' such as: *in the foreground, on the far left, right in the middle, to the right of the old lady, just behind him, some way away, in the distance*.

Books open. Now get Ss to work in pairs as in the rubric to describe their photos to each other.

Ex. 2

Classroom treatment

This exercise is designed to ensure that Ss are not too repetitious when commenting on visual material. Give Ss a few moments to think about how they would use the listed openers in comments about the photos, then invite contributions from individuals.

The target language here would be:
No-one would/could deny that ...
There's no doubt that/There can be no doubt that / Without doubt, ...
The family on the beach are obviously ...
There must be at least ... / It must have so much easier to ...
To my mind, ...
I have the feeling that ...
In my opinion, ... /I'm of the opinion that ...
As I see it, ...
It looks as if the children ...
The man seems to be doing something with ...
I get the impression that .../They give the impression of enjoying ...
Judging by the looks on their faces, ...

Ex. 3

Classroom treatment

Look together at the list of openers. These are long and quite formal. Ss should be given the chance to try and manipulate them comfortably and use them naturally. Some repetition or drill work will almost certainly be necessary. You might then ignore the given theme for a while and express some (slightly controversial?) opinions to individuals on a range of different subjects and see if they can use one of the openers in response.

Then get Ss to make their lists on their own as per the rubric. Here are suggested lists of family B pressures and pleasures:

Pressures

- high mortgage repayments
- children involved in petty crime, drugs
- greater threat of burglary / mugging
- media pressure
- threat to jobs
- problems of finding a job
- polluted streets and rivers, etc.

Pleasures

- television
- high-quality hi-fi
- convenience of a car
- air travel
- foreign holidays
- cinema
- cheap telephone calls plus other communication systems
- household gadgets and labour-saving devices

Ss then compare their lists with a partner's, as suggested. Encourage the challenging of particular items by partners and detailed explanation and exemplification where necessary. Remind them of the 'argument' language just practised and encourage its use in the paired exchanges. You might then bring pairs together to form fours to do likewise.

Monitor carefully what is going on and point out strengths and weaknesses afterwards.

Alternative treatment

If time allows, conduct the practice as a test with each pair in turn, you as assessor cum interlocuteur. Make notes during Ss' performance, give marks and discuss with them later.

Rounding off the Unit

Why not round off the Unit with a short quiz on the 20th Century? Ask teams in turn 'Which decade ...?' questions that might include these below. (Answers are given in years, but decade answers are expected from Ss — the Sixties, the Twenties, etc.)

In which decade

1 did man first travel in space? (1961)
2 was the Russian Revolution? (1917)
3 was Marilyn Monroe born? (1926)
4 did man first step on the moon? (1969)
5 did someone first fly across the English Channel? (1909)
6 was the European Economic Community founded? (1958)
7 did Lenin die? (1924)
8 did the Second World War break out? (1939)

Other questions might involve the history of the Ss' own country or countries.

11 All in a day's work

Warm-up

Choose one or more of these **alternative ideas**, all with books closed:

1 What are the implications of the expression '(It's) all in a day's work'? (It implies that certain jobs, however unpleasant, must be accepted as part of the day's routine.)

2 Prepare two sets of cards: A cards with professions; B cards with pros and cons of each profession. You need as many cards as there are students in the class. Give each student a card and ask them to find their partner. Examples:

A	B
Dentist	Clean, but bad breath
Vet	Varied, but can get bitten / fleas
Teacher	Long holidays, but homework to mark
King	Lots of money, but no private life
Gardener	Lots of fresh air, but hard on the back
Politician	Famous, but job is perhaps not very secure
Trapeze artist	Exciting, but dangerous
Midwife	People really need you, but you often have to work at night
Mountaineer	Get some good views, but can be very cold

3 Each student thinks of a way of completing this sentence 'I want to be a ...' and the others think of as many ways as they can of dissuading him/her.

4 Go round the class with everyone completing the statement 'When I was seven years old I wanted to be a ....'

5 Milling activity. Each student has a sticky label on his/her back with the name of a job on it. They have to ask other students 'Yes/No' questions to identify their job — 'Do I work indoors? Do I earn a lot of money?' etc. Suggestions for jobs: politician, king, conjurer, ballet-dancer, model, surgeon, professional footballer, midwife, cook, road-builder, cleaner, EFL teacher, zoo-keeper, etc.

Read and discuss

CAE Relevance: Paper 1 (Reading)

Background notes and vocabulary

'Plum Job for Brit in Paris'
nein: no, in German
pas du tout: not at all, in French
lagging behind: here, lower than
a bright spark: someone intelligent who is likely to go a long way
ousting: removing
counterparts: equivalents, people in similar jobs
the City: the financial area of London
arrondissement: French word for the district of a town
the Tube: London's undergound railway
head-hunting agency: an agency which helps companies to match people to appropriate top jobs
Unit Trust: a particular way of investing money

Exs. 1-5

Classroom treatment

1 Ask Ss to look at the photo and the title and to suggest what the article is likely to be about (a young British woman who gets a very good job in Paris).

2 Pair Ss and ask them to write five questions which they think the article may answer e.g. What job does the young woman do?

3 Allow the Ss only 30 seconds to skim the text. Working with the same partner they should then briefly compare what they picked up from their skimming.

4 Then give the Ss time to read the article but encourage them to read it as quickly as they can.

Having read the text, Ss in the same pairs should discuss questions 1-3.

Questions 4 and 5 can either be discussed in pairs and then written in class or be written as homework.

Answers
3 The possible answers are:

(1) goes in both directions
(2) liked the idea of working abroad

(3) there are several agencies in Paris

(4) everything else is dramatically different

(5) stays until 7 p.m.

(6) food, clothes and the beauty of the city

4 Possible answers are:

The idea of working abroad so far seems to appeal to young British people more than to other young Europeans.

Livia Sanders, a young Englishwoman, has had a very good job in Paris for a year.

She found it easy to find a job in Paris.

She does not earn more than in London but she enjoys the style of working more.

She also is enthusiastic about her life outside work.

5 Possible questions:

How do I go/set about finding accommodation in Paris?

How much would I have to pay for a flat/apartment in the city centre?

Do I need a work permit to work in France?

Will I get free health care?

Would I have to pay tax both in France and at home?

Extension if required

Extra questions for pair, group or class discussion — or as questions for additional written homework if desired, after completing the reading text:

Have you ever toyed with the idea of working abroad?

What appeals to you about working abroad?

Where in the world would you like to work and why?

What (if anything) puts you off the idea of working abroad?

Vocabulary: Overworked and underpaid!

CAE Relevance: All Papers

Ex. 1 Describing work and workplaces

Classroom treatment

1 In pairs and using dictionaries, Ss mark each word or phrase N (noun), V (verb) or A (adjective).

2 Check answers with the class as a whole.

3 Ask Ss in pairs to sub-divide the words in any ways they like and then to add new words to each group.

4 Ss now work in groups of three or four (each person in the group from a different pairing) to explain to

each other how they sub-divided the words and to say which words they added.

5 Whole class feedback on the activity.

Answers

The words are listed here in their most likely category but note that some could be included in more than one group. *Recruit*, *strike* and *picket* can be nouns as well as verbs for instance, *staff* is a verb as well as a noun, and *sabbatical* and *subsidiary* can be nouns as well as adjectives.

nouns	verbs	adjectives
profession D	recruit F	full time H
fee B	lay off F	part time H
vocation D	work to rule G	unemployed H
wages B	promote F	seasonal H
salary B	strike G	freelance H
commission B	earn B	self-employed H
expense account B	hire F	sabbatical I
shift D	retire F	subsidiary J
head of department A	resign F	salaried B
warehouse C	appoint F	
shareholder A	picket G	
receptionist A	headhunt F	
income tax B		
PA (Personal Assistant) A		
clerk A		
personnel officer A		
trade union E		
perks B		
pension B		
staff A		
headquarters C		

It is possible to subdivide the words in a number of different ways. The most obvious way perhaps is indicated by the following letters after each word.

A	people	F	hiring and firing
B	money	G	protest action
C	places	H	styles of work
D	types of work	I	type of leave
E	organisations	J	type of company

Ss then write three words on a piece of paper and pass it to the pair of Ss on their left for them to make up one sentence combining all the words on their list.

Ex. 2 Prefixes

Classroom treatment

Deal with the exercise as instructed in the CB.

Answers

Prefix	Meaning	Examples
re	again; back	re-write, return
sub	under	submarine, sub-editor
self	self	self-centred, self-controlled
under	under, not enough	underpaid, underworked
anti	against	anti-work, anti-war
pro	in favour of	pro-democracy, pro-revolutionary
in	in	insert, inside
in	not	incompetent, indirect
un	not	uncomfortable, undesirable
co	together	co-pilot, co-driver
super	above, extra	supersonic, super-intelligent

Homework

Ss should write a fairly short paragraph about their ideal job using as many of the words and phrases they have dealt with as possible.

Coursebook pp.68-69

Read, write and discuss

CAE Relevance: All Papers

Background notes and vocabulary

> 'Is It Time To Change Your Job?'
> *plucked:* here, picked at random
> *office-mates:* colleagues
> *aloof from:* distanced from
> *petty:* trivial
> *politicking:* intriguing to get a better position or to be in favour with the right people
> *divulge:* share, tell
> *workaholics:* people who are addicted to work (formed by analogy with the word 'alcoholic': compare also 'chocaholic')
> *grouse:* complain
> *CV:* abbreviation of the Latin expression 'curriculum vitae', which is a résumé of someone's life as sent in with a job application

Ex. 1

Classroom treatment

Ss read the questionnaire and mark their own answers.

Check that Ss have understood all the questions. Have them work in pairs and ask them to a) compare their

responses, and b) score their partner's responses.

Explain that they should mark the questions in the following way.

Key to the questionnaire

For saying True to statements 2, 6, 7, 8, 12, 13, 14 and 16 give a Y and for saying False to these statements give an N.

For saying False to statements 1, 3, 4, 5, 9, 10, 11, and 15 give a Y and for saying True to those statements give an N.

Now count the Ys and the Ns. If the Ys outnumber the Ns then it is time to change jobs, but if the Ns are greater then it is not time to change yet.

Ex. 2

Classroom treatment

Ask Ss to prepare their answers to this question individually before it is discussed with the whole group.

Answers

Positive	Pejorative
good	unsophisticated
team spirit	ignorant
hope	petty
encourage	politicking
open-handed	groan
outstanding	workaholic
enjoy	grouse
great	

Ex. 3

Classroom treatment

In preparing Ss to write for the 'Are you going to go to the top?' quiz, ask them first to consider what qualities are needed in someone on their way to the top — e.g. ambition, talent, diligence, ruthlessness, etc. This might help give them some ideas for their statements.

When each pair has compiled their statements, they should each administer them to two other students in the group and should tell those students whether, on the basis of their answers, they are destined for the top or not.

Ss should then report back as to whether they got consistent feedback from each of the sets of questions that they answered or not.

IMPORTANT: Take care to make this a light-hearted activity and to be sceptical about the results of such questionnaires in case Ss are upset at being told that they are not on the way to the top.

Language focus: Hopes, fears and reasons

CAE Relevance: All Papers

Ex. 1

Classroom treatment

Simply read through the task to make sure it is clear to everyone but do not discuss it in detail at this stage. It can, however, be highlighted that the exercises on the page give practice in the kind of language needed to complete the task.

Ex. 2

Classroom treatment

Ask Ss to discuss the sentences in pairs and then check through their answers quickly as a class.

Answers

I feel like an ice cream means 'I'd love an ice cream', whereas the second sentence means 'I feel as if I were an idiot'.

I'm afraid to do means 'I lack the courage to take a certain action', whereas *I'm afraid of doing something* expresses one's fear of certain things happening.

The same distinction can be made with *I'm frightened to do something* and *I'm frightened of doing*.

I'm anxious to do something means 'I'm keen to do it' or 'I want to do it' whereas *I'm anxious about* means 'I'm worried about doing it'.

In the first sentence *mean* means 'intend' whereas in the second sentence *means* means 'involves'.

I don't intend to means simply that 'I don't plan to' whereas *I have no intention of* sounds much more determined; the person is clearly not going to resign.

I'm going to see is often a personal decision that the speaker has reached; *I'm seeing* the boss has to include the word 'tomorrow' if it is to be clear that it has a future time reference but it is another common way of talking about fixed or arranged future plans. *I'll be seeing* can simply refer to something that the speaker feels is sure to be true without it actually being written in anyone's diary. You could say 'I'll be seeing the boss tomorrow' if, for instance, you always have lunch in the canteen at the same time.

I hope is a more general long-term wish whereas *I'm hoping* is used about something that the person is wanting and expecting at this very moment.

Ex. 3

Classroom treatment

Ss work individually to complete the questions. Check their answers. They then work in pairs to ask each other the questions. They then each report back to the class one thing they learnt about their partner's plans.

Answers

1 to; 2 at/for/to achieve; 3 to do; 4 setting; 5 of; 6 to; 7 going; 8 going

Ex. 4

Classroom treatment

Ss work on individual ways of completing their sentences. Then ask three or four students how they completed each sentence and put the most interesting example of each completion on the board.

Possible answers

Jo became a lion-tamer
– to see the world.
– in order to escape from the typing pool.
– in case she ever needed to find work in a circus.
– so as not to have to go to an office every day.
– so that she could conquer her fear of animals.
– so that her brother wouldn't call her a coward any more.
– with a view to setting up her own circus eventually.
– to avoid getting married.
– to get out of going to college.
– as a precaution against being unemployed.

Ex. 5

Classroom treatment

Set the question as homework, reminding Ss to revise the language practised on p. 69 before writing their answers. In setting up the homework, you might suggest that Ss may find it interesting in x years time to read something they wrote in their youth about their plans for the future. (See Introduction p.9.)

Possible model answer

I enjoy my working life as a teacher at the moment but I do not feel that I want to be doing exactly the same kind of work in ten or even five years' time. I need to feel that I am making progress and that I am continuing to learn myself as well as to teach others. I think I should like to stay at this school for another two or three years and then move to a different teaching post, one with more responsibilities, in another town.

After five years or so in that job I should review my possibilities. If classroom teaching is beginning to pall by that stage then I think I should try for a job in educational administration — who knows, I might even eventually become a headmistress! If I am still enjoying teaching as much as I do now then perhaps I could try to write a textbook in my free time. That way I should feel I was learning some new skills myself.

I sometimes worry a little about the poor pay which teachers get. It doesn't concern me too much at the moment when I am single and have no particular responsibilities. But maybe in the future it will become more of a problem. I hope that money, however, will never be a really significant factor affecting any job decisions that I have to make in the future.

Coursebook pp.70-71

Listen, discuss and write

CAE Relevance: Paper 4 (Listening)

Background notes and vocabulary

stand-offish: an informal way of saying aloof, unfriendly
Nobody would give a hoot what I did: a colloquial way of saying 'Nobody would care what I did'
ending up in a home: ending your life in a special kind of hostel for old people
creature comforts: physical things which are not strictly speaking necessary for life but do help to make it pleasant — ease of control of temperature within one's home, for example, or having a wide range of foods and services easily available

▷ 📼 **Tapescript (authentic recording)** (See Coursebook pp.153-154.)

Exs. 1-4

Classroom treatment

1 Briefly discuss the prediction questions as a class. Make sure that Ss know where Sri Lanka is — an island south of India. This should at least help them to predict comments about the weather.

2 Just before Ss listen, ask them to read the first two questions and to think about them, making notes if they wish as they listen.

3 Play the whole tape through once.

4 Have Ss in pairs compare their answers to questions 1 and 2 (as stated in 3).

5 Play the tape again stopping at appropriate points to ask additional comprehension and language questions, like these:

- What, in his first question, does the interviewer say is a stereotype characteristic of the British? ('Stand-offishness'.)

- Does Nelun agree that the British are 'stand-offish'? (No, just that they are more formal in their social relationships.)
- What positive and negative things about life in Britian does Nelun mention in her answer to the interviewer's second question? (Positive: there is more freedom and more privacy in Britain. Negative: life is very rushed in Britain.)
- What nationality is Nelun's husband? (British.)
- What does Nelun imply about the political situation in Sri Lanka. (It's troubled, perhaps unstable.)
- What does Nelun mean when she says 'the creature comforts may not be so good, but from the human angle, it's better'? (People may be materially richer, and people more comfortable in Britain, but people look after older members of society better in Sri Lanka.)

6 Set the scene for question 4. The aim of this exercise is to highlight the importance of making a magazine article interesting and informative for readers. One aspect of this is having good opening and closing paragraphs. The first paragraph must appeal in some way or readers will not go on reading. The final paragraph has to leave readers with some kind of strong final impression. At this point refer Ss back to the article on p. 66. What is included in the first and last paragraphs? What makes you want to read on after the first paragraph? The body of the writing must also be interesting and so the interviewer has to ask questions which are likely to lead to interesting answers. Make sure the Ss are aware of these points before they discuss the tasks set in 4 with a partner.

7 The opening and closing paragraphs could perhaps be set as homework.

Possible answers

Here are suggestions for possible first and last paragraphs for a magazine article about Nelun.

First paragraph
Would you exchange a hot sunny climate for Britain's damp and drizzle? Would you give up fresh pineapples and spicy curries for Del Monte chunks and fish and chips? Nelun Shamdas did just that when she decided to work in Cambridge rather than her native Sri Lanka.

Last paragraph
When it comes to retirement, however, Nelun would agree with the old saying, 'East, West, home's best'. And home is still where she was born and brought up, even though almost all her working life has been spent in greyer northern climes.

Additional classroom idea

It might be useful to copy some of your Ss' ideas for first and last paragraphs and use them as the basis for a lesson. Copy a number of examples of student ideas and circulate them among the class. Analyse the different techniques used to arouse interest at the beginning of the article and to round off the article at the end. Are all the techniques successful? If not, why not? Which ideas seem to work best?

Speaking

CAE Relevance: Paper 5 (Speaking)

Classroom treatment

1 Ss work in pairs on the questions beside the cartoons. Then compare answers with the class as a whole.

2 As a possible answer to q.1, perhaps teach the expression *The grass is always greener on the other side of the fence* (i.e. other people's lives always seem more interesting). Another possible answer to q.1 is that people always seem to get fed up with their own job however glamorous it might seem.

3 In answering q.2, practise 'The teacher wishes she were a film star/waitress/lion-tamer'.

4 Pairs or individuals list their five most important things for a work situation, e.g. work in open air, meeting people, etc. (see q.5). The other students try to suggest a job to match (e.g. ski-instructor).

Exam Practice: Paper 1 Reading

CAE Relevance: Paper 1 (Reading)

Background notes and vocabulary

scarred: physically marked (from *to scar*); compare with *scared* (from *to scare*) = frightened
nail-biting: very exciting
pile-ups: multiple car crashes
stunt woman: a woman specially employed to perform something dangerous for a film
Equity: a trade union for actors and actresses

Great Wall of China: ancient wall round the old border of China
into shot: into view of the camera (compare 'to shoot a film')
probationary period: initial time doing a new job; until one has successfully completed this time, one is not considered fully qualified (or a permanent member of staff)
Pinewood Studios: well-known British film studios
(to be) up to it (physically): (to be) capable (physically)
ITV, BBC 1: two British television channels
South of the Border, Jack the Ripper, London's Burning: the names of TV series
Supergirl, Superman IV: the names of two films
reek: to stink
well padded up: wearing plenty of protective clothing
creek: narrow inlet of water
bar-room brawl: a rough fight in a bar

Exs. a and b

Classroom treatment

Remind Ss that in Paper 1 they will have to match sentences or paragraphs taken out of a text with gaps in the text. Ask them how they would set about doing this. In other words, try and elicit some of the advice given in **a** before they actually read it.

Then read through the instructions in **a** with Ss as a class before asking them to do the exercise in **b** as homework.

Answers
a 7; b 8; c 1; d 10; e 11; f 4; g 2; h 5. (3, 6 and 9 do not fit.)

Rounding off the Unit

Why not round off this Unit with a free discussion about 'the ideal job/profession' — OR with a number of short talks on 'I wouldn't do *that* job if you paid me one million pounds!' (Ss talk for 30 seconds about a job they just couldn't imagine doing, without actually mentioning the name of the job or profession — other Ss listen and have to identify the job or profession.)

12 The persuaders

Warm-up

Here are two **alternative suggestions**, both with books closed:

1 Ask students to think of

a) something they want to sell (e.g. a cassette player, bicycle, old textbooks, etc.), *or*

b) a service they can offer (e.g. gardening, babysitting, cleaning at weekends, photocopying, computer setting, etc.) *or*

c) something they want (e.g. a part-time job, a secondhand bicycle, motorcycle or car, etc.) — and ask them immediately to write a small advertisement. Maximum number of words: 30.

The ad could be for a school, college or workplace noticeboard, or to go into the Personal column in an English language newspaper.

Go round checking and note any common errors that are being made.

After five minutes, ask a number of Ss to read out their advertisements.

2 Write up 'The Persuaders' on the blackboard/OHP. Then say: 'Quite a lot of people try to persuade us to do things in our lives: who *are* 'the persuaders', do you think? Write a list of such people.' Ss check with a partner, then the class as a whole. Which persuaders have most written? — Advertisers? Teachers? Politicians? Priests? Insurance salesmen? Others? Ask for reasons.

Alternatively, dispense with a 'books closed' Warm-up phase for once, and go straight into the 'Discuss and write' activity with books open.

Discuss and write

CAE Relevance: Papers 2 and 5 (Writing and Speaking)

Background notes and vocabulary

> *calorie:* a measure used when stating the amount of heat or energy that a food will produce, so *a low-calorie drink* is one that produces little energy

> *portable:* that can be (easily) carried or moved; quite small and light
> *the Amazon:* the river with the largest basin and greatest volume of water in the world, draining nearly half of South America, 5,500 km long
> *campaign:* a set of actions intended to obtain a particular result, often in politics or business, but here to clean up beaches around the coast

Classroom treatment

Ask Ss to work in pairs

a) to read the list of products and services,

b) to note down which emotions they would play on or appeal to for each, and then

c) to draft a first sentence for a short advertisement for each.

These first sentences should somehow reflect the emotion or emotions Ss have identified, and fictitious names of products may have to be invented — even for a first line.

When most of the class have completed the task, pairs then team up with other pairs to compare what they have written: a) emotions to play on or appeal to, and b) their draft sentences.

Finally, check with the whole class.

If you think the class might be unsure of what to do, discuss the first one or two products with the class as a whole. It might also be valuable to get the whole class to contribute to a list of emotions that advertisers commonly appeal to — fear, vanity, desire to improve yourself, sense of duty, guilt, etc. — and to scatter these on the board/OHP as reminders.

Possible answers

Products/Services	Emotions to play on or appeal to
• life insurance	> Fear — fear of death, accidents, etc.
• a new sports car	> Sense of adventure; social status
• a new low-calorie drink	> Concern about health — desire to live a clean and long life; vanity
• women's perfume	> Vanity, desire to attract
• a language course	> Desire to better yourself; desire for education
• a new portable computer	> Desire to keep up, to have the latest gadgets

- sun tan cream   > Vanity; health
- a new kind of bed for   > Desire for relief from pain
  people suffering from
  back trouble
- a guided tour up the   > Sense of adventure
  Amazon
- a seaside 'Clean Beach'   > Sense of civic duty
  campaign
- flying lessons   > Sense of adventure; doing
  something *new, different!*
  (Stand out from the crowd!)

Some possible first sentences

- **Life insurance:** What will happen to your family
  financially when you die?

- **A new sports car:** Do you feel any sense of adventure
  when you drive off in your old car?

- **A new low-calorie drink:** If you're concerned about
  your health, you need to think low-calorie!

- **Women's perfume:** Film stars like Joan Collins choose
  their perfume very carefully.

- **A language course:** Don't you wish you could have
  spoken Japanese when you went there last year?

- **A new portable computer:** The XYZ 94 Portable is the
  very latest.

- **Sun tan cream:** SUNSKREEN will bring out the tan in
  you — naturally.

- **A new kind of bed ...:** Your days and nights of back
  pain are *over* !

- **A guided tour up the Amazon:** You need a sense of
  adventure to journey up the Amazon.

- **A seaside 'Clean Beach' campaign:** Are the beaches
  near you filthy?

- **Flying lessons:** There's nothing more exhilarating than
  flying your own plane!

Look, discuss and write

**CAE Relevance: Papers 1, 2 and 5 (Reading,
Writing and Speaking)**

Background notes and vocabulary

AUTAN ('Meet me by the pool.')
This is one of a series of ads for 'Autan' insect-
repellent cream. They all use close-ups of insects'
heads.
the pool: here, the swimming-pool
deter: discourage, or prevent from acting

repellent (n.)*:* a substance that drives (sthg, esp,
insects) away, also used as adj.
ARIEL ULTRA
This is an ad for 'Ariel Ultra' washing powder. The
ad uses a close-up photo of part of the dial on a
washing machine.
Ultra: this prefix (meaning 'beyond, very') is
sometimes used with product names, as here, to
imply the very latest, the very best
WWF: World Wide Fund for Nature, the
organisation devoted to the protection and
conservation of wildlife throughout the world. Its
symbol is the panda.
NATUREST ('Rotten night?')
This is an ad for a herbal remedy to sleeplessness.
rotten: here, bad, unpleasant, restless
SAVE £££'s ON FAMILY HAIRCUTS
This is a typical 'money-saving' ad, many of which
appear in magazines. Very few people actually *read*
them! The attraction is in saving money on a low-
price article, and a free gift.
Save £££'s: Save lots of money
a snip: here, a bargain (but there is also a play on
words: *to snip* means *to cut*)
EUTHYMOL ('Dali's Tube')
This is one of a series of 'Euthymol' toothpaste ads.
The series depicts the toothpaste tube in different
art styles.
Dali's tube: a tube of toothpaste as the artist Dali
might have painted it. Salvador Dali (1904-1989)
was famous for his surrealist paintings. This is
reminiscent of his painting in which clocks and
watches 'droop' over the edge of things.
eucalyptus: the oil made from any of several types of
tall tree, such as the Australian gum tree, which keep
their leaves in winter, and which produce an oil used
for colds
thymol: an aromatic phenol, derived from the
natural oil of thyme (a herb) and used as an
antiseptic
Decidedly individual: Note this adverb-adjective
collocation
COMPUTEACH ('You must be SELFISH! To Get
a GOOD JOB in Computers')
Note the contrast betwen the pejorative 'selfish' and
the positive words 'self-disciplined', 'self-assured'
and 'self-motivated'.
self-starter: used here unusually to describe a
person: it is usually an (electric) apparatus for
starting an engine without turning it by hand

SPECIAL NOTE: It is not important for Ss to read everything in the advertisements. In some the copy is certainly too small. The important thing is for Ss to study them in view of the questions they have to discuss.

Exs. 1 and 2

Classroom treatment

1 Following the work done in the previous phase/ lesson ('Discuss and write'), Ss now have an opportunity (preferably in groups of three or four) to discuss the real advertisements on these pages. It might be advisable to discuss one of the ads with the group as a whole before letting Ss work on their own.

When groups have discussed all the ads, get each group briefly to report their opinions to the rest of the class. Then see if there is any agreement on which they thought was the best of all.

2 Ss work in pairs and begin to draft or write full advertisements for two or three of the products or services from the 'Discuss and write' phase. They can suggest any artwork or illustration(s) they would want with their ads. (See Introduction p.9.)

Ask Ss to try to finalise two or three ads as a homework assignment. You might display a selection in the classroom.

Possible answers to ex. 1

AUTAN
This is an ad for an anti-insect cream, or at least something (cream, tablets, or whatever) to repel biting insects. It's appealing to our fear of being bitten, and clearly aims to shock. Did you know that many small biting insects look as horrific as that?! Special language: *a long cool drink* vs *a long hot one. Your blood;* ... *bloodthirsty biting insect ...;*

ARIEL ULTRA
This is an ad for a washing powder. It's appealing to people who are concerned about the environment. It implies that, by using this washing powder you will be helping to save endangered species (the WWF symbol) and energy — by being able to wash cotton at a reasonably low temperature.

NATUREST
This is an ad for a herbal remedy for sleeplessness. It's appealing to a desire to get a good night's sleep! Special language: *Rotten night? Sleep more peacefully, more naturally.*

SAVE £££'s ON FAMILY HAIRCUTS
This is an ad for an electric haircutter so that you can do your own and the family's. Its appeal is in saving money.

Special language: save, *a snip, freegift, ... with free fluff remover*

EUTHYMOL
This is an ad for toothpaste. It's appealing to people who want something different, not just any old toothpaste!

COMPUTEACH
This is an ad for courses in learning to use a computer, perhaps even computer programming. It's appealing to people who want to get a better job, particularly in the computer world. Special language: *selfish, self-disciplined, self-assured, self-motivated, selfstarter; employment prospects; highly paid job; a valuable service Free of Charge*

Coursebook pp.74-75

Vocabulary: The right word helps persuasion!

CAE Relevance: All Papers

Ex. 1 'Positive' and 'negative' words

Classroom treatment

This is an extremely difficult area of vocabulary in English, but one in which Ss need to begin to grasp the effect (in speech or writing) of one word or phrase in place of another 'synonymous' word or phrase.

a Ask Ss to read the two headlines and ask a partner which he/she would use and why. Then get responses from the class as a whole.

Through brief discussion, or through your explanation, Ss must be aware that in the context of the two headlines, the phrase *freedom fighters* sounds more positive, more acceptable, and might even suggest that we could sympathise with them. Not so with *terrorists*, which sounds a rather blunt word, and therefore 'negative'. There is also a formality in the first through the use of the phrase *claim responsibility* as opposed to the informal *say they were responsible* in the second.

b Again Ss discuss these in pairs before a whole (but brief) class discussion. It's not so much that the words are positive or negative, but that the different words or phrases give a positive or negative impression on the listener or reader. And further, we often tend to use the more positive or euphemistic word or phrase in English to avoid giving offence — thus, for example, *unsightly skin blemishes* instead of the blunt phrase *ugly spots*, or the phrase *young offender* in place of the rather blunt (and now slightly outdated) *young criminal*.

c Ss work in pairs to match the words or phrases and to decide which word or phrase is which. Then they should use a thesaurus and/or a dictionary to look for other 'synonyms'. And finally check with the whole class.

This would be a good time to point out the problems of using an English Thesaurus which does not indicate for a foreign learner whether words have a positive or negative feel about them. However, while organised in the same way as a thesaurus, a Lexicon for foreign learners does (or should) indicate the use of different 'synonyms'.

d Set this as a homework assignment.

Possible answers

b People prefer to be described (if at all!) as *elderly, thrifty, chubby* and *slim* because these words have a pleasant positive feel about them. They don't like being described as *old, mean, fat,* and *emaciated* because these words are blunt, almost 'negative' in feel. The word *plump* is a euphemism for *fat,* but again would almost certainly not be used to a person's face.

c Ordinary, neutral or blunt > Polite or euphemistic [+ other 'synonyms']:

old > *elderly* [+ *aged* (neutral), *ancient* (for a person, negative, rude)]

to steal > *to abscond with* [+ *to pinch* (slang), *to take* (neutral)]

ugly > *unsightly* [+ *unattractive* (neutral)]

to sweat > *to perspire* [+ *to glow* (euphemistic)] There is a saying: 'Animals sweat, men perspire and ladies glow'.

a liar > *a fibber*

a smell > *an unpleasant odour* [+ *a stench, a reek* (strong, negative)]

drunk > *intoxicated* [+ *stoned* (slang), *inebriated* (formal)]

dying > *terminally ill* [+ *on his last legs, at death's door* (coll.)]

d 1 She absconded with (*or* took) some silver.
2 My stomach aches.
3 You don't read that (news)paper, do you?
4 The man was intoxicated.
5 This spoon's dirty/not very clean.
6 Their house smells a little/has an unpleasant odour.

Ex. 2 Describing the virtues and capabilities of a product

Classroom treatment

Before Ss do the exercise, write these two sentences on the board/OHP:

> *This tumbledryer dries very well indeed.*
> *That model/She photographs superbly well.*

Then say: 'What do you notice about these two sentences? Which is the subject of the sentence in each? ('This tumbledrier' and 'That model/She'.) And which is the object? (There isn't one.) But don't we normally need an object after the verbs 'dry' and 'photograph'? (Yes.) So how are the verbs being used here? (In a different way. In fact they are transitive verbs, which normally have an object, being used intransitively.) Advertisements often use sentences like this. This exercise will show you other typical combinations.'

Then ask Ss to do the exercise individually or in pairs. Check answers with the whole class and discuss the questions.

Possible answers

Various combinations are possible here. These are examples:

The 'Moveit 2000' cleans amazingly/incredibly/unbelievably well.

The 'Lifelike' prints/copies superbly/marvellously/fantastically.

The 'Washo XX' washes beautifully/fantastically/so cleanly.

The 'Dishes Galore ST10' washes/cleans beautifully/fantastically/so cleanly.

The [Ford] '2001 GI' rides/handles/drives so smoothly.

The 'Yusee' prints superbly/marvellously/fantastically.

The XV314 records superbly/amazingly well.

New 'Gleam!' washes/cleans superbly/marvellously/fantastically.

Our 'Barbe-Coke' burns so/very cleanly.

This cordless electric iron irons marvellously/beautifully/so smoothly.

Coursebook pp.75-76

Language focus

CAE Relevance: All Papers, but esp. Paper 3 (English in Use)

The tasks in this phase are essentially rewriting or editing tasks, much like the kind of thing Ss might be asked to do in the English in Use Paper. At the same time, however, the language practised will feed nicely into productive writing tasks and give Ss a sense of progress, achievement and direction.

At the end of this phase, then, we suggest that Ss might go back once again to the ads they wrote earlier in the Unit and improve them in the light of this Language focus work or choose two or three different ones from the list on page 72 and write longer ads for these in the light of the language they've practised.

Exs. 1-4

Classroom treatment

Through the rubric or your own explanation, make sure Ss know what they have to do in these exercises. Point out the language notes at the bottom of each section and suggest that they discuss in pairs why the words or phrases are grouped together. By looking at these first, they will be made aware of the kinds of changes they will have to make when 'editing' the texts. Then they can refer to the Grammar Commentary for further explanation, clarification or confirmation.

Before they start, you might ask them to glance quickly through all five ads and to say briefly what they are for.

Then let them work (individually or in pairs), reading and rewriting the draft ads according to the handwritten instructions.

Stop after each exercise to check with the whole class.

1 is concerned with the correct use of articles — *a/n*, *the* and Ø-article.

2 is concerned with describing quantities from *a minute number of* to *a vast amount of*.

3 is concerned with expressing quantities in % terms, with an appropriate adverb or adverbial phrase.

4 is a brief revision of the use or omission of defining relatives *which, that* and *who (whom)*.

Additional language (See Grammar Commentary CB p.145.)

There is one other structure that Ss may find useful in this Unit, and which is worth revising or teaching — inversion after negative adverbs. Here are some examples that they might see or use in ads. Point out how the word order is as for questions when the sentence begins with *Not only*, *Never*, etc.

Not only will you feel much better, (but) you will save money, too.

(= You will not only feel much better, but you will save money, too.)

Hardly/Scarcely had I started to use 'Washo' than I noticed the difference.

(= I had hardly/scarcely started to use 'Washo' before I noticed the difference.)

Never/Seldom have so many people been so grateful for such a simple cure.

Only then (when you have tried it) *will you appreciate* how good it is for your skin.

Expected changes underlined

1 Video 2000

Life nowadays is hectic. It takes time to go to the cinema or watch television. But with 'Video 2000' we store the programmes you want to watch when YOU want to watch them! We stock all sorts of programmes — plays, wild life, game shows, everything! So if politics interests you, or the news is a 'must' for you, we'll have all the programmes you might have missed!

First Class Travelling

The public is more discerning than you might think. That's why we've produced a new range of luggage which sets discerning passengers apart. Our information is that ...

2 Join the Charity Support Scheme!

There are quite a few people who say they support charities, but (very) few actually *do* anything! Too little is being done for many causes, and even that by a minute number of people. There are masses of worthwhile causes, and an enormous amount of work to be done. But charities need money. And the vast majority of people we talk to agree with us when we say that ...

3 NU-DEN

Over six million people can't be wrong! That's how many people in Europe use 'NU-DEN', the very latest method for cleaning your teeth! About/Roughly/ Something like/ Round about/Approximately half of the students in German colleges use it! And considerably more than half of the population of Holland uses it! But far less than 10% of the population in this country uses it — as yet! Don't get left behind.

4 Timeless

What do you give the man or woman who has everything? Something (that/ which) no one else has thought of, that's what! Something(that/which) they don't even know they need! And the present that/which gives pleasure every time is timeless — to be precise, the 'Timeless' digital watch for men and women.

Coursebook p.77

Listen, discuss and write

CAE Relevance: Papers 2 and 4 (Writing and Listening)

▷ 📼 **Tapescript for exs. 1 and 2** (See Coursebook pp.154-155.)

Exs. 1 and 2

Classroom treatment

1 As a brief prediction exercise, ask Ss to look at the four pictures and say or note down what they think the radio advertisements will be for.

Then play the tape to let them tick or write down which pictures match which advertisements. Ask for reasons for their answers, and check how good their predictions were.

2 Before playing the tape again, ask Ss to read through the questions to be discussed. Then play the tape, stopping after each ad to discuss the questions, either in pairs or small groups or with the class as a whole. (See Possible answers below.) When trying to spot accents, get students at least to *try* to say what they think is special about a Scottish accent, or an American accent, etc.

Answers

1 Ad 1 Pic **b**; Ad 2 Pic **d**; Ad 3 Pic **a**; Ad 4 Pic **c**

2 Whether Ss think the ads are effective is of course a matter of opinion. However, here are some suggested answers to some of the other questions:

Ad 1: Appealing to young businessmen; suggests life will be easier with a car phone — will avoid frustration — and is relatively cheap. Some nice phrases: 'You wouldn't believe the difference it's made', 'That's way under anyone else's prices', 'Can you afford to miss out?'

Accents: All standard British English

Ad 2: Appealing to young people starting (or changing) career. Nice use of jokes. And 'Camtown 12345. And you don't need a course to learn that!'

Accents: First speaker — regional accent (London?); second speaker standard British

Ad 3: Appealing to the average listener, esp. people with children. Appeals to people's interest in wildlife. Some nice phrases: 'It's right on your doorstep,' '... in perfect safety', 'an experience you'll want to repeat.' (We often use the expression 'An

experience you'll want to forget' in English.)

Accents: First man and woman Welsh; man giving all the information, American.

Ad 4: Appealing to anyone who wants a secondhand car. Appealing to pride in owning at least a 'fully guaranteed' used car, if not a brand new one. Nice phrases: 'That could be you', 'We've got them all ... and price to suit all pockets', 'WYSIWYG ... What You See Is What You Get'.

Accents: Woman driving away, and Ray Grant, both Irish; second woman, standard British.

Ex. 3

Classroom treatment

Ss now work in pairs to write a script. This should be prepared in class, with you monitoring ideas and language, and completed as a homework assignment. (See Introduction p.9.)

At the end of this lesson, or in the next (following homework), Ss might be encouraged to read out or 'act out' their ads to the rest of the class. Or they might record their efforts for others to listen to, especially if they have used a small number of speakers and have tried to add some simple sound effects!

Coursebook p.78

Exam Practice: Paper 2 Writing

CAE Relevance: Paper 2 (Writing)

Background notes and vocabulary

> *Business and Marketing Course:* a course designed for people wanting to go into business and selling or advertising
>
> *cosmetics counter:* the table or flat surface on which goods are shown or at which people in a shop are served, here where perfume, lipstick, face-cream, etc. (cosmetics) are sold
>
> *to pump:* here, to force the smell back into the shop with a pump
>
> *to site:* to put, place or position
>
> *lingerie dept. (= department):* the department in which they sell ladies' underclothes
>
> *to cram:* to fill (something) too full
>
> *v.* = very
>
> *esp.* = especially
>
> *checkout:* the desk in a self-service shop where you show the goods you've chosen and pay for them

assoc. = associated
faraway (adj.): distant, here with a sense of exotic
packaging: the way food and other articles are
packaged ready to sell
environmentally friendly: friendly towards (i.e.
won't damage) the environment

Exs. a and b

Classroom treatment

a As a brief 5-10 minute introduction to this task, ask
Ss to read what they have to do (i.e. the instructions
in **b**) and then cover the page and tell you in their
own words what they have to do. Elicit various
suggestions as to how to do the task. One 'method'
might be: i) read the letter extract and underline the
main points or summarise in a sentence what the
writer wants; then ii) read the lecture notes and
underline, circle or jot down relevant information
which will answer the letter writer's queries.

Before Ss begin this task, remind them that in a task
like this they must decide a) what to say, b) how to
organise their ideas, and c) how to say it effectively.

b In pairs, Ss should i) read the letter extract and agree
on what the writer wants, ii) read the lecture notes
and pick out and note down or summarise what
points will be useful, iii) decide the best way to order
the different ideas in their reply, and iv) begin to
draft the reply. (See Introduction p.9.)

Point out that the notes are typical of the kind that
people/students take at lectures — with lots of
words missing (*a, the, they,* verbs, etc.) — and that
any of the points used in the reply must be expanded
into full grammatical sentences.

Possible reply to the letter

Different Ss will clearly take different points from the
notes according to what they think will be of value to
the letter writer. However, here is a sample of the
friendly informal letter they might produce. It's about
260 words.

Dear [Kathy],

Thanks for your letter which arrived yesterday. How nice
to hear from you after all this time — especially with your
news. Yes, you're right, I did do that course, and I've found
out my old notes, some of which might be of help.

As you're going to open a small shop selling, as I
understand it, highly select clothes and gifts, not all the
notes I have will apply to your situation. However, for what
it's worth, here are some tips for you.

First impressions are vitally important, so I'd suggest
putting bright things (some clothes and quality gifts) near
the door. Lighting's important too, so it's a good idea, for
instance, to install soft lighting on 'soft' or soft-coloured
items, but strong colours to exaggerate some of your
brighter articles — perhaps orange lights onto orange-
painted craft gifts (or whatever you're selling). I'm sure you
know what I mean. And one thing you mustn't do is to cram
shelves with gifts or clothes rails with clothes. Spread them
out so that customers can see what you've got and so that
they look more 'individual'.

By the way, have you thought about any background
music? If you're going to have any, from what you say in
your letter, I'd suggest soft soothing music, not loud pop.
The music should match the quality image.

And the final thing is packaging. When people buy
quality goods, they like to see them in rich colours —gold,
rich dark green and so on.

Hope these tips are of some use to you. All the best in
your new venture!

Write soon,

Love,

Rounding off the Unit

Why not round off the Unit by getting Ss to tell each
other about advertisements on television, on radio and
in newspaper/magazines which they think are (or
were) particularly memorable and/or effective?

13 Travel broadens the mind

Warm-up

Here are two **alternative suggestions**, both with books closed:

1 Get Ss to consider the place they are in now — their home town or 'adopted' home town — as a tourist attraction. Divide the class into five groups, to reflect the five major continents: Africa, America North and South, Asia, Australasia and Europe. Say to each group: 'How would you market/publicise this town for the people from your given continent?' Then give five minutes for them to plan how they would 'present' the town to their particular market. Allow time afterwards for each group to report their thoughts and for general discussion to follow.

2 Issue maps of the world or atlases. In groups, and in 5-10 minutes, Ss plan a round-the-world trip (but which way, following which route and including which stop-over places?) and then report their plans to the rest of the class, who may challenge with: 'But then you wouldn't see ... / you'd miss ... / you'd spend ages just ...' Which group has the most attractive-sounding world trip?

Read, edit and write

CAE Relevance: Papers 2 and 3 (Writing and English in Use)

Background notes and vocabulary

hydrofoil: a type of large motor-boat which raises itself out of the water as it moves
olive groves: groups of olive trees, planted or natural
pine forests: forests of pine trees; pines are usually tall trees with thin sharp leaves that do not drop off in winter
a stone's throw: an idiomatic expression meaning 'a short distance (from)'
amenities: the things/conditions in a town, hotels, etc. that one can enjoy and which make life pleasant
shrubbery: (part of a garden or countryside planted with) shrubs (small bushes) forming a mass or group

Ex. 1
Classroom treatment
This draft brochure piece is of course about a totally fictitious country, island, hotel. (You might, however, at some point ask Ss if the location reminds them of anywhere they have visited.)

Give Ss two minutes to read the text, ignoring for the moment the phrases given for substitution. Check comprehension, either with straightforward questions: 'How many ways can you get to the island? What sort of vegetation is there on the island?' etc. — or with a quick 'Correct my statements' exercise: 'The hotel is on the mainland... No? On an island? Oh, ah yes, an island to the north of the mainland... No? Oh, near the southern tip. I see. And it can only be reached by boat... ' etc.

Alternatively, Ss form pairs: get S1 in each pair to read the piece to S2 who has his/her book closed. Then check how good a picture the 'listeners' have of the place.

Alternatively, get Ss to read the text and then quickly to sketch a map of the area following the information they have read.

Then draw attention to the phrases below the text and go through the task rubric with the class. This relatively easy task might be given added spice by your imposing a time limit, (time is going to be at a premium in the exam!) say three minutes. When checking, spend some time discussing whether the substitution has improved the piece, made it more readable, more or less formal, etc.

Model substitutions
halfway > midway
within easy reach of > with easy access to
in the middle of > amid
surrounded by > encircled by
is situated > is located
quite near > just off
a stone's throw > within a mile
five miles > eight kilometres
20 minutes by air > a 20-minute flight
a short stroll from > within walking distance of

Ex. 2

Classroom treatment

Use the first visual for classwork and set the second as homework. Groups of four to five (an editorial staff) could work on the first visual. Remind Ss of the sort of language that sells holidays — how spectacularly beautiful, easy and convenient everything is — then set the task. They should be encouraged to think of the task as more than a 200-word essay. Is there going to be more artwork? With captions? Will there be headings? Will there be a photo top left? In other words, get them not only to write but also to design a page.

Coursebook pp.80-81

Read, write and discuss

CAE Relevance: Papers 1 and 2 (Reading and Writing)

Background notes and vocabulary

> 'Travels with Grandma'
> *BritRail pass:* a special card/ticket that allows the holder to travel anywhere in Britain for a fixed period and for a fixed sum of money
> *soap opera:* a regularly broadcast TV series built around a particular set of characters; the situation is often domestic and often sentimental; *Dallas* has been the most (in?)famous example of recent years.
> *dysentery:* a disease affecting the intestines, causing gripping pains and diarrhoea
> *The Red Cross:* an international organisation, founded in Switzerland, whose aim is to relieve suffering and help those in need
> *Bangkok:* capital city of Thailand
> *Waterloo:* the scene (in Belgium) of the final action (18.06.1815) of the Napoleonic Wars
> *bronchitis:* an inflammation of the mucous membrane in the lung's bronchial tubes
> *skinned:* here, had the skin rubbed off
> *drag:* literally 'to pull along', colloquially used as a noun (as here) to describe something or someone boring or annoying as in 'What a drag!'/'He's a drag!'
> *Karachi:* former capital, but still chief town and port of Pakistan
> *pooh-pooh:* here 'to make light of', rather than the stronger definition 'to dismiss with contempt'

> *Hyderabad:* situated on the river Indus, the capital of the Sind province of Pakistan
> *mail:* Am. English for 'post' or 'send'

Classroom treatment

As a warm-up, give groups of Ss a certain age for them to imagine themselves at (16, 21, 29, 40, 55, 70, etc.). Ask them to consider what a trip around the world would mean to them at that age. Why would they do it? How would they spend their time? What do they think would be the highspots of their journey? Ss then tell the rest of the class the above information/opinions.

Focus attention on the text. It's long. As per rubric, give Ss a short time (1-2 minutes in this case) to scan the text to answer the given questions.

Answers

The countries they have visited together (at least 21 countries) are some in South-East Asia, Hongkong, Thailand, Burma, Malaysia, Singapore, [Northern] India, Nepal and Pakistan.

Alone, the writer has visited Europe and Latin America.

Alone, Grandma has been to England, Scotland and Wales.

Exs. 1-4

Classroom treatment

Many well-documented techniques exist for dealing with lengthy texts:

- You might get Ss reading to each other in pairs, listener with book closed.
- You could read parts of the passage to Ss (books closed), pausing occasionally to see if they can suggest what comes next.
- You could break the piece up into chunks and when each section has been read,
  a) check comprehension with simple direct questions,
  b) ask Ss to make questions for factual answers you give them,
  c) invite cross-class question and answer on what has been read,
  d) 'Correct my statements' exercises,
  e) completion exercises,
  f) 'transfer of narrator' exercises in which Grandma tells her story, gives her impressions, etc.
- You could, on the other hand, just ask Ss to read silently and then work in pairs to answer the questions and do the exercises that follow.

Ex. 1 clearly has direct exam relevance to Paper 1.

Ex. 2 is practising the important skill of paraphrasing and is solid preparation for parts of Paper 3.

Ex. 3 is partly practising retrieval of factual information and partly training interpretation and inference.

Ex. 4 would best be set as homework, especially in a multi-lingual class, where Ss do not share a common country and therefore cannot collaborate on the writing task.

Expected or possible answers

1
1. paragraph 2
2. paragraph 1
3. paragraphs 6 and 9
4. paragraph 7
5. paragraph 3
6. paragraphs 5 and 6
7. paragraph 6
8. paragraph 7

2
1. most of England
2. not ready to give up by any means
3. made her ill
4. she can normally manage to walk six miles a day without any problem
5. make a fuss about / make this thing seem important
6. an amount of money that seemed right in those circumstances
7. an expression that means meeting one's match, having to face a severe 'final' battle, as Napoleon did at Waterloo
8. in a metaphorical sense ('drag' can mean a bore) and in the main, 'real' sense of the word (Grandma had to be pulled along)
9. she laughed it off, didn't take it seriously
10. the only thing I would ask (you to do)

3 Some possible answers in this open-ended exercise:
1. She was adventurous, brave, courageous, determined, tenacious, modest, and self-effacing.
2. She suffered from glaucoma, she couldn't stretch her feet wide properly, she was allergic to a lot of different food, she wasn't able to walk far, and she was somewhat overweight and feeble.
3. She got dysentery several times, bronchitis once, suffered foot problems, broke her foot, skinned her knees, and twisted an ankle.

Coursebook pp.82-83

Language focus

CAE Relevance: All Papers, especially Paper 4

▷ ▣ **Tapescript for ex. 1** (See Coursebook p.155.)
Exs. 1 and 2

Classroom treatment

To introduce this practice on expressing directions and locations, say to the class: 'You don't know where I live, do you?' and proceed to give them directions from the school to your actual home if practicable or a fictitious one if not. Mention street names only sparingly. See if in their mind they can 'place' the destination you describe: Ah yes, I know, it's in one of those roads leading off the main road out of town going east, isn't it? (Accurate directing and accurate understanding of directions can be much more difficult than Intermediate coursebooks often suggest.)

Focus attention on the map and run through the rubric. Play the tape. Ss mark in pen/pencil the route described. Check afterwards visually and verbally.

Play the tape again and Ss make notes in order to contextualise the given phrases.

Ss check what notes they have and what they remember with a partner and then with the rest of the class.

Expected answers

'headed south, *down through* Normandy'; 'went *across* the Channel' / 'back *across* the Channel'; 'which we never actually *got to* in the end'; 'we drove up *towards* Paris' / 'sort of heading *towards* Orleans' / '*towards* Rouen'; 'we drove east, *along* the Loire' / 'and then back *along* the A13'; 'climbing *up and down* gorgeous old staircases (and *along* endless corridors)'; '*through* the Loire valley'; 'kept *away from* the main roads'; 'going *round and round* in circles'.

Exs. 3 and 4

Classroom treatment

3 If Ss have had problems with what has happened so far, take time to remind them of

a) locating expressions like *in the far north, a few miles west of..., to the east of..., across the river from ...* ; and

b) directing expressions such as *down as far as ..., up into the Alps, on down until we came to ...* .

Get Ss to draw their sketch map and then practise with a partner. As always, remind the 'listener' in the pair what an important role he/she has in terms of reacting, empathising and questioning.

4 This should be quite relaxing consolidation of what has been practised earlier, Ss working in pairs or small groups.

Read, summarise and then listen

CAE Relevance: Papers 1 and 3 (Reading and English in Use)

Background notes and vocabulary

> *Kavos:* a small village on the Greek island of Corfu
> *Homeric:* like those Homer (Greek poet c. 700 B.C.) would have described
> *Eden:* The Garden of Eden — Paradise
> *quid:* a slang word for pound(s) (£ sterling)
> *pub grub:* slang expression for the meals, often simple, that one can buy in an English public house
> *Sunday roast:* a traditional British Sunday meal of roast meat and vegetables
> *chip butties:* sandwiches with chips as the filling — a 'poor man's' snack
> *bouncers:* men, usually big and strong, whose job it is to keep order in a club or disco etc., and to make sure unwanted clients do not stay long
> *ouzo:* a Greek drink of aniseed-flavoured spirits
> *tequila slammers:* strong cocktails with a base of tequila, a Mexican liquor
> *brawling:* fighting or quarreling noisily and roughly
> *make quick bucks:* (slang) to earn a lot of money (dollars) quickly
> *Costa(s):* the Spanish word for 'coast'; here it refers to the popular coastal region of Spain —the Costa Brava, Costa del Sol, etc.
> *Benidorm / Benicasim:* holiday resorts on the east coast of Spain

▷🖭 **Tapescript for ex. 2** (See Coursebook p. 155.)

Exs. 1 and 2

Classroom treatment

1 Give Ss three minutes to read the extracts, then set them the initial task of writing three summarising sentences in pairs — a five-minute activity. Monitor and ask selected summaries to be read out to the class afterwards. Check that the gists of all extracts

have been understood. You might at this stage, or later, ask which of the extracts Ss think best sums up the problem of global tourism. Here it serves as a good lead-in to the listening task.

2 Set the scene for the listening by focussing attention on the rubric. Point out that in this phase they are not required to show their personal opinion but simply to label the extracts according to what the speakers say about them.

Play the tape. See what Ss have achieved so far in terms of labelling. If there is general agreement, play the tape again just for confirmation, stopping regularly for 'Yes, that's obviously the first one they're talking about, because ...'. If there is some disagreement, play the tape again to settle any dispute and point up the clues which make the correct answer correct.

Correct answers
The labelling of the paragraphs: 1 G; 2 F; 3 A; 4 E; 5 B; 6 D; 7 C.

Coursebook p.84

Vocabulary : Travel broadens the mind

CAE Relevance: All Papers, especially Paper 3

The three exercises in this section should be done in pairs, threes or fours. They may prove difficult and Ss should have the support of others to take them through. 'So we're all in the same boat!'

Ex. 1

Classroom treatment
Before or after the exercise, get Ss to try and explain the difference between the seven target items: a very challenging task because a number of them, of course, overlap.

Correct answers
1 trip; 2 flight / voyage; 3 excursion / trip; 4 journey / travel; 5 travels

Ex. 2

Classroom treatment
Ss may not have thought about this 'problem' before, in which case it might be unfair to launch into the exercise immediately. On the other hand they might be pleasantly surprised to find their 'feeling' sees them through. Though not 100% true, 'widen' does tend to

be used for physical changes and 'broaden' for more abstract ones, but ...

Correct answers

We would normally choose to:

widen a road; broaden a discussion; widen a gap; broaden your experience; broaden your horizons; broaden your mind; widen the angle

Ex. 3

Classroom treatment

Most of these items are inexplicable collocations; in their small groups, Ss might recall most of the 'correct' collocations, and if ideas are then shared among the class, consensus should be reached. It is important that by doing this exercise Ss appreciate the problems they are confronted with at this level, rather than feel they have solved the problem of collocation at a stroke by completing these 14 items.

Correct answers

1 brain; 2 mind; 3 brain; 4 mind; 5 mind; 6 head; 7 brain; 8 mind; 9 mind; 10 mind; 11 mind; 12 head; 13 head / mind; 14 mind

Exam Practice: Paper 3 English in Use

CAE Relevance: Paper 3 (English in Use)

Classroom treatment

By this stage in the course Ss will have begun to develop a feeling for register and style. To check this, you might prompt them in the preliminary questions like this:

1 Will you say: *You should* ... or *You are strongly advised to* ...? Why? *Each passenger will be issued with* ... or ... *You will be given* ... ? Why?

2 Which future form do you think will be most often used? (*will* simple future, because it's a semi-formal representation of the arrangements on paper, and not that immediate!) Why do you think passive forms will be used a lot? (to avoid we ... we ... we ... and allow 'you' to be the main subject.)

3 What other types of word are missing? (forms of the verb *to be*, personal pronouns/adjectives, relative pronouns, conjunctions, modal verbs)

Set the writing task as a timed piece of work and impose a time limit of 15 minutes.

Model handout

At 08.45 all members/you should congregate at the Sunshine Tours desk, where you will be met by our representative, Mr Jack Lord. You will all be given/He will give you all a holiday information pack before boarding/you board the (aero)plane. Window seats have been reserved for all our clients, which will ensure a breathtaking flight (for everyone).

On arrival at Doka Airport, you will be taken by airport bus on a short journey to the main terminal, where there will be a maximum 15-minute wait. Your luggage will be collected and transported to your (chosen) resort separately. You will be taken to the resort on our own coach via Tomkin Valley and the (quite) incredible Bayo Gorge. Your luggage will be delivered to your villa door within fifteeen minutes/a quarter of an hour of your arrival. You will be provided with keys (to the villa) as you get off/alight from the bus.

Inside the villa, the kitchen is/will be fully equipped with crockery, cutlery and basic provisions. The fridge is/will be fully stocked. If you require/need any assistance, there is a/press the /feel free to press the button above the socket in the kitchen.

Rounding off the Unit

Why not round the Unit off by asking Ss to describe in concrete terms any particular way in which travel has broadened their own mind?

OR Why not take into the class 20 or 30 postcards (you must have hundreds!). Distribute them to Ss. In pairs Ss 'reminisce' about the time they spent in the places shown on their cards. The postcards should be passed steadily round the room, improvisation continuing with each new 'picture' the Ss receive.

14 A chapter of accidents

Warm-up

Here are three **alternative activities**, all with books closed:

1 Discuss briefly with Ss what is being done in their own area/country to preserve the national heritage.

2 Ss write down all the words that Prince Charles makes them think of (if they know anything about him).

3 Give this brief dictation about Prince Charles:

> Prince Charles is the heir to the British throne. He was born in 1948 and, unlike any previous British monarchs, attended school and went to university. He studied history and anthropology at the University of Cambridge. He is married to Princess Diana and they have two children, William and Harry. He is a not untalented artist and has also written two books, one a children's story and the other about architecture.

Look, listen and discuss

CAE Relevance: Papers 4 and 5 (Listening and Speaking)

Background notes and vocabulary

> *St Paul's Cathedral:* Cathedral in the City of London, designed by the famous architect, Sir Christoper Wren, and completed in 1710
> *Nelson:* (1758—1805) British naval hero. His most famous victory was the Battle of Traflagar (1805). Buried in St Paul's Cathedral.
> *Wellington:* (1769—1852) British soldier and statesman. Most famous battle — the Battle of Waterloo (1815). Tory Prime Minister from 1828 to 1830. Buried in St Paul's Cathedral.
> *Sir Winston Churchill:* (1874—1965) British statesman, Prime Minister during the Second World War (from 1940 to 1945) and again from 1951 to 1955. Like Nelson and Wellington, he was given a state funeral in St Paul's.
> *incendiary bomb:* a bomb that causes destruction by making fires start

> *Guildhall:* the Town House of the City of London, the place where the Mayor of London presides
> *mausoleum:* building which contains the grave of an important person
> *balustraded drum:* the architectural term for the circular drum-shaped structure with columns around it on which the dome, or cupola, of St Paul's is placed
> *parish church:* church serving a particular small religious area
> *Canaletto:* Italian artist (1697—1768), well-known for his scenes of Venice and London.
> *Mona Lisa:* Famous painting by Leonardo da Vinci. Now in the Louvre in Paris.
> *La Défence:* new financial quarter of Paris
> *Notre Dame:* Cathedral on an island in the river in central Paris
> *St Mark's:* Cathedral in the heart of Venice
> *St Peter's:* Cathedral in Rome, the church of the Vatican and the main church for Roman Catholics
> *Pirelli Building:* Pirelli is a major Italian company, making, among other things, tyres

▷ 🔊 **Tapescript** (See Coursebook pp. 155-156.)

Ex. 1

Classroom treatment

Read the introduction to the listening text with the class. Briefly discuss the question in the introduction: Ss will probably expect Prince Charles to have fairly traditional views but it does not, of course, matter if they have different expectations.

Ss listen to the text once and answer question 1.

Expected answer

Charles has a great respect and reverence for St Paul's and he deplores the modern architecture around it. He feels like this because he thinks of St Paul's as being a kind of symbol of the nation and thus feels that the architecture around it should harmonise with it and not belittle it.

Ex. 2

Classroom treatment

Read q.2 with the Ss and ask them to make notes as they listen to the speech a second time.

Expected answers

Things Prince Charles does to make his speech effective:

- uses questions
- makes a joke
- draws comparisons
- speaks slowly and clearly
- uses dramatic pauses
- uses strong words e.g. 'appalled', 'devastated'
- uses dramatic inversion: 'Not only did they wreck ...'
- uses repetition of sentence structure:'That familiar dome ....', 'That skyline ...'
- refers to own experience: 'I well remember the cold March morning ...'
- addresses the audience directly: 'ladies and gentlemen', 'your predecessors'

Ask Ss how the pictures on the page relate to points made in the speech.

As a footnote, the speech Prince Charles made on this occasion had a strong effect. Plans were later changed to come into line with the views that he (and others) had expressed.

Coursebook p.86

Think and write, then read and discuss

CAE Relevance: Paper 1 (Reading)

Background notes and vocabulary

> This text comes from a quality newspaper article about Venice.
> **the Adriatic:** the sea, part of the Mediterranean, on which Venice stands. Venice was once one of the most powerful trading ports in the world.
> **subsidence:** land becoming lower than it used to be
> **dredging:** cleaning by dragging something along the bottom of the canals to drag up all the mud and rubbish that is there
> **midges:** insects that love damp places and biting people
> **thrive:** do very well
> **critical:** here, serious
> **silted-up:** blocked (with *silt* = mud and sediment)
> **can be restored to her former glory:** can once again become as glorious as she used to be

Exs. 1-4

Classroom treatment

1 Brainstorm onto the board/OHP all the words which Ss come up with when they think of Venice.

2 Ask Ss to look at the title and the picture and to predict what the text is going to be about.

3 Allow the Ss 10-15 seconds to skim the first paragraph and check whether their predictions were accurate or not.

4 Allow Ss 15 minutes to read the text and to write their comprehension questions. Tell them that they can use their questions either to find answers to points that they themselves do not understand or to test their partner's comprehension — as they prefer. Ss ask their questions in pairs while you monitor, noting points that need to be discussed as a class later.
It might be necessary to do some extra vocabulary work. Get Ss perhaps to mark words that are unfamilar and then to guess their meaning from the context before checking in a dictionary.

Home preparation

Ask Ss to read the Grammar Commentary for this Unit and to prepare exs. 2 and 3 on p. 87 as homework.

Coursebook pp.87-88

Language focus: What happened to it?

CAE Relevance: All Papers

Exs. 1-3

Classroom treatment

Read the task in 1 with the Ss and make sure all the topics on offer are understood but do not discuss the task further at this point. You should make it clear that exs. 2-7 will give Ss practice in the kind of language they will need to write their composition.

Check the homework (exs. 2 and 3).

Answers

2 *is being destroyed:* present continuous (passive) because it describes something that is happening now

raced in: past simple — one event in the past

has been done: present perfect (passive) is talking both about the past and the present together. 'Until now' is understood.

is sinking: present continuous — something that is happening at this moment

will continue: future with *will* — prediction

used to be flooded: used to — something that happened repeatedly in the past

was done: past simple (passive). *It's time you/something ...* must be followed by a past tense form

thrive: present simple — something that happens repeatedly (every summer)

had become: past perfect — something that happened before something else in the past (the authorities managed to agree)

will have noticed: future perfect — here, making a prediction about something that is now past

3 a are visiting / have been visiting / have visited / will be visiting; is being held
   b were gliding; heard; singing
   c will have sunk
   d arrive; shall/will try/am going to try to arrange

Ex. 4

Classroom treatment

Check that Ss understand all the verbs listed. Check particularly *to found* (= to establish, NOT the past tense of *find*) and *to besiege* (= to surround a place with armed forces). Then allow Ss five minutes to prepare their answer to this exercise. Correct the ex. with the Ss, dealing with any problems.

Expected answers

1 lies; 2 was founded; 3 built; 4 was besieged; 5 died; 6 suffered; 7 were completely destroyed; 8 have been done; 9 resemble; 10 have been consulted/were consulted; 11 involved; 12 has taken; 13 to make; 14 look.

Ex. 5

Classroom treatment

Ask Ss what they will always find in a passive form (a part of the verb *to be* (or *get*) plus a past participle).

Ask them to underline all the verbs in the passive in the text on p. 86.

Check that they have found them all.

Ask Ss why the passive is sometimes preferred to an active form. When the agent is unknown or unimportant; when the intention is to focus on the object rather than the subject of the verb. Ask why they think the passive is used a lot in this text.

Finally, ask Ss what other kinds of texts frequently use passives. (Scientific texts and law reports, newspaper articles, explanations and instructions, etc.)

Expected answers

is being destroyed; has been done; used to be flooded; was done; is being faced; had to be done; had to be done; are being dredged; are being repaired; can be restored

Ex. 6

Classroom treatment

Ask Ss if they had any queries on reading the notes on causative *have* and *get* in the Grammar Commentary. Deal with any problems that may have arisen.

Ss work in pairs discussing question 6. Have a short feedback session with the class afterwards.

Ex. 7

Classroom treatment

Check that Ss understand all the connectors listed in the box. Pay particular attention to the difference between *after* and *afterwards* — *after* is a preposition or conjunction and *afterwards* is an adverb — and to *eventually* which is similar in meaning to 'finally' or 'in the end'.

Check too that Ss are clear about the difference between *in time* (any time before the appointed time) and *on time* (exactly at the appointed time).

Ss then do the exercise individually or in pairs.

Check their answers.

Expected answers

a Wherever; b At first/At the beginning; c at the end; d as soon as; e then/ afterwards; f in time; g eventually/in the end/finally

Ex. 8

Classroom treatment

Ss return to q.1 on p.87 to discuss which topic to write about. Set the writing for homework.

Model answer

A Heroic Rescue

Dan Jones was a geologist on his first trip in the Arctic. He had one companion, Fred Forrest, an experienced Arctic scientist. Dan had felt lonely and homesick for most of the three months he had been working there. Above all, he was terrified of polar bears. Fred had shown him some flares which he had made to frighten away any bear which came too close to their camp. These were large torches which, when lit and thrown at a bear, were guaranteed (almost) to send it running for cover.

At first they did not see any bears near the camp but in the last two weeks they seemed to have been coming closer. Fred explained they were being drawn unusually far south in the search for food. Dan had now only three days to go until the end of his stay and he could hardly wait to go home.

Working about a hundred metres from the camp Dan heard Fred scream 'Get the flares!'. Looking up in horror, he saw a bear with its gigantic paw raised to strike Fred's head.

He raced to the camp house and grabbed some flares. Then he hesitated for a second. Surely there was no chance of saving Fred now? Might it not be better just to barricade himself inside the hut? To throw the flare would mean going outside again and perhaps exposing himself to other bears which might be lurking in the vicinity. He hesitated for only a second and then quickly lit a flare, ran outside and threw it at the bear. Fred was lying motionless on the ground and the bear's foot was on his head. The bear reared up at the sight of the flare, looked angrily at Dan and then ran off. Holding onto a second lit flare Dan went up to Fred and examined him. He was unconscious and losing a lot of blood but was still breathing. Dan carried him back to the camp and radioed for help.

A helicopter from the nearest base could not reach them for another twelve hours. All night, as he did his best to nurse Fred, Dan could hear — or thought he could hear — bears padding round the camp. After being lifted by the helicopter, Fred recovered in hospital and Dan received a medal for bravery. Fred returned to the Arctic the next year. He begged Dan to accompany him, but Dan refused.

Vocabulary: A torrent of words

CAE Relevance: All Papers

Exs. 1-3

Classroom treatment
Draw Ss' attention to the title of the Unit which also uses an expression of the type practised here. This is mainly revision of some basic partitive constructions. There is further practice with partitives in Unit 20.

1 Ask the class the question. Ss should know the answers — a) a flock of sheep, and b) a block of flats.

2 Have Ss discuss this question in pairs and then check their answers.

3 Discuss this exercise with the class as a whole.

Expected and possible answers
2 a chain of shops; a range/chain of mountains; a bunch of keys; a bed/bunch of flowers; a gang of robbers; a herd of cows; a pack of cards; a fleet of ships; a pile of books

3 a bunch of bananas/grapes; a pack of thieves/lies/wolves; a pile of letters/work/ newspapers/magazines

```
              Coursebook p.89
```

Exam Practice: Paper 4 Listening

CAE Relevance: Paper 4 (Listening)

▷ 📼 **Tapescript**

TUTOR: Unit 14. Look at page 89, Exam practice **a**. You're going to hear four people talking about experiences they've had. Listen and do the exercises. One.

WOMAN 1: My aunt and I were driving along the High Street when suddenly another car dashed straight out of a side street into our front wing. Fortunately no one was hurt but my aunt's car was a write-off — and she'd only just bought it too.

TUTOR: Two.

MAN 1: It was her maiden voyage and not only I but also all the rest of the crew were pretty inexperienced; I suppose we didn't read the charts properly and we went on the rocks about half an hour after we'd left port.

TUTOR: Three.

WOMAN 2: We'd been to the cinema and were coming home with some fish and chips and in a really good mood. What a shock when we turned the light on in the living-room. Things were all over the floor in a terrible mess. They don't seem to have taken very much, but it's horrible to think of someone being there doing something so spiteful.

TUTOR: Four.

MAN 2: The children were playing football out in the garden. Garry gave the ball a really strong kick and that was it. A huge hole in the French window. It would happen on a really cold day too.

TUTOR: Unit 14. Look at page 89, Exam Practice **b**. You're going to hear six people reading extracts from autobiographies relating to experiences of disasters. Listen to do Task One. Then run the tape back to do Task Two.
One.

MAN 1: The winds had been terribly strong all night and it had been raining heavily too and so I suppose I shouldn't have been surprised to see the river had overflowed its banks and was almost up to our front door when I looked out in the morning. I'm amazed now that I wasn't scared but in fact it was incredibly lovely. The wild clouds scudding across a brilliant blue sky, the bare dark trees dramatically etched against the sky. My main feeling was not panic or fear but just a sad regret that I didn't have enough talent as an artist to capture the scene.

TUTOR: Two.

WOMAN 1: When I came back and saw flames leaping from the kitchen window, I guess I should have rushed inside the house and tried to save some of our belongings but somehow I just couldn't summon up the enthusiasm. I had never liked the house and did not particularly want memories of what had happened there. No one was inside and I certainly couldn't be bothered to stir myself for mere objects.

TUTOR: Three.

MAN 2: It was quite a frightening experience I suppose in retrospect but at the time I felt so tormented in myself that the destructive power of the wind seemed to fit my mood perfectly. We were both angry and if I'd had the strength to tear off roofs and root up trees, I'd happily have done so.

TUTOR: Four.

WOMAN 2: I was in bed and just falling asleep when suddenly it felt as if the whole building was shaking. At first I thought I was having a nightmare and then I realised that the building really was shaking. They'd been predicting one for ages and now it had come. We'd all had instructions about what to do and I did on auto-pilot what I'd been told so many times but I was terribly scared. I kept remembering TV film of bodies being discovered under rubble ten days later and I was terribly shaky.

TUTOR: Five.

MAN 3: As a geologist I was actually very pleased to have the opportunity to see one happen. It wasn't as though we were in any danger. We had quite a reasonable view from our hotel looking across the bay. I was actually sitting on my balcony looking at it when it started erupting and I got some great shots with my telephoto lens. After a few days things had cooled down enough to go and have a rather closer look.

TUTOR: Six.

WOMAN 3: I'd always enjoyed snow as a child but this was completely different. I suppose it was the wind that made it so alarming and it was coming down so fast as well. I couldn't see a thing and knew that there were hardly any houses in the neighbourhood. I rushed off in one direction after the other and felt as if I was going round in circles. I forgot everything I'd ever learnt about what to do in conditions like that and if Jim and the dogs hadn't found me, goodness knows what might have happened.

Ex. a

Classroom treatment

1 and 2 Ss discuss the questions in pairs. They should come up with the idea of trying to predict vocabulary items, so that they are in effect describing each picture.

3 Ss listen to all the texts for part **a** and decide which fits where.

Check to see whether Ss got the correct answers.

Answers
Speaker 1 — Picture B

Speaker 2 — Picture C

Speaker 3 — Picture E

Speaker 4 — Picture A

Picture D was not described.

Classroom treatment

4 Ss listen to each section in turn and check which vocabulary items they predicted were actually used. Were there other items not predicted which gave the game away? If so, which?

5 Have Ss in pairs make up a similar statement about picture D and then read out their statements to the rest of the class.

Ex. b

Classroom treatment
Do this exercise under exam conditions.

- Give Ss time to read the task.
- Play the tape twice.
- Give them time to check their answers.
- *Then* check the answers with the whole class and deal with any questions about the texts.

Answers
Task One
Earthquake — Speaker 4; Tidal wave — Not mentioned; Hurricane — Speaker 3; Drought — Not mentioned; Fire — Speaker 2; Blizzard — Speaker 6; Flood — Speaker 1; Volcano — Speaker 5

Task Two
Panicky — Speaker 6 (Blizzard); Afraid — Speaker 4 (Earthquake); Hysterical — Not mentioned; Contented — Speaker 5 (Volcano); Puzzled — Not mentioned; Lacking in energy — Speaker 2 (Fire); Overcome by a certain beauty in the experience — Speaker 1 (Flood); At one with nature — Speaker 3 (Hurricane)

Rounding off the Unit

Why not round off this Unit by getting each S to describe a disaster as if they had experienced it themselves? It might almost be a competition to see who can make the most dramatic story.

15 All work and no play ...

(The phrase *All work and no play ...* is the first half of the English proverb *All work and no play makes Jack a dull boy,* which means that a person who spends all his or her time working and has no time for leisure will be dull and uninteresting. As in the title of this Unit, it's often shortened to *All work and no play ... .*)

Coursebook pp.90-91

Warm-up

Here are two **alternative suggestions**, with books closed:

1 Ask the class: 'Where does the title of the Unit come from? What does it mean? Do you agree? Is it always true, do you think? Can you give us any examples?'

2 Say to the class: 'People say that 'play' (sport, pastimes, hobbies, etc.) is just as important as work. Write down five advantages of 'play' and order them from most important to least important.' Each S compares his/her list with a partner, then with a group — then the class tries to come to some agreement.

Read, look and speak

CAE Relevance: Paper 5 (Speaking)

Background notes and vocabulary

> *theories abound:* i.e. there are lots of theories: *to abound* = to exist in large numbers
> *to juggle:* to keep (several objects) in the air at the same time by throwing them up quickly and catching them again; used here metaphorically
> *a myriad:* a great and varied number e.g. a myriad stars (literary)
> *light entertainment:* entertainment simply to amuse; a TV 'light entertainment' programme consists of short acts by e.g. dancers, singers, comedians, ventriloquists, jugglers, etc.
> *(to be) at a loss:* (to be) unable or uncertain what to do, think or say
> *catch up (on):* to come up to date (with something)

Exs. 1 and 2

Classroom treatment

1 First, read and study the introductory paragraph ('Theories abound ...') with the class, or ask them to read it silently — and ask Ss to tell you what the questionnaire is going to be about.

Then Ss work in pairs, very much as opinion poll researcher and member of the public. S1 reads out, slowly and carefully, the questions and options in Part A and ticks the appropriate boxes as S2 gives his/her verbal answers.

NB: S2 has book closed or covers page 90.

Having completed Part A, S1 then closes his/her book or covers page 91 while S2 reads out the questions in Part B for S1 to give verbal answers.

Optional: When they have completed Part B, they then change again for S2 to quiz S1 on Part A, and again for S1 to quiz S2 on Part B.

At any time throughout the questioning, the person being quizzed may ask for a repetition or further clarification.

Round off the whole activity by getting the class (verbally or through a show of hands) to complete or help you complete on the board/OHP, a chart which will summarise all the responses from the class.

As a follow-up homework assignment, Ss might write a summary report of the survey, quoting some of the figures. (See Unit 12 again.)

2 This should be a very brief discussion to round off the lesson. First, Ss work in pairs asking each other the questions about the three activities (jet-skiing, playing chess and playing a musical instrument), and then briefly discuss the questions as a class.

Coursebook pp.92-93

Language focus: Whether you succeed or fail — enjoy it!

CAE Relevance: All Papers

Background notes and vocabulary

unusual weekend breaks: it is becoming quite popular in Britain to go away and stay in a hotel for a weekend, and many hotels offer special cheap rates for these weekend breaks. This pages features weekend breaks that are more than just staying in a hotel. And some are for longer than a weekend.

geographical spread: the way they are spread out in different places in the country

aromatherapy: one of the modern 'alternative medicines', this one using aromatic (= pleasant-smelling) oils to reduce tension and solve other problems

belly dancing: performing a sexy dance that makes use of the movements of the belly — one of the few phrases in English where we can use the word *belly* in place of the more acceptable word *stomach.*

calligraphy: the art of producing beautiful writing by hand

decoy duck: the (usually wooden) figure of a duck which is used for attracting wild birds within range of guns

woodcarving: cutting wood to a special shape

to elope: to run away secretly with the intention of getting married, usually without parental approval

Gretna Green: a village in Scotland, just inside the Scottish/English border, where couples can get married without parental permission

falconry: the art of training falcons (birds of prey) to hunt, and the sport of hunting with falcons

bird of prey: any bird that kills others birds and small animals for food e.g. owls, falcons, eagles

graphology: the study of handwriting as a guide to a writer's character

graphologist: someone who specialises in the study of handwriting as a guide to character

herbalism: another 'alternative medicine', this one treating diseases with medicines made from herbs

holistic approach: an approach which takes into account the whole body when diagnosing illnesses and health problems, not simply the part(s) affected

kite: a frame of very light wood or metal covered with paper or cloth for flying in the air, often as a plaything, at the end of a long string

lapidary: cutting precious stones, polishing them and cutting patterns etc. in them

▷ 📼 **Tapescript for ex. 2** (See Coursebook p.156.)
Ex. 1

Classroom treatment

To break down the activities here into manageable parts, we suggest you might deal with exs. 1-3 in one 45-50-minute lesson, and exs. 4-6 in a second lesson. Even then, it might be advisable to ask Ss to read page 93 (*A-Z of Unusual Weekend Breaks*) as a pre-lesson study task, and to think of the clean writing of the letter in ex. 6 as a homework assignment.

If Ss have read the text for homework, first check comprehension e.g. 'What are some of the things you can do on an unusual weekend break? What *is* kite making? Where can you go and do it? etc.

If Ss have *not* read the text for homework, ask them to read it silently and help each other to understand. Encourage the use of dictionaries, or you help with difficult vocabulary as and when necessary. Check comprehension (as above.)

Then get them (again with the help of a dictionary if necessary) to think of some unusual weekends beginning with the letters M-Z. Get as many responses as you can from the class, the more amusing or outrageous the better! (This could be a team game.)

Answers

A few possible unusual weekends for M-Z:

Meditation/Murder, Novel writing/Narrow-boat cruising, Organising dinner parties/Origami, Parapsychology/ Plastering, Quick cooking for two, Riding, Subaqua weekend, Table manners/Tracing your ancestors, Unicycle riding/ Upholstery, Ventriloquism, Wrestling, Xylophone playing, Yachting/Yoga for the Family, Zoo management

Ex. 2

Classroom treatment

Introduce the tape and ask Ss to read the questions. They then listen and answer the questions. You might ask more questions e.g. 'Why did the woman accuse the man of being cynical? Why did the man say he would be no good at doing anything like calligraphy?'

If time allows, Ss might conduct conversations about other weekends on page 93, beginning 'I've just come back from one of those weekend breaks. It was great fun/marvellous/dreadful/a total waste of time!'

Then conduct a brief general class discussion on whether Ss would like to go on the calligraphy course or not, and why/why not.

Expected answers

a The woman went on a calligraphy course.

b She learned to do beautiful handwriting.

c Yes, she enjoyed it very much.

Exs. 3-6

Classroom treatment

3 Working in pairs or groups of three or four, Ss try to persuade their partner(s) to go on one of the unusual weekend breaks. As the aim is to get Ss to produce fairly free conversations, it might be advisable to study the boxed language with Ss before they begin. In particular, point out and briefly practise (in the second box) the patterns with adjectives *important, essential,* etc., and the different constructions (in the third box) with *It's no use, It's not worth,* etc. followed by the *-ing* form.

4 Ss should first think and make notes about any unusual hobby they have or have had experience of. Then, working in groups of three or four, Ss describe their hobbies to each other. As the aim is to get Ss to produce fairly free conversations, it might be advisable to study the boxed language with Ss before they begin. In particular, highlight and practise past tenses and past tense sequences, and ways of expressing past success or failure with *managed to do, succeeded in doing,* etc. As an example, and using language from the box, tell the class about one of your own hobbies, when you started it, how long you've been doing it, what you found easy or difficult, etc.

5 Ss work in pairs for this brief phase, but before they begin, ask them to think for a few minutes and make some brief notes. They then tell each other how to start by saying something like: 'I'm going to tell you about rock climbing. One of the best ways to get into it is to join a good club … . Of course, you'll never learn to be a good rock climber unless you can tie knots easily …'

Again, an example from you will give a clear idea of what and how much Ss are expected to say.

6 Before Ss begin this task, make sure they understand the situation. Ask them to read the rubric and then to tell you what they have to do. What kind of letter must they write? So will they write in a formal or informal style?

Then they must choose between 'an activity weekend break' and 'a new hobby'. If they choose the former, suggest they use one of those on page 93; if a hobby, then they might use one that they or another S has used in ex. 5.

Ss should begin this letter individually in class and complete it as a homework assignment.

Coursebook pp.94-95

Vocabulary: Bring it off with a simple verb!

CAE Relevance: All Papers, especially Papers 3 and 4 (English in Use and Listening)

▷ 📼 Tapescript for ex. 1 (See Coursebook pp.156-157.)

Ex. 1 Verbs with the same form as nouns

Classroom treatment

Introduce this phase by writing these on the board/OHP and asking Ss to complete the sentences in their own way:

I had no time for play when … / I didn't play …

Then ask how the word *play* is different in the two sentences. (In the first it's a noun, in the second a verb.) Explain that they are going to look at a lot more words like this.

Quickly ask individual Ss to suggest sentences using the words given (*a boot / to boot, a thumb / to thumb,* etc.) before getting them to work in five groups (A-E) to see how many pairs of words they can come up with in the categories given. Set a time limit for this activity (say, five minutes?) — otherwise you and they are likely to be there for a long time!

NOTE: When they are reporting their lists, Ss should not only give the words for the rest of the class, but also show they know how the verbs are used, since many are used in a special idiomatic way or with a meaning somewhat divorced from the meaning of the corresponding noun. (Dictionaries will help.)

Answers

Some possible pairs of nouns and verbs:

A *parts of the body:* head/to head (a ball), scalp/to scalp (someone), shoulder/ to shoulder (one's way through a crowd), elbow/to elbow (one's way through a crowd), finger/to finger (something), arm/to arm (e.g. with a knife), toe/to toe (e.g. to toe the line), foot/to foot (the bill), palm/to palm off, thumb/to thumb (e.g. pages)

B *tools and appliances:* hammer/to hammer, screw/to screw, shovel/to shovel, rake/to rake, fork/to fork (over), plane/to plane, brush/to brush, knife/to knife

C *materials and substances:* iron/to iron, water/to water, paint/to paint, butter/to butter, oil/to oil, wine/to wine (as in 'to wine and dine someone'), steel/to steel

D *clothes and footwear:* collar/to collar, skirt/to skirt, buttonhole/to buttonhole, boot/to boot, cuff/to cuff, tie/to tie, lace/to lace (up), belt/to belt, coat/to coat (something with oil, for example)

E *the garden:* rake/to rake, weed/to weed, plant/to plant, bloom/to bloom, fork/to fork (over the soil), shovel/to shovel, grass/to grass, leaf/to leaf (through)

Listening: Classroom treatment

a Make sure Ss know what they are going to hear and what they have to do before you play the tape for the first time. Play it for Ss to write down (in any note form they like) what the different speakers are describing or talking about. Check answers with the whole class.

b Play the extracts again, this time pausing frequently (after each sentence, if necessary) to allow Ss to listen for and write down any verbs that have the same form as their corresponding noun. Check answers with the whole class.

Follow-up activities might be:

1 Ss work in pairs and try to 'repeat' to each other what the speakers said on tape — using their notes and lists of verbs; or

2 Ss act at being e.g. a gardener, or a shoeshop assistant, etc. — and tell a partner about their job using as many appropriate nouns and verbs from this phase as they can.

Expected answers

a The first is talking about practice sessions with his rugby team.

The second is a book collector talking about what people do at book fairs.

The third is a man talking about parachuting.

The fourth is the mother of a girl who goes riding and has her own horse.

The last is a man talking about rally driving.

b Verbs used by the speakers:

1 coach, boot, palm, head; 2 fake, thumb, finger;
3 shoulder, step, phone; 4 foot, pay, shoe, pocket;
5 buttonhole, soup (up), corner, garage

Ex. 2 Phrasal verbs with *off*

Classroom treatment

Explain that there are many ways to learn and understand phrasal verbs. Here, a number are grouped under the particle *off*, which can indicate distance, disconnection, departure, etc.

Different Ss will probably know some of these verbs, but not all Ss will know all of them. Exploit this by getting Ss to work in pairs or threes to study the verbs and write short sentences with them to bring out their meanings: they can help each other or use dictionaries if they get stuck. They will not really need to make their own sentences with *come off, take off, hit ... off* or *pay off* (with a meaning of 'success') as the examples are already in short sentences — although they could write others if they wish.

Check the sentences produced and correct and explain where necessary before getting Ss to do the editing task in class or as a homework assignment.

Answers

knock off (NOT 'strain off'), *put us off* (NOT 'cut us off'), *turned/switched off* (NOT 'knocked off'), *set off* (NOT 'pulled off'), *pulled off* (NOT 'come off'), *bring off/pull off* (NOT 'lift off'), *paying off/taking off* (NOT 'ringing off'), *hit it off* (NOT 'rang it off')

Write

CAE Relevance: Paper 2 (Writing)

Classroom treatment

This is similar to the open-ended writing task that Ss might find as one of the options in the second part of Paper 2 Writing — although this will be shorter.

We suggest the task should be discussed, prepared thoroughly and begun in class, then set as a homework assignment. Ss should write about 150 words.

Ss read the instructions and then check comprehension with questions like this: 'Have you got to write a letter, or an article? What *have* you got to write?' (Part of a magazine ad.) 'What will you stress?' (That it's a week or weekend activity course for people who need a break from work.)

Ss then think of an 'unusual' activity for a weekend/week, what it might involve, where it will take place, how much it will cost, what accommodation will be offered, what the week or weekend will contain (i.e. the course programme), and how they might attract the reader's attention. (You might read out the sample below as the kind of thing they should aim to write.)

Remember the suggested procedure for drafting, editing and clean writing (see Introduction p.9).

Answers

This is a sample of what students might aim at

Do you need a break from work?

Of course you do!

And the best way to begin to relax is to get away and take up

GUITAR PLAYING FOR BEGINNERS

— a five-day course in any week from April to October.

No previous knowledge or experience needed.

An elementary knowledge of music might be useful — but it's not essential!

And it would be an advantage if you could bring your own (or someone else's) guitar — but again that's not vital.

The course will take you from simple theory to simple melody and chord playing — in easy stages, and with no pressure. No tests, no exams. You'll be doing it for your own enjoyment. And very quickly we'll help you play what you want to play — classical, pop, jazz. And the vast majority of our participants succeed in mastering the basics in next to no time.

Fees: £350, including full-board accommodation and free loan of a guitar for the duration of the course if you can't bring your own.

Exam Practice: Paper 5 Speaking

CAE Relevance: Paper 5 (Speaking)

Exs. a and b

Classroom treatment

Remind Ss that in Phase C of Paper 5 they will be asked to discuss and try to solve a problem of some kind, usually based on a picture or pictures. The important point is that they have to try to come to some agreement, or 'agree to disagree', in two minutes. They may not have to describe the picture or pictures they are given, but they *will* need to express opinions, agree and disagree with each other, etc.

a To encourage Ss to think of some of the language they will need for the task, ask them to suggest what we can say to express an opinion, etc. Get them to suggest as many different phrases as they can. (This could be a whole-class or group activity.) Examples:

to express an opinion: *I think/reckon/believe (that) .../ It's my opinion/ belief that ... / As far as I'm concerned, ... / In my view, ... / To my mind, ...*

to express a strong opinion: *I firmly believe .../ I believe quite strongly that .../ I'm of the firm belief ... /*

There's absolutely no doubt in my mind that ... / I'm absolutely convinced that ...

to agree with an opinion: *Yes, of course. / Well, yes, you're quite right, of course. / Agreed. / Fine.*

to agree partly: *Well, yes, but ... / All right, but ... / Well, that's all right as far as it goes. But what about ...?*

to disagree politely: *No, I'm sorry, I can't agree with that/I can't really accept that ...*

to disagree forcefully: *No, I just can't accept that (as an argument)./ No, I can't possibly agree with that.*

to disagree not so politely: *Oh, come on! That's rubbish / ridiculous! And you know it.*

to introduce an example: *(Let's) take, for example/for instance ... / Let me give you an example of what I mean.*

to add an extra point to a discussion: *OK, but what about ...? / But there's something you've/we've forgotten, I think.*

to ask for a repetition: *(Sorry,) can you repeat that, please?*

to ask for an explanation: *(I'm sorry,) what do you mean by that exactly? / I'm not sure I (quite) understand what you mean/what you're getting at.*

b Ss now look at the Gambols cartoon and discuss in pairs whether this shows the best way to get away from 'the noise and bustle of the city'. Suggest that they think of advantages and disadvantages of such a holiday. Give two or three minutes for this activity, as they would have in the exam.

Pairs report their decision to you or to another pair. If different pairs have come to different decisions, they might form groups of four to discuss the question again for a further two minutes and try to persuade the other pair of their point of view.

c Finally, discuss how easy or difficult Ss found it to keep going for the allotted time. If any pairs found it difficult, discuss strategies for keeping a discussion going e.g. playing devil's advocate, asking each other open questions, describing personal experiences, etc.

Rounding off the Unit

Why not round off this Unit by getting the class to discuss and try to come to an agreement on an ideal lifestyle which balances work and play?

16 Body matters

Warm-up

Here are two **alternative suggestions**, both with books closed:

1 Set up a 'boasting' game, in which each student has to outdo the previous speaker in terms of how healthy they are. Demonstrate and then encourage chains/exchanges like this:

   A: I jog for an hour a day.
   B: Well, I jog for an hour and a half a day, *and* I have bran for breakfast.
   C: Well, I jog for two hours a day, I have bran and nuts and wholemeal bread for breakfast, *and* I never drink more than a glass of wine.

   Each 'round' finishes when a 'contestant' is unable to better the previous speaker. At this point start another 'round' and continue until all Ss have had a chance to contribute.

2 Write on the board/OHP (some of) the following abbreviations (without their explanations). They are all to do with health and the world of medicine.

   GP (= general practitioner / 'family doctor')
   TB (= tuberculosis)
   MS (= multiple sclerosis)
   WHO (= World Health Organisation)
   ECG (= electro-cardiogram)
   MO (= Medical Officer)
   A1 (= OK, healthy)
   BO (= body odour)
   AIDS (= auto-immune deficiency syndrome)
   REM (= rapid eye movement)
   SRN (= State Registered Nurse)

   Ss in pairs or small groups use dictionaries to find out their meanings. They then pool their newly-acquired knowledge with the rest of the class.

Read, edit and discuss

CAE Relevance: Papers 1 and 3 (Reading and English in Use)

Background notes and vocabulary

The two illustrations here, 'Headache' and 'Panic Avenue' are by the artist Andrzej Dudzinski
buzzword: see Possible answer for ex.3
(everyday) hassles: a colloquial word meaning irritating difficulties
a surfeit of: too large an amount of (something)/ too much
it's not on: it's not acceptable behaviour
to belt (the boss): to hit (the boss) hard

Ex. 1

Classroom treatment
Go through the rubric carefully with Ss, making sure they understand the situation completely. Remind them of the clues that will help them relate one paragraph to another as they did in Unit 10 ('Supertots' text).

Give the class 10 minutes to try and complete the task, working alone. Then get Ss to compare their results with a partner's for two minutes. Finally, let groups of five or six develop to see if further light can be shed on any remaining problems.

Alternatively, you might stop the first ten-minute activity after three minutes to check that Ss have isolated the three 'intruding' paragraphs correctly.

Answers
The correct order of the paragraphs: A, F, D, H, G, L, C, N, K, O, M, J, P.

Paragraphs B, E and I do not belong.

Ex. 2

Classroom treatment
Make Ss aware of the freedom they are offered in this exercise (there are no *correct* answers!). You may need to give the first underlined section as an example. For example (para. E):

Sweating before an interview or before you have to make a speech in public can be just as natural as sweating from intense heat; the stammering we experience when we are nervous is no less real than a permanent physiological feature which produces a stutter.

Possible answers

G changing nappies, cooking for a family of six, doing housework, dealing with clients, answering customers' complaints

H if the family splits up, when you have an unexpected visitor, if you have a road accident, when there is some sudden damage to your house

I cheese, ice cream, margarine; cream, yoghurt, milk

K hot flushes, loss of concentration, headaches, eye strain, irritability

N outbursts of temper, periods of depression, bitterness, nostalgia, self-pity,

irrational behaviour; skin rashes, colds, teeth and gum problems

P self-control, expressing yourself clearly, handling problems, getting on with superiors/juniors

Ex. 3

Classroom treatment

Best to set these six questions as pairwork or groupwork and let Ss discuss their ideas. Let pairs etc. pass on their ideas to other pairs and so on, before doing a shortish feedback with the class.

Possible answers

a A buzzword is a fashionable word or phrase esp. related to a specialised subject, thought to express something important but often difficult to understand. Other examples of buzzwords: economic upturn, serial killers, a no-win situation, a here-and-now circumstance, a communicative activity.

b-d Open-ended

e Inability to face life's demands.

Well, you see, when your mummy, for example, suddenly hears that your granny is ill and your Uncle Harry is dying and your daddy has lost his job, it's normal if she feels, well, you know, if she cries a bit and well, generally gets a bit worried.

f Open-ended, but these prompts from you might help:

i) black coffee, paracetamol, another alcoholic drink, sleep, a cold shower, liquids of any kind, cold tea with lots of sugar

ii) leaning back, lying down, a cold key down one's back, pinching the nose, holding a cold cloth on the back of the neck

iii) staying in bed, whisky and hot water, hot lemon drink, aspirin

iv) sleeping pills, counting sheep, going to bed late, TV, radio

v) friends, a long walk, reading, TV, a holiday, last-minute revising, a party, reading yourself to sleep

Ex. 4

Classroom treatment

This is best suited to a homework exercise. If done in class, one piece could be done as a class effort with the paragraph built up on the board, one with Ss working alone (and then comparing paragraphs with partner(s), and a third with Ss working in co-operation with one or more partners to produce a version. (See Introduction p.9.)

Model paragraphs

Before E

Some people do not believe that 'illnesses' brought on by tension are as 'real' as illnesses that come from viruses or germs. This is absolutely untrue.

Before B

Many people who drink heavily believe that alcohol removes our inhibitions and allows us to be our true selves; after drinking we can dance on tables, say things we would never dream of saying sober, show a side to our character we would never dare to reveal in everyday life. To a certain extent this is true.

Before I

Nowadays a lot of people say that fat is bad for you, they go on fat-free diets and are horrified if they are served something that has a very high fat content, like fish and chips. In a way they are right to feel like this.

Coursebook pp.98-99

Language focus

A number of different points are raised and practised in this phase. Try to diagnose where the emphasis should be placed in your lesson — by thinking about recent errors made by your Ss, for example.

CAE Relevance: All Papers, especially 2 and 5

Ex. 1 Possibility and potential

Classroom treatment

Write these three sentences on the board: *He may come on Friday. He'll probably come on Saturday. He'll definitely come on Sunday.*

See how many ways Ss can express the different ideas, for example:

- He might come on Friday. It's possible that he'll come on Friday. I wouldn't be surprised if he came on Friday.

- He's (quite) likely to come on Saturday. The chances are he'll come on Saturday. There's every likelihood of him coming on Saturday. He may well come on Saturday.
- There's no way he won't come on Sunday. He'll certainly come on Sunday. I would be absolutely amazed if he didn't come on Sunday. He's bound/ sure to come on Sunday.

Though not giving them all the answers, this will probably lead Ss comfortably into the exercise. Let them do it in pairs or threes, then check with the whole class.

Model sentences

1 a) A headache caused by tension is likely to be as bad as one ...

b) A headache caused by tension is potentially as bad as one ...

c) There is no reason why a headache caused by tension shouldn't be as bad as one ...

d) A headache caused by tension may well be as bad as one ...

e) It's possible that a headache caused by tension will be as bad as ...

OR It's possible for a headache caused by tension to be as bad as ...

2 a) Ask a dozen people and there is little doubt that you will get ...

b) Ask a dozen people and in all probability/the probability is that you will get ...

c) Ask a dozen people and you are unlikely/it is unlikely that you will get twelve similar answers/more than two answers the same etc.

d) (If you asked)/Ask a dozen people and it would be no surprise if the answers were all different/ no one couple gave the same answer.

e) Ask a dozen people and it's almost sure you'll get/and you're almost sure to get twelve different answers.

3 a) Nowadays the major sources of stress are almost certainly the boss ...

b) Nowadays the chances are that the major sources of stress ...

c) Nowadays there is every chance that the major sources of stress are .../ every chance of the major sources of stress being ...

d) Nowadays the likelihood is that the major sources of stress are/will be/ there is every likelihood of the major sources of stress being the ...

e) Nowadays the odds are on the major sources of stress being the .../the odds are that the major ...

4 a) It's possible that friends have/will have the skills ...

b) Perhaps friends have/will have the skills ...

c) Friends might well be able to help you with the skills ...

OR It might well be that friends have/will have the skills ...

d) There is a possibility that friends have/will have/of friends having the skills ...

e) There's a good chance that friends have/will have/of your friends having the skills ...

Ex. 2 Ellipsis

Classroom treatment

Although they will have seen hundreds of examples of this in their reading, this may be an unfamiliar concept for Ss. Stress how common a feature it is in spoken and, particularly, in written English. A few 'authentic' sentences from a recent newspaper, read out to the class, would help here. Demonstrate on the board such pairs as:

Children brought up in the country learn to ...

Children who are brought up in a town learn to ...

Children planning a career in teaching should ...

Children who plan/are planning a career in teaching should ...

When the concept of ellipsis has been illustrated like this, ask Ss to look back at the asterisked sentences on pp. 96-97 and to expand them in the same kind of way.

The next exercise (with the 8 prompts) should be reasonably easy. Do the first two items with the class, then set the rest of the exercise as paired work with class feedback afterwards.

Answers

Answers to sentences on pp. 96-97

Para D: He defines stress as an imbalance between the demands that/which are made ...

Para E: A headache which/that is caused by tension can be just as bad as one which/that is caused ... : ... is no less real that the diarrhoea that/which is caused ...

Para F: The best definition of the word is probably the one that/which is offered ...

Para I: Four important vitamins are provided only by foods which/that contain fat.

Possible sentences for prompts 1-8

1 People suffering (who suffer) from angina have a much better chance of recovering/being cured than such people 20 years ago.

2 Men not used to strenuous physical exercise should not take up this sport.

3 Babies born prematurely are normally smaller than average.

4 The dose prescribed should not be exceeded.

5 Exercises specially designed for the back are better than general aerobic exercises.

6 Diets based on scientific research often seem to have less success than those made up by the particular individual.

7 Women planning to go back to work soon after having children should inform their employer well in advance.

8 Those allergic to dust should avoid working in a factory or similar environment.

Ex. 3 Giving advice

Classroom treatment

Go through the rubric with Ss. Study together the model sentences given below. Elicit other forms used to give advice. These should include the following:

If I were you, I'd ...; Why don't you ...?; What about ...?; Perhaps you ought to/should ...; If ..., you'd better ...; You could always ...; Perhaps it wouldn't be a bad idea to ...

Discuss the range of formality/informality that is present in the compiled list and those in the text on page 99. Almost certainly Ss will have come up with more informal expressions than those in the book. Point out how the importance of the advice is expressed through sentences/clauses beginning *Otherwise ...; ... because ...*

Can Ss think of other ways of explaining why a certain course of action is advisable? *... so that ...; ... in case ...; ... in order to ...; ... so as not to ...; because of ...,* etc.

Focus attention on the pictures. See if in speech Ss can a) say which is right and which is wrong, b) why, and c) what potential dangers there are in doing 'it' the wrong way.

Paired practice can reinforce what has been done above with one student advising the other directly. This will make the use of *If I were you, ... Or you could ...,* etc. particularly apt.

Then ask Ss to write a couple of paragraphs, trying to 'formalise' the language used in their discussion.

Vocabulary: A bump on the head — and a sprained ankle!

CAE Relevance: All Papers

Classroom treatment

You may like to pre-teach/check some of the less common vocabulary in this exercise before the game commences. Try to elicit as much as possible from Ss themselves; run through various parts of the body and see if they can list some of the things that can go wrong with each part. For example: T: feet. S1: blisters, S2 sore feet, S3 ingrowing toenails (toenails that grow into the toes), S4 Athlete's foot, etc., thereby covering some of the vocabulary in the exercise and bringing in still more.

Alternatively, get the members of the two groups to check the meaning of 'their' unfamiliar words in dictionaries. (The drawback here is that the other group may be unable to respond to certain 'challenges' through simply not knowing a word addressed to them.)

Depending on the size of class, conduct the game as two teams 'challenging' each other in turn as per rubric, or divide a big class into teams of, say, four, and let two or three games run concurrently.

There is a good opportunity here to check on Ss' use of *did, was doing, have done, have been doing* . You would have a remarkable class if Ss even at this level were not quite regularly misusing these tenses. Monitor and pass comment after the activity.

Coursebook pp.100-101

Listen and decide

CAE Relevance: Paper 4 Listening

▷ 📼 **Tapescript** (See Coursebook p.157.)

Classroom treatment

This is in part a continuation of the vocabulary development work on page 99 and you may choose to pre-teach/check a few items likely to be unfamiliar: *blood vessel, stomach cramps, abdominal pains, dislocate, run-down, a shooting pain.*

Alternatively, warn Ss that there is quite a heavy vocabulary load, but play the extracts without prior help or guidance, in more or less examination conditions, allowing Ss to hear the tape twice before checking answers.

As usual, Ss should be encouraged afterwards to pinpoint the 'clues' which helped them match correctly. Refer to the Tapescript on page 157 if you want to draw Ss' attention to any vocabulary items.

Answers
A3, B6, C2, D8, E4, F1, G5, H7

Tip Strip

Classroom treatment
In this Unit we have the first of five Tip Strips — hints and advice on each of the exam Papers in turn. Before doing the Exam Practice here as a timed test, get Ss to read through the Tip Strip. Get feedback: what advice and warnings are included? how is the positioning of the questions and text important? which tips do they find it easy/difficult to follow in practice?

Note that in these last five Units there is no other preliminary work on the Exam Practice section.

Exam Practice: Paper 1 Reading

CAE Relevance: Paper 1 (Reading)
Classroom treatment
Set the exercise 'Eating Out? Watch Your Health!' as a fifteen-minute test. Some of the headings include tricky idiomatic language, but best at this stage of the course that Ss get used to dealing with such problems, trying to deduce and infer meanings.

Background notes and vocabulary

Sauce for the goose may not be sauce for the gander: a slight variation on the saying 'What's sauce for the goose is sauce for the gander', which means that what's good enough for one person is good enough for another

Fortune favours the not-so-brave: the saying is 'Fortune favours the brave', which means 'those who are brave or courageous do well in life'.
Never too crowded!: the difficulty here is appreciating that this means it is impossible to have a restaurant too crowded = the more crowded the better.
ill-kempt: an unusual negative of well-kempt, which means literally well-combed but in common usage, well-kept. The common word for 'ill-kempt' is 'unkempt'.
gargantuan: enormous, gigantic
sushi: a Japanese snack of cold rice, flavoured and garnished

Correct answers
The best headings for the eight paragraphs, in order:
D, A, H, B, I, G, C, E. Headings F and J do not belong.

Rounding off the Unit

To round off, why not revise some of the 'health and illness' vocabulary presented in this Unit (and elsewhere) with a brainstorming game, in which teams compete together?

Either ask each team in turn to give you five of the following:

a) things you'd find in a school first-aid box
b) common sport's injuries
c) foods heavy in cholesterol
d) common allergies
e) children's illnesses
f) ways of losing weight
g) jobs a nurse does daily
h) departments or wards of a hospital
etc.

Or give categories like those above and teams take turns to supply an example, the last team to supply one winning the point.

17 Love makes the world go round

Warm-up

No warm-up activities are suggested for this Unit as the first activity could be seen as a warm-up in itself, but if something is desired you could:

a) ask students how old they were when they first fell in love and how many times they have been in love;

or

b) ask students if they know any apt quotations about love — they could try to translate something from their own language(s) if they like.

Read, discuss and write

CAE Relevance: All Papers

Ex. 1

Classroom treatment

Ss work in pairs on this exercise and then compare their answers with those of other Ss and with the originals. Stress that even if they don't know the sayings, they should complete the sentences with something meaningful.

You might ask Ss to try to explain (briefly) what each saying means.

Answers

Here are the original ways of filling in the gaps in the sayings:

Warm <u>hands</u>, cold heart.

'Tis better to have loved and lost, than <u>never to have loved at all</u>.

Love me, love my <u>dog</u>.

Love will find a <u>way</u>.

One cannot love and be <u>wise</u>.

When <u>poverty</u> comes in at the window, love flies out of the door.

All's <u>fair</u> in love and war.

The course of true love never did <u>run smooth</u>.

Lucky at <u>cards</u>, unlucky in love.

Love is <u>blind</u>.

Exs. 2 and 3

Classroom treatment

2 Ask Ss if there is anything they themselves dislike in the list on the page.

Then ask them individually to compose their own lists of things they love. When they have finished, they should walk round the room comparing their lists with those of other students and asking each other supplementary questions if necessary.

3 Look at the question with Ss and discuss what kind of writing is likely to get first prize — something that is well-written, has a striking opening and a strong conclusion, for instance. Set the task as homework.

Listen and speak

CAE Relevance: Paper 4 (Listening)

▷▣ **Tapescript (authentic recordings)** (See Coursebook pp.157-158.)

Exs. 1-3

Classroom treatment

1 Ss listen to the tape and answer question 1.

2 Ss listen again to each speaker individually and discuss this question as a class after each part of the recording.

3 Ss discuss this question in twos or threes.

4 If you wish to, you might finally ask Ss what they think the people in Picture **b** might have said about love.

Answers to ex.1

Speaker 1 — Picture **c** (girl looking sad), Speaker 2 — Picture **a** (climbers), Speaker 3 — Picture **d** (unloading bags of grain for famine relief)

Vocabulary: whatsitsname? and what a slip-up!

Ex. 1 I'd like a whatsitsname

Classroom treatment

Ask Ss if they can give a name to the things Sue and James are describing here (= a food-processor and a lawnmower).

Ask them to make a couple more sentences of the same type using ideas from the pictures (e.g. I want a thing for making toast with *or* I want something to carry my papers to work in).

Then ask Ss in pairs to think up three or four more sentences of this type. They must have some object in mind but they don't actually need to know the English word (or even the word in their own language) for the object.

Ss then read out their sentences to the rest of the class and the other Ss try to give the proper word for the objects being described. Points could be given to Ss who *can* provide appropriate words.

Answers
Wedding presents in the picture:

A case to carry papers in. (A briefcase.)
A machine/thing for mowing grass/the lawn with. (A lawnmower.)
A spoon to serve spaghetti with. (A spaghetti server/spoon.)
A bike for exercising. (An exercise bike.)
A thing to open tins with or A thing for opening tins with. (A tin-opener.)
A thing for drilling holes with. (An electric drill.)
A thing to make toast with. (An electric toaster/A pop-up toaster.)
A thing to open bottles with. (A bottle-opener.)
A thing to stand hot pots and pans on. (A trivet.)
A thing for crushing garlic (with). (A garlic crusher.)

Ex. 2 What a slip-up!

Classroom treatment
Explain what is meant by a compound noun and check the meanings of the words in the introduction to the exercise.

Read the text aloud to Ss and ask them to underline all the compound nouns as you read.

Ss in pairs then discuss the meanings of the compound nouns. If they do not know the meanings, they should try to work them out from the context and from the way the words have been formed.

Check the meanings, discussing how well Ss managed to work them out.

Answers

slip-ups	=	errors
crack-down	=	tightening of controls
cover-up	=	attempt to hide
outlets	=	shops/places where its products are sold
turnover	=	here, changes
holdups	=	delays

walkout	=	strike
breakdowns	=	failures (in something)
feedback	=	a report
set-up	=	organisation
input	=	contributions
downfall	=	fall from his/her position
setbacks	=	problems
upturn	=	improvement
output	=	production

Read and discuss

CAE Relevance: Paper 1

Background notes and vocabulary

'Marriage by Arrangement'
(NOTE: Most of the more difficult words and expressions are explained in the answer to question 7.)
Coventry: British industrial town in the Midlands
papers: here means scientific articles
ardent: full of warm emotion
anniversary: day on which something special happened in a previous year
courtship: friendship between a boy and a girl prior to marriage

Exs. 1 and 2

Classroom treatment
1 Ss discuss the pre-reading questions in threes or fours.

2 Ask the Ss to read the text as quickly as possible. Do not allow more than three minutes for this.

Ask Ss to discuss the questions in pairs.

Check Ss' answers and discuss any additional problems which Ss may have had with vocabulary in the text.

Answers to ex. 2
1 The author's main argument is that there is something to be said for arranged marriages.

2 Here are the missing sections from the text: 1 went out for three months together before the wedding; 2 of whom my parents approved; 3 into our future together with our four eyes; 4 buying designer party clothes and dancing; 5 would not need to cook for several years; 6 of disillusionment with the way things are going in the West; 7 they are pretty or clever enough and depending on men to prove to them that they are; 8 I am not a prisoner of the romance industry.

3 Marriage in Western society is very unstable — more so than in traditional Eastern societies.

Fathers in Eastern countries know their children and want the best for them.

Romance is quite different from marriage.

Marriage is for life and should not be based just on physical attraction.

You can have a more relaxed social life if you're not worried all the time about finding a spouse.

4 Many of the points in the answer to 3 above are implicit criticisms of Western marriage.

7 *soap operas:* TV series which are shown at least once a week and are based on the same characters and their continuing family and working lives
devotion: dedication, commitment to each other
flash in the pan: something (exciting) which is quickly over and cannot be repeated or developed
passionate: full of strong emotion
fiancée: girl a young man is engaged to
gazing: looking fixedly
wreck: ruin
marriage bureau: an agency which arranges marriages
coercion: compulsion
to have a lot of say: can give an opinion and it will be listened to
to play games: pretend things that are not true

Classroom treatment

Here is an **additional exercise** on the text which might be useful.

It uses language from the article but the necessary prepositions have been missed out. Read it out, write it up or photocopy it for Ss and ask them to supply the missing prepositions. If they are unsure, they should look at the article again.

Jane was brought _____ in the house next door to Jim. They were both good _____ tennis and, when they were teenagers, they spent most of their weekends at the tennis club together. Their parents approved _____ their friendship and everyone assumed they would eventually get married. However, one day a tall, dark, handsome stranger called Martin came to work at Jane's office. They soon started going _____ together. Jim was sure that something terrible would happen _____ Jane. He looked _____ Martin as a dangerous liar who would trick Jane into loving him. He thought she would not be able to see _____ his false words of love and feared that she would become a prisoner _____ his charms. Jim told Jane that she needed

someone whose love _____ her was deep and true and based _____ a shared background and interests. He asked Jane to marry him. Jane said ...

Ss should then decide how Jane answered Jim. They should write down what she said to him and then compare what they wrote with what others wrote.

Coursebook pp.106-107

Language focus

CAE Relevance: All Papers
Exs. 1-3
Classroom treatment
Ss work through exercises **1** to **3** in pairs.

In a feedback session deal with any problems that have arisen and any points that the Ss do not all seem to be clear about.

Set ex. **4** for homework. Then in class on the day you are due to collect the homework, allow Ss another five minutes to check their writing before handing it in.

Answers

1 1 **a** suggests that a trouble-free marriage is possible for everyone but **b** that it is possible for no one.

2 **a** suggests that all men could in fact make her an ideal husband whereas **b** suggests that no man could fill that role.

3 **a** means that good champagne is available, whereas **b** suggests that one good brand of champagne is available, and **c** that more than one good brand is available there.

4 **a** means that the speaker likes some but not others, **b** emphasises that there are no English boys that the speaker likes, and **c** says that the speaker doesn't like English boys in general without being quite as emphatic as **b**.

5 **a** means that he needs love in general (and so no article is required), whereas **b** specifies what kind of love he needs with a following phrase and so the definite article is needed before the word *love*.

6 **a** means that he wrote poetry in general and **b** that he wrote one particular verse or poem.

2 Here are the most probable ways of completing the sentences.

a Love is what makes the world go round.

b I haven't done (the or any) tidying-up for ages.

124

(*any* emphasises the fact that no tidying-up at all has been done.)

c I like (- *or some or* any) tall dark, handsome men.

(- makes a general statement, *some* says a number of them but not all, and *any* says all of them).

d She is in love with youth (or a youth, some youth or the youth).

(*youth* means the state of being young, *a youth* means a young man who has not been referred to previously, *some youth* means a young man but I don't know precisely which one and it also perhaps suggests disapproval, *the youth* means the youth we have just been talking about.)

e What is the meaning of life without love?

f This statement is all right as it stands as a newspaper headline but normally it would need expanding to: 'A crackdown at the/a hospital has angered the/some nurses' — depending on whether the readers already know which hospital is being referred to and whether all or only some of the nurses are angered.

3 Possible exchanges about the photo:

A: Who's the lady in blue standing beside the bridesmaid on the left?

B: Oh, she's the aunt who brought the groom up when his mother died.

A: Who's the man with glasses standing at the back on the right-hand side?

B: The one with glasses? Oh, he's the uncle who later sailed round the world single-handed.

A: What's the building they're standing in front of?

B: It's the church (that) the bride went to (or where the bride went) when she was a child and where she always wanted to be married.

Extra activity
Here is an extra exercise on ellipsis you might wish to use to consolidate what was done in Unit 16.

Ellipsis — What's missing?

Write this sentence on the board/OHP. There are two small words missing from it. What are they? ('which was' i.e. 'The food which was delivered ...')

'The food delivered to Ethiopia last weekend should save many lives.'

Ask Ss to lengthen these sentences in the same way:

a Any young person going out on their first date feels pretty excited.

b He's madly in love with the girl wearing a white T-shirt.

c If asked out, don't hesitate to accept.

d When not sent any Valentines, teenagers can feel quite rather miserable.

e While determinedly working to help Amazonian Indians she fell for a handsome young Brazilian doctor.

Now ask Ss to shorten these sentences:

a Any woman who is married to a politician must have a difficult life.

b The volunteer workers who were held up at the border for two days have now been allowed to proceed to their destination.

c The girl who is sitting at that table over there is stunningly beautiful.

d While I was working in the Sudan I met a lot of interesting people.

e When she is invited to dance she always refuses.

Writing for Section A of Paper 2

CAE Relevance: Paper 2 (Writing)

Classroom treatment
Read the introduction at the top of the first column and then look at the task with the Ss as a class, asking them

1 to underline all the information from the input which they need to make use of, and

2 to consider the question of which style should be used.

Highlight the fact that both pieces of writing requested are formal but that the letter to a rejected candidate should be reasonably positive and friendly.

Set the writing for homework.

Answers
This is the kind of answer that students should be aiming at. It must be stressed, however, that students may with equal justification choose to offer the job to another applicant.

a) The Report
We interviewed four candidates, each of whom had certain points in their favour. They were all physically fit and all seemed to be caring, genuine people.

Suzanne has demonstrated determination in her swimming career. She has had no experience of working with children, however, and wishes to commit herself to working for only six months before going to university.

Peter has experience of teaching young children and has certain practical skills like carpentry which could be useful. He has travelled relatively little, however.

Anna has had some experience of both working with children and travelling but her main motive in applying for the job seems to be dissatisfaction with her own life rather than a vocation to help others.

Kim is young but has already shown initiative by hitch-hiking round the world. She has a good idea of what conditions can be like in developing countries. As an orphan herself, she has a particular understanding of the children she would be dealing with.

All things considered, I would recommend offering the job to Kim.

b) The Letter

Dear Suzanne,

Thank you for your application to join our project. You have many qualities which would be of great value to us but in the end we decided to offer the job to someone with more experience of working with children. The person we chose is also anxious to spend at least three years with the project.

We could, however, offer you a job on another project for the summer before you go to university if that would be of any interest to you. The job is that of sports instructor on a camp we run for children in Northern Ireland. The work partly involves helping children improve their sports skills; there is also, however, an important caring role as some of the children have psychological problems arising from the difficult situation in which they live.

We look forward to hearing from you.

Yours sincerely,

Tip Strip

With books closed, ask Ss what advice they would give to someone about Paper 2 of the CAE. Try to elicit from them as many of the points from the Tip Strip as possible. Put their ideas on the board/OHP.

Then ask them to look at the Tip Strip and to see which of their ideas are not mentioned there and which are included there which they did not think of.

Coursebook p.108

A final exclamation!

CAE Relevance: Papers 4 and 5 (Listening and Speaking)

▷ ▣ **Tapescript** (See Coursebook p.158.)

Ex. 1

Classroom treatment

Ss spend five minutes in pairs discussing which of the expressions they know and what they mean and considering any other expressions they have heard.

Check the meanings as a class and discuss any other exclamations the group comes up with.

Expected answers

Well I never (did)! expresses surprise.

Not on your life! refuses something in horror.

How dare you! expresses horror or disgust at someone's behaviour.

You must be joking/kidding! is said when you do not believe (or pretend that you do not believe) what someone is saying.

For goodness'/heaven's sake! suggests exasperation or annoyance.

Congratulations! is when someone has done something particularly well. (N.B. It is not used for birthdays unless it is a particularly special one, a 100th, for instance.)

Fantastic!/Great!/Marvellous! all express admiration or enthusiasm.

How ghastly! expresses horror and *ghastly* can, of course, be replaced by a huge variety of adjectives to express different emotions.

Bless you! is used after someone sneezes or sometimes by a religious person wishing you well.

Exs. 2 and 3

Classroom treatment

2 Listen to the tape and ask the Ss to respond in appropriate ways.

Discuss the responses the Ss give.

3 Ss work in pairs thinking up two or three more situations like those on the tape. Ss should then work in fours (separately from their original partner) testing the other Ss in their group with the situations they have thought up.

Possible answers to ex.2

2 Congratulations!   3 Not on your life!   4 Well, I never (did)!   5 How dare you!   6 Well, well!
7 How dreadful!   8 Fancy that!

Exam Practice: Paper 2 Writing

CAE Relevance: Paper 2 (Writing)

Exs. 1 and 2

Classroom treatment

Discuss with Ss how to choose a task.

It is important to choose one that they have both ideas and language for to do properly.

It is important to feel comfortable about the kind of style that they are being asked to write in.

The tasks that look easy may actually be less so in practice — and vice versa. So advise Ss to think carefully about the implications of the question before making a final choice.

Set a composition as homework or, if preferred, ask Ss to write a timed composition in class.

Answers

These are the kind of answers students should be aiming at:

1 The Letter

Dear Anne,

Thank you for your lettter. How wonderful that you are in love with a man who loves you. Still the course of true love never does run smooth, as they say.

You ask me what I think. Of course, our cultures are very different and there are many things that you might find hard to get used to in this country just as I'm sure your boyfriend would not find everything easy in your country. But surely there are difficulties in any marriage and each partner has to work to overcome them. At least you enter a marriage with someone from a different culture aware of the difficulties that may lie ahead. In more ordinary circumstances couples may feel that they will never themselves experience any difficulties and so are shocked when the first little problem crops up, as it is of course bound to do some time.

If I were you, I wouldn't rush into anything. Why not come over here and work for a while before deciding whether to go ahead with marriage or not. It will give you a proper chance to get to know your boyfriend as well as help you to work out just how much of a problem the cultural differences might be. It will also show your parents that you are behaving sensibly. If you still feel as you do now after, say, a year, both sets of parents may well be more prepared to support you in your marriage plans.

Anyhow, good luck! I do hope it all works out for you both.

With much love,

2 The Brochure

How would you feel if your children were not getting enough to eat?

How would you feel if your children were unlikely ever to learn to read and write?
How would you feel if you had no doctor to turn to when your children were ill?
How would you feel if you could not provide your children with a roof to keep them dry and warm?
How would you feel if your children faced a future of famine and disease?

Any parent would feel the same.

All parents want to protect their children, to give them food and shelter, to keep them healthy and happy and to offer them a future that is filled with hope.

Yet many parents throughout the world have to suffer the pain of hearing their children beg for something to eat when they have nothing to give them. Many parents have to suffer the pain of not knowing what to say when their children ask why life is so unkind.

Our charity, aptly called 'The Future of the World', aims to help children throughout the world. We seek to provide food, shelter and medical care for children in developing countries. We seek to help children who are suffering in industrialised countries too. We fund a range of projects whose only common link is that they aim to make the world a better place for children. You know how you love your children. Share a little bit of that love with less fortunate children.

Please give generously.

Every gift, however small, helps the future of the world.

Rounding off the Unit

Why not round off the Unit by setting a competition relating to the compound nouns studied in the Unit? Give tasks like these and check each one as you go:

1 Write down three words ending with the particle 'out'.
  (Examples: *breakout, workout, walkout, turnout, fallout*)

2 Write down five words ending with the particle 'up'.
  (Examples: *line-up, slip-up, break-up, run-up, turn-up, hold-up, set-up*)

3 Write down five words beginning with the particle 'out'.
  (Examples: *outlook, outbreak, outcome, output, outset, outburst*)

The first S to complete a task correctly earns a point. Any S who can then use one of the words correctly in a sentence (verbally) can also earn a point.

18 There's no accounting for taste

(The phrase *There's no accounting for taste* ... means: you can't, or it's not possible to, explain or give reasons for different people's taste in clothes, music, reading, etc. Compare: *There's no knowing/saying/telling what he'll do next* = It's impossible to know/say/tell what he'll do next.)

Coursebook p.109

Warm-up

Here are two **alternative suggestions**, both with books closed:

1 Ask Ss to try to define 'taste'. They might like to write their own definitions, then check with you and the class, and/or with different dictionary definitions.

Refine further by asking Ss to define 'good taste' and 'bad taste'. Ask Ss to write down (and then discuss) examples of what they consider to be bad taste — in terms of behaviour, clothes, home decoration, etc.

Then, what other words can they think of connected with 'taste': write lists and try to explain e.g. tasty, tasteless, distasteful, a tasting (Note particularly: 'tasty' to describe food, 'tasteful' to describe clothes, etc.)

2 Initiate a short general discussion on keeping up with 'fashion' e.g. When you go to buy clothes or shoes, a music cassette, CD or video, or have your hair done, etc., do you like to buy or have 'the latest'? If so, why? If not, why not?

Alternatively, dispense with a warm-up phase and go straight into the 'Read, look and discuss' activity.

Read, look and discuss

CAE Relevance: Papers 1, 2 and 5 (Reading, Writing and Speaking)

Background notes and vocabulary

These articles and descriptions all appeared in the British consumer magazine *Holiday Which?*. Note the deliberate humour and irony in the style in sentences like 'Delight your friends and impress your neighbours ...', 'Bring yourself good luck ...'

These short descriptions are written in a style typical of brief descriptions in some mail order catalogues.
flaunt: to show for public admiration (something you're proud of)
Big Apple: a nickname for New York
Eiffel Tower: the 320-metre tower in Paris designed by Alexandre Gustave Eiffel, the French engineer, in 1899
replica: a close copy
Daisy the cow: 'Daisy' is one of the names traditionally given to a pet or favourite cow in Britain
within earshot: within the distance up to which a sound can be heard
mantelpiece: the shelf part of a fireplace on which English people traditionally place mementos, small ornaments, etc.
Indonesian: from Indonesia, a republic in the Malay Archipelago, comprising the Sunda, the Moluccas, and West New Guinea
balsa wood: the light strong wood from a tropical American tree, used esp. to make floating objects such as rafts

Classroom treatment

Ask Ss to read the introductory paragraphs ('Taste is something ...') and then to tell you what it says about 'taste'.

They then look at the mementos and read the descriptions and decide which should be given First, Second and Third Prizes in the fictitious competition. (They are all real mementos and all appeared in a *Holiday Which?* magazine report. The magazine is a popular British consumer magazine which reports on holidays round the world, value for money, investigates holidaymakers' complaints, etc.)

Ask Ss now to think of another memento they have seen, or have bought, or have even been given by a well-meaning friend or relative (in good or bad taste), and ask them to write a brief description like the ones on the page.

Perhaps you can find a cheap memento of your local town or city (in suitably bad taste!) to give as a prize for the best?

You might round off the phase with a brief class discussion: 'Why is it that so many souvenirs and mementos of places people visit are so dreadful/so tatty/so tasteless/in such awful taste?' OR 'What kinds of mementos or souvenirs do you like to bring home from places you visit?'

Coursebook pp.110-111

Language focus: It might be a good idea if you read the reviews

CAE Relevance: Papers 1 and 3 (Reading and English in Use)

Background notes and vocabulary

> 'REVIEW — Your Weekly Guide ...'
> This is fairly typical of the arts and entertainment review pages in some British magazines which consist of brief reviews of current books, plays, films, etc. written and compiled by a small team of reviewers. In this case, while all the review paragraphs and three of the items they refer to are fictitious, three of the items referred to are fact (*Fantasia, Jimmy's* and *The Trials of Life*).
> *intriguing:* fascinating
> *Fantasia:* famous Walt Disney film described in the review
> *Jimmy's:* a British television documentary series about the work done at the famous St James's Hospital in Leeds in the early 1990s. The hospital is affectionately known as 'Jimmy's'.
> *The Trials of Life:* the book by David Attenborough (famous for many TV films and books about wild life) which paralleled a TV series with the same name

Ex. 1

Classroom treatment

Ss should *not* read the Review text on page 110 before the lesson as they will be studying it in some detail through exs. 1-8 on page 111.

Explain that the 'Review' is a page which has been printed and which a designer has pasted together (titles and paragraphs), but which still has to be proofread and checked again before it is final. The printer has made mistakes and whoever pasted the bits together has put the reviews under the wrong headings.

Ss must read the whole text very carefully (not necessarily for meaning), but just to find the printing/

spelling mistakes! Although they will not be allowed to do so in the exam, you might suggest they use dictionaries here to help.

Answers

Preferences: re~~vue~~ = review, a~~sess~~ = assess, ~~intriging~~ = intriguing

Fantasia: da~~mming~~ = damning, ~~sinchronised~~ = synchronised

Jimmy's: pr~~ograme~~ = programme

The Trials of Life: pr~~ase~~ = praise

The Urban Symphony: ~~planed~~ = planned, ~~absolutly~~ = absolutely

Images of Space: pr~~ommote~~ = promote

Ex. 2

Classroom treatment

Now Ss must read again, but this time more carefully for meaning in order to match the review extracts with the headings Music, Books, Theatre, etc.

When most have finished, check with the whole class.

Answers

MUSIC: *The Urban Symphony play Bach*
BOOKS: The Trials of Life by *David Attenborough*
THEATRE: Preferences by *Anna Carr*
CINEMA: Fantasia (*Disney*)
VISUAL ARTS: *Curzon Warren's* Images of Space
TV & RADIO: Jimmy's (*ITV*)

Exs. 3-8

Classroom treatment

Exs. 3-8 now concentrate on some of the language used in the reviews, so you might check further general and specific comprehension with questions like these:

Which of the reviews were positive? In other words, which reviewers praised what they had read, or seen, or watched? (Those who wrote about *Preferences, Fantasia, Jimmy's*, The Urban Symphony, and *Images of Space.*)

And if you believe critics and reviewers, which of the things wouldn't you see, or read, or watch? (I wouldn't bother to read *The Trials of Life* .)

If you were one of the following people and you read these reviews, how would you feel, and why? a) Curzon Warren, b) a doctor at Jimmy's, c) Anna Carr, d) a member of The Urban Symphony, e) David Attenborough.

Each of exs. 3-8 focuses on a different language point, with the 'Review' text as the starting point in each case. Ss have to scan the text to find the example and then work from there. They can work individually, in pairs, groups or as a class. They might refer to the Grammar Commentary while doing the exercsies, or as a check on all the points at the end of the phase.

Expected or possible answers

3 He/She absolutely adores listening to an orchestra playing live in a concert hall.

Possible sentences from Ss:
I (really/rather) enjoy listening to classical music.
I (quite) like playing tennis.
I (absolutely) love going to modern art exhibitions.
I (absolutely) adore buying new clothes.
I (really) hate being told what clothes to wear.
I (absolutely) loathe watching football.
I (just) can't stand/can't bear going to art exhibitions.

4 'What I like most about going to the theatre is allowing myself to be taken in ...' (*Preferences*)

and 'What I like most about this classic cartoon is the way visual images are synchronised with famous pieces of classical music.' (*Fantasia*)

'The thing I thought was so good about the programme was the fact that not once did you lose this sense of 'realness'.' (*Jimmy's*)

Possible sentences from Ss:

What I dislike most about a lot of modern sculpture is the way it never seems to resemble anything I can recognise.

The thing I think is good about most big cities is the fact that there is always so much to do and see.

5 The critic of *Jimmy's*. He/She wrote: 'I'd rather watch this again on Thursday evening than watch anything else on TV.'

Possible sentences from Ss:

I'd rather see *Fantasia* this week than go and see that new play. I'd prefer to do that because I like Disney films.

6 (*Preferences*) 'I wish I hadn't been asked to review this play.'

The critic of *The Trials of Life* regrets having read the book. He/She wrote: '... this is a book I wish I hadn't bothered to read.'

Possible sentences from Ss:

I wish I hadn't gone to see that dreadful film.

I wish I hadn't read/hadn't bothered to read that book.

7 The critic of The Urban Symphony play Bach wrote: ' ... I suggest it might be a good idea if you were to attend this special concert.'

It might be strange to write 'Why not attend ...' or 'Why don't you attend ...' because a) these two formulae are often used quite informally and spoken between friends,

and b) the verb *attend* sounds formal or written — we'd probably say 'Why don't you go to ...'.

8 The critic of The Urban Symphony play Bach wrote: 'Obviously it's completely up to you what you do this coming Saturday evening, ...'

He/She might have written: It's your decision what you do, but ..., OR You can choose what you do, but ...

Write some reviews

CAE Relevance: Paper 2 (Writing)
Classroom treatment
For this lesson, bring in (or ask Ss to bring in) a current (English or native language) newspaper or magazine with a 'What's On' column and/or a Reviews section. Ask Ss what films are showing this week, what plays or art exhibitions are on, and what new books have been published. Then ask them to pick two or three and think about whether they want to recommend them to readers or not.

They then begin drafting their reviews using as much or as little of the language from the page 110 Review as they wish. Go round the class encouraging, suggesting ideas, questioning, answering questions and correcting where necessary. Ask Ss to complete three short reviews as a homework assignment.

What's the difference? — if any!

Classroom treatment
This should be a short phase to round off this part of the Unit. Ss might best work in pairs and refer to the Grammar Commentary after they have discussed the pairs or groups of sentences.

Possible answers
1a is what *I* want to do (= I want to leave), 1b is what I want *you* to do (= I want you to leave). (The structure changes from *I'd rather do* ... to *I'd rather you did* ... with a change of subject.)

2a *She* wants to stay, 2b she'd like *them* to stay/she'd be happy if *they* stayed, and 2c means the same as 2b).

3a means: I would really like to see a change in your (reading) habits. 3b means I'm sad that you don't read much. 3c) means You didn't read much in the past; I'm not very happy about that now.

4a seems to be a simple suggestion, one of many possibilities perhaps. 4b means that it many not be ideal, but there's no better alternative.

5 There is very little difference between a) and b) here. If anything, a) seems to be an unsolicited suggestion, whereas b) might be said in answer to a request for advice.

6 There is little or no difference between a) and b) here.

7a) and 7b) mean just about the same, with the subject gerund replacing the *it*-construction. Compare: It's stupid to buy cheap mementos. / Buying cheap mementos is stupid. (If there is a difference, the gerund *-ing* seems to make a more general statement. 'It's stupid to buy ...', for example, more often refers to a particular (this) situation.)

```
Coursebook pp.112-113
```

Vocabulary

CAE Relevance: All Papers, esp. Papers 4 and 5 (Listening and Speaking)

▷ 📼 **Tapescript for ex. 3** (See Coursebook pp.158-159.)

Ex. 1 'Beauty is in the eye of the beholder'

Classroom treatment

1 The aim here is to make Ss aware again of the range of vocabulary items available to them in English when talking about taste, making judgments, comments or criticisms, and expressing likes and dislikes. Ss work individually or in pairs to list the words in two groups. They might even try to order them in terms of beauty and ugliness.

2 Give Ss two-three minutes to discuss the pairs of pictures freely.

3 Play the tape as often as necessary to let Ss hear how two English people express their opinions. While listening, Ss might again work in A/B pairs, A writing down how speakers say they like something, B noting down how the speakers express their dislikes. (Note: To express their likes and dislikes, most of the time both speakers simply use 'I think ...' with a variety of the adjectives from the box at the top of page 112. Ss should listen for these rather than try to find different grammatical structures.) Check with the whole class afterwards.

Possible answers

1 Group 1: beautiful — attractive, appealing, well-proportioned, exquisite,   gorgeous, stylish, elegant, aesthetic, well-made, splendid, superb, pleasing   to the eye, excellent

  Group 2: ugly — hideous, ghastly, abominable, awful,

repulsive, grotesque, formless, horrendous, dreadful, ill-proportioned, crude, unaesthetic, clumsy

3 The speakers express their likes and dislikes with 'I think ...', 'To my eye, ...' and 'I like ... because ...' plus the words 'attractive', 'comfortable', 'well made', 'pleasing to the eye', 'dreadful', 'elegant', 'aesthetically made', 'dumpy (old chair)', 'clumsy', 'stylish', 'completely and utterly abominable', 'superb', 'fantastic', 'dynamic', etc.

Ex. 2 What a difference a preposition makes!

Classroom treatment

1 Read out the sentences and ask Ss if they can briefly explain what each means and how they are different.

2 Explain that there are other pairs of phrases (like *make a fuss of/make a fuss about*) where the preposition is important. Tell them to read the short article quickly and tell you what it's about. Then they should read it again and circle or underline the prepositions that are wrong. Check with the whole class and ask for reasons.

3 Finally, Ss write sentences about themselves, friends or family using the phrases given. Again, check with the whole class.

  (You might give the following as further examples of expressions in which the preposition is vital:

  hold an exhibition of (paintings) vs hold an exhibition for (someone or a cause); take a look at (this) vs take a look over (the place);

  an argument/a battle/a case for/against;

  I have no taste for modern art vs She has good taste in clothes vs I had a taste of ...)

Possible answers

1 make a fuss of = to pay a lot of attention to ; make a fuss about = to get excited, annoyed or angry about

2 'to take a look over' should be 'to take a look *at* '

  'a collection of oil paintings of' should be 'a collection of oil paintings *by* '

  'to hold exhibitions of themselves' should be 'to hold exhibitions *for* themselves'

  'to take care over its new talents' should be 'to take care *of* its new talents'

  'they hold exhibitions for new paintings' should be 'they hold exhibitions *of* new paintings'

  'the artist has a taste in life' should be 'the artist has a taste *for* life'

  'she has so little taste for clothes' should be 'she has so little taste *in* clothes'

3 Examples of what Ss might produce:

People make too much fuss about breaking things.

She always makes a fuss of her grandchildren when she see them.

We're holding an exhibition of antique silver this month.

We're holding the exhibition for charity.

They took care of me when I had no money.

Take care over what you say — she's very sensitive.

She has no taste in music at all. / I'm slowly getting a taste for aubergines.

Tip Strip

Why not ask Ss to read this Tip Strip at home (and before doing the Exam Practice on p. 114) and look back though the course at the different English in Use tasks they have done? Then check in the next lesson what they have read. Ask if there are any other points they should remember which are perhaps not mentioned in the Tip Strip.

Coursebook p.114

Exam Practice: Paper 3 English in Use

CAE Relevance: Paper 3 (English in Use)

Background notes and vocabulary

> *alu'minium:* (AmE a'luminum) a silver-white metal that is a simple substance, light in weight and easily shaped
> *do your bit:* (colloquial) to make a contribution
> *recycle:* (of something that has already been used) to pass through a system of treatment so that it is fit to use again
> *(the) sheer (size):* pure; nothing but; utter
> *compress:* to crush
> *Wallmounting screws provided:* screws are provided to mount or fix the Can Crusher onto a wall
> *compact:* (adj.) neat, small, filling a small space
> *shredder:* a machine which tears or cuts paper (such as secret papers to be thrown away) into very small pieces which cannot be read

> *stay that way:* i.e. stay/remain confidential
> *bulky:* having great size or mass in comparison with weight
> *mere:* (adj.) no(thing) more than
> *easy-empty:* (adj.) which can be emptied easily
> *mains:* i.e. mains electricity

Exs. a and b
Classroom treatment

a Explain that this task does not actually involve rewriting a whole text in a different register, but in reading a text or texts, then reading a second text with blanks and completing those blanks.

Ss first read the instructions in **b** and answer the questions 1-3 in **a**.

b Ss now do the task individually or in pairs. They should read the 'Crush a can ...' and 'Compact Desktop Shredder' texts quite carefully so that they are fully conversant with the contents. Then they read the text at the bottom of the page and fill in the blanks, constantly referring to the two texts above.

a Possible answers

1 Read the catalogue descriptions and complete the blanks in the chatty letter.   2 What individual Ss will do depends on how they want to tackle the task: Read and study the texts in detail? Read the letter at the bottom? Read the two short texts quickly (for gist)?   3 No more than two.

b Answers

2 According to; 3 not only; 4 but; 5 to; 6 down on; 7 the wall; 8 by hand; 9 lots of/piles of/masses of; 10 put on/place on/sit on; 11 (much) smaller; 12 quieter/ less noisy; 13 much/considerably/far; 14 doesn't include; 15 have to/need to

Rounding off the Unit

Why not round off the Unit by asking Ss (in groups or as a class) to say how they would decorate and furnish a brand new apartment (if money were no object)? Prompted by others, they should be forced to defend their taste, or lack of it!

19 *I didn't read what it said!*

Warm-up

Here are two **alternative suggestions,** both with books closed:

1 To introduce the theme of written warnings and instructions, read out to the class a number of signs and notices and Ss write down where they would expect to see/find them. Suitable examples would be:

- Cheques will only be accepted with a banker's card. (In a shop)
- Not less than 60% meat. (On a pack of sausages, pâté, etc.)
- Trespassers will be prosecuted. (On a gate, door, fence)
- Store out of reach of children. (On a bottle of medicine)
- Keep clear. (On a garage door, outside a house, by a drive)
- Printed matter. Do not bend. (On an envelope)
- To be taken three times daily after meals. (On a bottle of medicine)
- Keep your distance. Baby on board. (On rear window of car)
- Doctors say no to cuts. (A newspaper headline)
- 20p off your next purchase. (On the packet/tin of supermarket product)
- For Office Use Only. (On an official form)

2 To introduce the language of instructing which is a focus of the Unit, invite Ss to instruct you in how to do the following:

bowl a ten-pin-bowling ball / knit / tie a tie / put a plug on a lead, etc.

Ss are immediately confronted with the problem of finding verbs like *press, twist, push, bend,* which are going to recur in the Unit.

Listen and decide

CAE Relevance: All Papers, esp. Paper 4 (Listening)

▷ 📼 **Tapescript** (See Coursebook p.159.)

Classroom treatment

As per rubric, start the activity with Ss in groups thinking of what instructions, warnings or general information they might expect to find on the containers listed. If eight seems too many, get one group to write down some ideas for A-D, and the other group for E-H. Then groups report back to the whole class on what they have come up with.

Play the tape and check how many containers and voices Ss have been able to match. Do not supply correct answers yet; let there be dispute and argument, justifying and quoting, even if the results are inconclusive. Play the tape again, stopping after each speaker, to check whether first ideas were correct, who's changed his/her mind, what clues there were, etc.

If you are able to lay your hands on suitable realia, tins, tubes, bottles, etc. with labels etc. in English, round off this activity usefully with Ss in pairs looking at 'their' products, reading bits out to each other, helping each other with meaning, before passing on to the pair on the right and receiving a 'new' product from the pair on the left. When they have studied six or seven products, see how much they can recall.

Answers

The matching should be: 1 B; 2 G; 3 D; 4 C; 5 E; 6 H; 7 A; 8; F.

Vocabulary: The right word

CAE Relevance: All Papers

Ex. 1

Classroom treatment

Focus attention on the verbs *scratch, scrape,* etc. See how many of the actions Ss can demonstrate or mime. *Either* show the meanings of the unfamiliar ones *or* , more usefully perhaps, get Ss to use dictionaries and let them show the meaning/usage. Before setting the exercise, run through the verbs, Ss suggesting nouns which would often be the object after each of them. For example: *scratch* — your head, your arm, your cheek, your foot, a record, etc.

Ss do the five-item exercise individually, compare answers with a partner, then jointly write sentences including the verbs not used: *graze, rub, caress.* Check answers with the class and have some imaginative example sentences read out.

Focus attention on the second part of each sentence. What do Ss notice? Point out the use of adjectives (*desperate, worried*), participles (*regretting, showing*) and noun [phrases] (*brush, bleach, a look of pure contentment*). Such constructions are often a stylish way of avoiding the introduction of a second or third main clause: He scratched his head and/because he was feeling totally confused and he regretted ...

Answers

1 scratched, 2 scraped, 3 wiped, 4 scrub, 5 stroking.

Ex. 2

Classroom treatment

As in 1 above, see how many of the listed verbs Ss recognise, can illustrate or exemplify. They can then use dictionaries to find out the meaning/usage of the others. As a check, before they do the exercise, ask which of the verbs would often be used by an interior decorator, for example: *dip the brush gently into the paint ...* , *soak the old wallpaper thoroughly before scraping it off*, etc. Ask which of the verbs would often be heard in the kitchen, for example: *sprinkle the grated cheese over the ...*, *pour the excess fat away*, etc.

Ss do the exercise individually, compare answers and then write sentences jointly with the verbs not used: *immerse, plunge, drench, pour*. Answers are checked with the class as above, and some example sentences heard.

Point out finally the use of the *-ing* form in the second part of all five sentences. Ss should be familiar with the gerund after *before*, but some might be surprised at the present participle after *if*. The ellipsis at work here — *you are* being omitted — was dealt with in Unit 16. You might refer back to it.

Answers

1 dip; 2 soak; 3 squeeze; 4 rinse; 5 sprinkle.

As a creative **follow-up activity**, divide the class into fours and write up on the board/OHP the following lines:

1 pat   tap   strike   hammer   knock
2 chop   slice   grate   trim   saw
3 drill   pierce   prick   rip   tear
4 twist   screw   stir   fold   bend

S1 has to compose a five-item gap-fill exercise for his/her five verbs (*pat, tap*, etc.). S2 does the same for his/her verbs (*chop, slice*, etc.) And so on. A very tricky —

though rewarding — task, as a number of the verbs are sometimes interchangeable and Ss must find contexts in which they are not. When they have written their exercises, they should be passed around the group for the others to do. In this way, Ss are challenged by three more five-item exercises, in addition to having composed their own 'unambiguous' one. Good fun.

Coursebook pp.116-117

Read, match and listen

CAE Relevance: Papers 1, 3 and 4 (Reading, English in Use, and Listening)

Background notes and vocabulary

'How To Keep A Happy Car'
Shirley Conran: British writer, was Woman's Editor of the Observer Colour Magazine and of the Daily Mail. Her publications include *Superwoman* (1975), *Lace* (1982), *The Magic Garden* (1983) and *Savages* (1987).
Automobile Association (AA): one of the two major road organisations in Britain, dealing with everything from insurance, legal matters and foreign travel to breakdown services and weather reporting
anti-freeze: a substance which, dissolved in the coolant of an engine, reduces the freezing point, thereby preventing it from freezing
dip-stick: the long thin metal measure used to determine the depth of oil in the oil reservoir of a car
bearing: part of a machine that bears the friction set up by a moving part
crow's feet: tiny creases in the skin at the outer corner of the eye, caused by ageing

▷ 📼 **Tapescript for ex. 2** (See Coursebook pp.159-160.)

Ex. 1

Classroom treatment

To introduce the text, you might spend two-three minutes on the subject of cars. A quick vocabulary check, perhaps, on parts of the car. Go round the room with Ss each supplying a 'part' until no more are forthcoming. **Alternatively**, get Ss in groups quickly to list five-ten 'jobs' that should be done regularly on a car to keep it in good order. This will naturally preview quite a lot of the tricky vocabulary in the text.

1 At this stage in the course, this exercise might be best done as timed 'exam practice'. Give 10 minutes for Ss to read the text and do the exercise. Then check, see if Ss can justify their choices and deal with any problems.

2 In a more relaxed mood, get Ss to work in pairs, matching the six pictures to references in the passage. Quick check and feedback afterwards.

Answers

1 The six sentences A to F, belong as follows: 1 D; 2 E; 3 B; 4 F; 5 A; 6 C

2 The five pictures relate to the following passages:

Pic 1 — Check water level (in radiator); Pic 2 — Treat yourself to a new pair of windscreen wipers before each winter; Pic 3 — Check the level of oil with the dipstick; Pic 4 — Before a long drive, check … tyre pressure; Pic 5 — Make sure that the terminals … (on the battery) … are free from dirt and corrosion.

Ex. 2

Classroom treatment

Make sure Ss understand their task and encourage the taking of brief notes while listening to the tape. Play the tape, and then get Ss in threes to make a list of as many things the man did wrong as possible. At this stage, just ask the groups how many 'mistakes' they have found. Play the tape again for Ss to add to their list if necessary.

Expected answers

Ss should have a list of 'mistakes' that includes these points:

- Has always ignored the burning smell the car makes.
- Hasn't checked water in radiator recently; has probably never put any in.
- Puts tap water in battery, not distilled water.
- Fills battery right to the brim with water.
- Opened the radiator cap too soon, without waiting for it to cool down.
- Doesn't check oil, waits for service.

Ex. 3

Classroom treatment

This should not be treated as an examination or test exercise. Get Ss in pairs or threes to read through the passage again together, armed with pencils or highlighter pens, and underline or mark any words, phrases, sentences, paragraphs that they find at all amusing.

Discuss with the class then how they would describe the humour. Is there irony? Sarcasm? Mockery? Satire? Is her main target the condescending attitude men still have to women drivers? Or is she laughing at her own sex?

Possible answers

Ss who are very easily amused might find humour in any or all of these references:

Most women feel that a car should appreciate in value and give as little trouble as emeralds. (Mocking women's ignorance?)

Sweet of them. (Sarcasm.)

… you should care for your car as you do your face …

Make sure that the terminals — the knobs where the thick wires join the battery — are free from dirt. (Is she seriously explaining what terminals are, or treating women as a lot of men do/would?)

… the engine room of your engine … (Playing with words)

Plugs in bad condition make you very prone to breakdowns. (Unusual choice of phrase might make one smile.)

The fragrant smell of burning buns sniffed while the car is running … (Relating car problems to something nearer women's normal field of experience — the kitchen!)

… have it investigated: it may mean that an engine bearing is wearing badly and needs immediate attention. Worn engine bearings lead to a gradual wearing down of the engine. (Her simplistic style here reminds one of adults talking to children. Is she again mocking men patronising women?)

Just as some things, like shoes, men or scrubbing brushes, need renewing from time to time, … (In no particular order!)

Treat yourself to … (One thinks of a new wardrobe, not windscreen wipers!)

Not only do you risk developing crow's feet … but it is dangerous to drive with a dirty windscreen … (What are her priorities?!)

To summarise, most of the gentle humour seems to stem from the stance the writer takes as a not particularly mechanically minded woman, who rather resents the patronising way men treat her and other women when it comes to cars. While mocking male attitudes, however, she gently makes fun of women too.

Coursebook pp.118-119

Language focus

CAE Relevance: All Papers

Ex. 1 Dramatising

Classroom treatment

Before Ss do the exercise, refer them to the Grammar Commentary on p. 145.

Do the first item with the class, inviting suggestions for a), b) and c). This will ensure all Ss know exactly what they have to do. Set the rest of the exercise as pairwork, to be done orally or on paper, depending on which you feel is more useful to the class at this stage. Check with the whole class at the end. Get Ss to write similar 'disaster' sentences with any of the prompts which they had trouble using. Suggest contexts if necessary.

Model sentences

1a No sooner had I turned the thing than this great burst of steam gushed up.

1b As soon as I turned the thing, this great burst of steam gushed up.

1c The minute I turned the thing, this great burst of steam gushed up.

2a Before I could turn the tap back on, water started spurting out everywhere.

2b I was on the point of turning the tap back on when water started ...

2c I was about to turn the tap back on when water started ...

3a While I was rolling out the pastry, I smelt this ghastly smell.

3b Just as I was rolling out the pastry, I smelt this ghastly smell.

3c I was in the middle of rolling out the pastry when I smelt this ghastly smell.

4a Having finally got the screws in, I realised the whole shelf was at an angle.

4b It wasn't until I'd finally got the screws in that I realised the whole shelf ...

4c I didn't realise the whole shelf was at an angle until I'd finally got the screws in.

5a You see, I had never worked with electricity alone before.

5b Never before had I worked alone with electricity, you see.

5c It was the first time I had ever worked alone with electricity, you see.

Ex. 2 Processes

Classroom treatment

1 Make sure Ss know what they have to do, then give them three-four minutes — all work should be done at some speed by this stage in the course — to rewrite the paragraph. Warn them that word order might be something of a problem. Get Ss to compare their version with a partner's, then hear a model read out to the class. Discuss the differences in tone and also which they would prefer to read if having to follow instructions.

2 Ss work in pairs for the first part of the task, S1 telling S2 (who has book closed) how to make the ice cream. S2 should be encouraged to take an active part in the activity, asking for repetition/clarification, reacting with interest/excitement, objecting that there must be/they know a better/simpler way.

For the writing task, pairs should work together to produce the formal recipe. (See Introduction p.9.)

As a follow-up to both phases of this exercise, encourage Ss to tell their partner another recipe they know well and then write it up for homework.

Model answers

1 The water level should be checked and topped up with distilled water to 1/4 inch over the plates. This is a service which should be provided by any garage. The battery should be topped up, but not overfilled. (If fluid seeps out at the top, the case may be corroded.) Ensure that the terminals, i.e. the knobs where the thick wires are joined to the battery, are free from dirt and corrosion. They should be cleaned with a little wire suede brush or even, irrespective of what onlookers think, with a toothbrush, then lightly greased.

[Comment: A paragraph such as the one above sounds slightly stilted at times; the formality is not quite suited to something so practical and 'physical'. The original is surely easier to follow with more concise, short, to-the-point instructions.]

2 The target language for the first phase would be along the lines of:

Well, as far as what you need goes, equipment and so on, you've got to have a stainless steel bowl, plus a small saucepan, you know, a milk-type saucepan, er, and ... what else? ... a spoon, big spoon, ...

The target language for the second phase would be:

The egg yolks and sugar are whisked in the bowl until the mixture is light and creamy. The milk should be scalded briefly in the saucepan and then the cocoa stirred in. When this has been thoroughly mixed, the yolks are poured in. The bowl is then placed over a pan of simmering water and the mixture stirred for ten minutes. When it has thickened slightly, it should be removed from the heat and the cream and vanilla (can be) stirred in. The mixture is then left to cool, poured into the ice cream container and frozen in the ice cream maker.

Listen, then tell each other

CAE Relevance: Papers 4 and 5 (Listening and Speaking)

▷ 📼 **Tapescript** (See Coursebook p.160.)

Ex. 1

Classroom treatment

Ss look at the list of eight things and write down the ones they think they will hear when the man starts talking. (This naturally focusses their attention during the listening phase.) Ask them to 'justify' their choices by saying how they think he will have used, shall we say, a paper-clip. What will he have used the adhesive tape for? And so on.

Play the tape and Ss see how accurate their predictions were.

Play the tape again, to let Ss focus on the narrative techniques used. (They are going to have to do something similar themselves soon!)

Answers

The items the man actually mentions using are:

1 a hammer: 'hammered in the nail'

2 (doesn't say he used a screwdriver on the screw, but presumably he did)

4 adhesive tape: he mentions strong tape ('no chance') so he must have tried

7 a nail: 'hammered in the nail'

He didn't use an electric drill (3) to make a hole — only 'a corkscrew-looking thing'.

He tried a clip that was on the picture rail, but not paper clips (5).

He doesn't say anything about a saw (6) or a tape measure (8).

Ex. 2

Classroom treatment

It may be advisable to give Ss one more example of the sort of speaking 'task' set them here. Recall or invent an episode from your own do-it-yourself past — burnt cakes, unwearable dresses, all-too-easily-collapsible furniture, etc. — to tell the class about. Then give Ss a minute or so to remember (or make up) a similar 'disaster' to tell their partner(s). Refer them to the list on page 119, but they may prefer to choose something

different. This activity would benefit from some built-in repetition. If Ss move around the room, they will have the opportunity to tell one story at least twice, before perhaps trying another. Nothing more natural than an opening gambit: *I was just telling Maria about the time I ... .* And the story would no doubt improve with the retelling.

Tip Strip

Before doing the Exam Practice as a CAE test, spend some time on the Tip Strip. Before they look at it, Ss might be asked to predict what it will say. What *are* the difficulties of Paper 4? What *can* you do to partly, if not wholly, overcome them? What will normally be the character of the four passages they will hear? How many times will they hear each piece?

Ss then read the Tip Strip to see if it includes all their ideas and if it includes anything else. (See also notes in Units 16, 17 and 18 of this Teacher's Guide.)

Exam Practice: Paper 4 Listening

CAE Relevance: Paper 4 (Listening)

▷ 📼 **Tapescript**

TUTOR: Unit 19. Look at page 119, Exam Practice. You're going to hear eight people talking about problems they remember having in various situations. On page 119 you see a list of those situations. Match the speakers with their problems. Write 1 beside the first problem you hear described, 2 beside the second, and so on. One.

MAN 1: I was doing about 60 when suddenly it came off in my hands; you can't imagine. And no sooner had that happened than the windscreen just shattered, just like that.

TUTOR: Two.

WOMAN 1: When I tried to roll it out, it all just stuck to the rolling pin, all a gooey mess, quite inedible.

TUTOR: Three.

WOMAN 2: When I tried it on, it made me look as if my waist was bigger than my hips. And I'd just taken it off again when I saw this huge rip right across the back, so, well, into the bin it went.

TUTOR: Four.

MAN 2: Well, one of my friends thought it looked like a nuclear power station, somebody said it was like an

Eastern temple after a hurricane, and all it was supposed to be was our little bungalow.

TUTOR: Five.

MAN 3: I don't know, it looked so easy. I mean all you've got to do is wrap it once round and then bring it round between the legs and pin it, isn't it? Well, I was doing that for about half an hour. Cry, I thought he'd never stop.

TUTOR: Six.

MAN 4: It looked a piece of cake, the lump of clay on the wheel, and the demonstration made it sound quite straightforward; once the wheel started moving round, the clay went completely out of control; elegant vase or mug, forget it; primitive ashtray maybe.

TUTOR: Seven.

WOMAN 3: For a start the vowels are completely different from ours, utterly unpronounceable, and you get about three or four consonants all stuck together that would turn your mouth inside out, if you ever got near to saying them correctly. I gave up as soon as the first week was over.

TUTOR: Eight

WOMAN 4: I washed it in hot water, cold water, rubbed it, scrubbed it, soaked it. Nothing, couldn't shift it.

Classroom treatment

Give the Exam Practice as a test. Let Ss briefly study the rubric. Play the tape. After a shortish pause, play the tape again. Then check answers and discuss difficulties. Play (parts of) the tape again if there is still dispute.

Answers

The correct matching of problems and speakers: A5, B4, C8, D2, E1, F3, G7, H6.

Rounding off the Unit

Why not round off this Unit with a variation of an old parlour game? As Ss may be due to sit Paper 5 imminently, give them some practice in creative improvisations.

Each S receives three or four objects from you. (If they are broken or damaged, so much the better.) After a short time for thought, they then tell a partner a story in which all three or four objects play a key part.

This activity can go on as long as you want it to, by having the objects passed around the room after each pair of stories.

20 Into the future!

Coursebook pp.120-121

Warm-up

Here are three **alternative suggestions**, all with books closed:

1 General group and/or class discussion on the question: Are you (or were you) looking forward to the next/21st Century? Why?/Why not?

2 In answer to the question 'What do you think life will be like in the next century?', different pairs of Ss might be asked to prepare brief notes on one of the following, then perhaps try to talk for 30 seconds or tell another S or pair what they think:

the family/family life, travel, public transport, work, leisure and entertainment, shopping, the world map (e.g. United States of Europe?, United States of South America?), holidays, language/languages, music, education, fashion/clothes, space travel, etc.

3 Ss write down the names of some of the other Ss in the class. They then make two or three predictions for each of them — imagining what their lives will be like in thirty years' time e.g. She will probably be an eminent politician; She will have at least six children; He will have played football for his country; etc. The rest of the class must then try to guess who the predictions refer to.

Look, read and discuss

CAE Relevance: Papers 1 and 5 (Reading and Speaking)

Background notes and vocabulary

'Japanese city of the future'
prise sby away from: drag or force somebody away from
satchel: a small bag of strong cloth or leather, usu. with a band (or bands) for carrying over the shoulder or on the back
dart out: rush or run out
shopping precinct: an area in a town (often enclosed) containing only shops
Aeropolis: presumably 'the city in the air' (compare *metropolis*)

come up with: to think of (a plan, an answer, etc.); to produce
blueprint: a photographic copy, in white on blue paper, of a plan for making a machine or building a house; here, it implies a grand plan
edifice: (fml. or pompous) a large, fine building, such as a palace or church
Mount Fuji: a nearly symmetrical volcanic cone (3,778 m.) in south central Honshu, Japan. The volcano has been dormant since 1707.
jet stream: a narrow current of high-velocity westerly winds, close to the tropopause, which in turn is the level separating the troposphere and the stratosphere, occurring at an altitude of 8-16 km.
a host of: a large number of
penthouse: a small house or set of rooms built at the top of a tall building, often considered very desirable to live in

Exs. 1-3

Classroom treatment

1 Ask Ss what they think the article will be about and what information it might give, just from the title and photo. Note various predictions on the board/OHP.

2 Ss read the article. Check comprehension and how good their predictions were.

3 **Alternative procedures**

   a Ss read the text again individually and list some advantages and disadvantages of living in Aeropolis, which they then compare with a partner and then a group or class.

   b Ss read individually and list **either** advantages **or** disadvantages. They then compare with a S who has done the opposite. Then group or class discussion.

   c **Debate:** Divide the class into two halves, A and B. Group A discuss and list as many advantages as they can think of, Group B discuss and list disadvantages. Then hold a formal debate: 'This House believes that the Aeropolis proposal is a recipe for disaster.' (If there is not time for a formal debate, perhaps set aside a special lesson for it following this one, or later in the Unit.)

Answers to ex. 3

Some possible advantages:

- everything is 'under one roof'
- no need to travel large distance to work, school, shops, etc.
- could have a real 'community' feel about it

Some possible disadvantages:

- begin to feel isolated from the rest of the world
- danger of a major disaster through fire, earthquake, high winds, etc.
- possible threat from terrorists threatening to blow the building up unless certain demands are met

As a brief follow-up, ask Ss what they can remember about the space hotel in Unit 5. Are there any ways in which the space hotel and this city of the future are similar?

Look, speak and write

CAE Relevance: Paper 2 and 5 (Writing and Speaking)

Background notes and vocabulary

'Goodbye Tracey, hello Robot'

Tracey: This was a very common girl's first name in Britain in the 70s, 80s and early 90s, so your checkout girl at the supermarket was quite likely to be a Tracey.

supermarket checkout: see notes to CB Unit 12, p.78

all but: (adv.) almost, nearly

bane: a cause of bad things (esp. in the phrase *the bane of my life*)

variable pricing: different prices charged on the same items at different times of the day or week

'loyalty card': a card showing that you are 'loyal' to that supermarket

trolley: a low four-wheeled cart that you push round a supermarket by hand

bar-code scanner: a device that scans or reads the bar code on an article in a shop. There is a bar code on the back cover of this book.

liquid crystal displays: here, computerised systems. These are already used in thermometers that you can place against a patient's forehead or hang on the wall to see whether a room is the right temperature (particularly for old people)

pad (of plastic sheets): a number of sheets fastened together along one edge (as in *a writing pad, a pad of paper*)

Classroom treatment

This is something like the kind of task Ss might be asked to do in the first part of Paper 2 Writing.

First, ask Ss what they like and don't like about supermarket shopping. This should help to preview some of the language to come e.g. *checkout, (supermarket) trolley, aisles, bar codes,* etc. Then read the title, sub-title and beginning of the article with the whole class, explaining where necessary, and checking comprehension.

Ss then work in pairs to read, check meanings, and make notes on what changes are planned to make supermarket shopping easier in the future. Before Ss start writing, get them to tell you as a class what is proposed, what might or will happen — and point out a) how often passives are used with modals here — *this may be done, that can be done,* etc., and b) how they will have to change many of the present tenses in the illustration captions to future forms when they are writing. (See Introduction p.9.) Ss then draft and clean-write the rest of the article, possibly as a homework assignment. Advise Ss that they do not need to include all the fine detail of the changes that are planned.

Answer

Here is an example of what students might aim to produce:

The checkout system is the bane of supermarket operations. In order to reduce queues to a minimum in the future, a number of technological devices are going to be introduced. How often have you had to wait because the checkout girl doesn't know the price of something? Well, in future, electronic shelf edge labels will be linked to checkout scanners so that prices shown will be the same as those charged. They may well also introduce variable pricing and 'loyalty cards'.

Some of the most important things they are proposing, however, are fitting trolleys with hand-held bar-code scanners and liquid crystal displays so that customers will only have to handle items once, and introducing 'intelligent' trolleys which will record a customer's route around the supermarket. And to make life even easier in future at the checkout, customers will be able to pass purchases over a laser scanner themselves and goods will also be packed automatically. All you will have to do is place your goods on a large pad of plastic sheets and when a predetermined weight is reached, a machine will automatically form a bag around the items.

Coursebook pp.122-123

Vocabulary: Looking forward to the future — with more than a touch of concern

CAE Relevance: All Papers, but esp. Paper 3 (English in Use)

▷ 📼 Tapescript for ex. 3 (See Coursebook p.160.)

Ex. 1 Three-word phrasal (or phrasal-prepositional) verbs

1

Classroom treatment

Either ask Ss to read these together and discuss the questions, then check with the whole class,
or read out the sentences, stopping after each to let Ss rephrase them or explain the verbs, and then discuss how *let in on* and *prise away from* are different from the others. (Note: *prise away from* and *come up with* appeared in the 'Japanese city of the future' text on page 120.)

Answers

came across as = gave the impression of being, seemed to be; *get round to* = finally do; *let you in on* = tell you; *looking forward to* = waiting with anticipation to do; *prise ... away from* = get somebody away from something by force

let somebody in on and *prise somebody away from* are both transitive verbs (i.e. they must have an object after the verb): the others are all intransitive.

[If Ss need more examples, here are some more **transitive three-word phrasal verbs**:

take (sby) up on (e.g. He <u>took</u> me <u>up on</u> my offer), *do (sby) out of, let (sby) in for, play (sby) off against (sby else), put (sby) down as, put (sthg) down to, put (sby) up to, take (sthg) out on (sby)*

And here are just a few more **intransitive three-word phrasal verbs**:

catch up with, come down with (= begin to suffer from), *cut back on, date back to, get on with, go along with* (= agree with), *go down with* (an illness), *look down on, look up to, stick up for*

Remind students that if a verb follows a phrasal-prepositional verb, it will be a gerund, whatever the preposition, even *to* e.g. *I'm **looking forward to** meeting you. / He tried to **talk me out of buying** the car. / He couldn't **wriggle out of doing** the job.*]

2

Classroom treatment

Before reading the draft, ask Ss to look at the verbs in the box, to check what they mean and to break them into two groups — transitive and intransitive e.g. *boil down to* but *talk somebody out of.* They may use dictionaries for this. Ss do the exercise individually, in pairs or as a class.

Answers

Replacements for the verbs and phrases underlined:

... <u>put it down to</u> old age ...; We can no longer <u>shy away from</u> the fact ...; learn to <u>put up with</u> ...; the West has <u>come in for</u> ...; have to <u>face up to</u> the fact ....; it's time we <u>snapped out of</u> ...; We can no longer <u>wriggle out of</u> ... ; If scientists could only <u>come up with</u> ...; If scientists continue to <u>monkey about with</u> ...; It's difficult to <u>talk just one person out of using</u> more energy ...; Our children will no doubt <u>come/run up against</u> problems that we ....; <u>frightens the life out of me</u>; What it all <u>boils down to</u>, ...

3

Classroom treatment

Play the tape as often as necessary here to let Ss do the exercises. (While they may well have to listen to a number of short extracts like this in one part of Paper 4 Listening in the exam, this is not a test.)

Answers

a) Speaker 1 thinks we have a rosy future if people can break out of some of their old attitudes.

Speaker 2 is worried that crime will become a greater problem in the future unless we do something now.

Speaker 3 is worried about the environment in the future.

Speaker 4 thinks that people in future will have a lot more leisure time to fill.

Speaker 5 thinks we must find a cure for AIDS.

Speaker 6 thinks the next millenium will be marvellous — 'a sort of rebirth'.

c) Speaker 1 — *break out of, get along with*; Speaker 2 — *come in for, clamp down on, crack down on*; Speaker 3 — *clean up after*; Speaker 4 — *go in for*; Speaker 5 — *come up with*; Speaker 6 — *look forward to, come up to*

4

Classroom treatment

You might ask for suggestions from the class as a whole for completions for the blanks ('...'s) in the speech, but this might best be set as a homework assignment.

Possible completed speech

Ladies and gentlemen,

You can put it down to old age if you like, but whatever the reason, I've been wondering recently more and more about the future. And I've been thinking about all those problems that *must* be solved if our children are to have any future at all!

One thing that concerns me is the terrible gulf between rich and poor. We can no longer shy away from the fact that the rich must help the poor in this world by giving aid in as many ways as they can. And in doing so, it may well be that people in rich countries will have to learn to put up with a slightly lower standard of living.

In recent years, the West has come in for a great deal of criticism for not doing enough to relieve poverty and famine in countries in Africa and Asia for example. All governments of the world, but especially those with money, have to face up to the fact that they owe it to their poorer relatives to help them achieve a better standard of living. I say it's time we in the western world snapped out of our complacency and did something. We can no longer wriggle out of our responsibilities towards our neighbours in the world or our children's future. If we don't do something soon, there will be no future to look forward to — for any of us.

And then there are other major world problems. If scientists could only come up with a solution to the AIDS problem, they could prevent the deaths of thousands of men, women and children in many countries across the world.

If scientists continue to monkey about with the environment, our children will face greater problems than we have ever seen and than we could possibly imagine.

When it comes to conserving the world's energy and natural resources, it's difficult to talk just one person out of using more energy, let alone the whole population of a country!

The future is as uncertain as the past. Our children will no doubt come/run up against problems that we have never even dreamed of.

Just thinking of the future of the world frightens the life out of me.

What it all boils down to, I've decided, is that we have to start thinking globally.

Ex. 2 Partitive structures: 'A touch of concern'

While the first part of this (together with a brief mention of common partitives like *a lot of/a mass of/a host of/a (large) number of people/problems etc.*) should be revision for most Ss, ex. 2 introduces certain partitives which will no doubt be new.

1 Classroom treatment

Ss work as fast as they can, dragging up from their memories and past English lessons(!) and listing as many different partitive phrases as they can. Check with the whole class. Don't get too bogged down in specific (and often rare) phrases such as *a pride of lions* !

Possible answers

a) Others with uncount nouns: a loaf of bread, a glass of wine, a lump of cheese, a piece of wood, a bar of chocolate.

b) Others to show shape or amount: a curtain of fire, a tuft of hair/grass/ wool, a bundle of hay, a mound of sand, a plank of wood, a block of wood, a pad of paper, a ball of string, a bar of soap/chocolate, a clump of trees.

c) Others to show groups: a crowd of people, a team of experts, a shoal of fish, a pride of lions, a pack of dogs/wolves, a host of angels, a fleet of cars, a block of flats, a swarm of bees. [You might remind students of these: a chapter of accidents, a catalogue of disasters.]

d) Others to refer to containers and contents: a bottle of wine, a carton of milk, a packet of tea, a box of matches, a cup of tea.

e) Others to refer to one thing of a type: an item of news, a piece of luggage, a sheet/piece/pad of paper, a branch of medicine, a field of study.

2 Classroom treatment

As many of the partitives in this group may be new for many Ss, you might ask them to cover the page and listen to the following sentences as examples. Nearly all the partitives mean 'a small amount, a little bit'. Get Ss to listen, repeat and then rephrase the sentences *without* the partitives. They will often be able to use *some* or *any* in their place.

*There wasn't **a grain of truth** in what he said.*

*The police were sure the man did the crime, but they didn't have **a shred of evidence**.*

She played the whole piece at the concert without **a trace of nerves**.

It's only April, but already there's **a hint of summer** in the air.

*His son's in **a spot of trouble** with the police, I'm afraid.*

Ss then do the exercise and check back with you.

Possible answers

1 There wasn't a scrap/shred of evidence ...; 2 There isn't a grain of truth ...; 3 They had a spot of bother ...; 4 The criminal didn't show a trace of remorse. 5 There was a hint of irony ...

Coursebook pp.123-125

Tip Strip

Before Ss read this Tip Strip (in class or at home), why not briefly ask them to discuss what it's like to be an examiner in an oral exam, and perhaps to put themselves in the examiner's shoes and say what he or she is looking for?

(See also notes in Units 16-19 of this Teacher's Guide.)

Language focus: 'A rosy future?'

CAE Relevance: All Papers, esp. Papers 2 and 5 (Writing and Speaking)

Classroom treatment

The aim of this phase is to present (or revise) and practise language which will feed into the writing task — a piece entitled 'I predict ...' for a magazine — *and* into the final Exam Practice phase to follow. All the language should be practised orally in A/B pairs — with A being an optimist and B a pessimist. In general, the language here is reasonably formal and perhaps more appropriate to writing, but the magazine piece itself to be written at the end should be serious and fairly formal in tone. (In fact Ss might practise the language here orally and then come back to planning and writing the piece *after* doing the Exam Practice.)

Deal with any problems as they arise and, at the same time, advise Ss to consult the Grammar Commentary as necessary. The following should be highlighted in the different parts. (Sentences that Ss might produce, or that you might give as examples, are given below.)

Ex. 1 Future forms with *will* and *might*

Highlight the certainty of *will* and the less certain *might* (or *will probably*). And quickly revise *By then ... will/might have done* and *By then ... will/might have been doing + for some time*.

Ex. 2 Impersonal/Introductory *it*

Point out the use of a *should*-clause after *it* + adjective in sentences like these:

It's only natural that such things should happen, but ...

It's ridiculous that people should have to work so hard, but ...

Ex. 3 Joining ideas with *whereas, while, apart from,* etc.

Practice here concentrates on using *whereas ..., while ..., apart from ..., let alone ..., on the other hand,* etc. to compare situations.

As a final thought, Ss might find the following adverb-adjective collocations useful when writing their piece for the magazine: *desperately/dreadfully short of [food], seriously under-nourished, pitifully/woefully inadequate [conditions]*

Answers

Examples of some of the things Ss might say:

Optimist: I think the world has a rosy future. I predict that by the year 2050 ...

1 Most people will be enjoying a good standard of living./ We will have solved the problem of AIDS./We will have been living in peace for a long time.

2 It's only natural that disasters and accidents should happen, but I'm sure we'll be able to deal with them better.

It's absurd that people should have to spend much of their life working, but I think that in the future we'll be able to ...

3 Whereas the West has masses of food, many countries have too little, so in the future we're going to have to learn to share a lot more.

Pessimist: I think the future looks grim. I predict that by the year 2050 ...

1 There still won't be peace in the world. /Thousands will be living in poverty in this country./We will have used up most of the earth's oil reserves. /We will have been fighting AIDS for years, and still not found a cure.

2 It's understandable that people should want to change things, but I don't think things will be any better in the future.

3 Apart from having too many mouths to feed in the future, we will have created deserts in many parts of the world, so millions will die of starvation.

Exam Practice: Paper 5 Speaking

CAE Relevance: Paper 5 (Speaking)

Background notes and vocabulary

This cartoon was drawn by Peter Brookes, a well-known and well-respected English cartoonist who contributes regularly to *The Times* and other publications. Drawn in the style of Albrecht Dürer, the 16th-century German artist, it portrays a 1990s version of the Four Horsemen of the Apocalypse, which have traditionally been Plague, Famine, War and Conquest. Brookes has replaced Plague and Conquest by AIDS and Pollution to bring it up to date.

famine: (a case of) very serious lack of food

apocalypse: any prophetic writing or utterance, esp. one concerned with the end of the world

Exs. a and b

Classroom treatment

This is to give some practice for the Section C 'problem-solving' phase.

a This prediction exercise is to get Ss thinking about the picture and the task. To help them, give some background to the cartoon (see Background notes) and/or ask what they think the cartoonist's message is. Then get them to think of and write down questions that an examiner might ask — *not* comprehension questions, but questions to discuss.

b Now ask pairs of Ss to discuss these questions (and check how many predicted them in some form or other):

Does this cartoon give too pessimistic a view of the future? And even if it does, which of the 'riders' or 'horsemen' do you think poses the greatest problem for Mankind in the future? Why?

Allow two minutes before asking each pair whether they agreed and what they thought. Then, if time allows, open up the discussion to the whole class.

Rounding off the Unit and the Course

Why not round off this Unit and the course by getting Ss to summarise the content of each of the 20 Units from memory and mention any details (facts and figures? language? photos or cartoons? etc.) they particularly remember? The Unit title in each case should be sufficient to jog memories and generate a few minutes' comment on each one.